Collins
English for Exams

SKILLS FOR THE TOEFL iBT® TEST

Listening and Speaking

Collins

HarperCollins Publishers
77-85 Fulham Palace Road
Hammersmith
London W6 8JB

First edition 2012

Reprint 10 9 8 7 6 5 4 3 2 1 0

© HarperCollins Publishers 2012

ISBN 978-0-00-746060-1

www.collinselt.com

A catalogue record for this book is available from the British Library.

Editorial Services: Content*Ed Publishing Solutions, LLC

Writing Services: Creative Content, LLC

Typeset in India by Aptara

Printed in Italy by Lego

Academic Word List © Coxhead, Averil 2000

Contents

How to Use This Book   v

Overview of the TOEFL® Test   vi

Guide to Listening   1

Overview

Challenges and Solutions

Lesson 1:   Main Idea Questions and Detail Questions   13

Lesson 1A: Main Idea Question Overview
Walk Through
Get It Right: Tips and Tasks for Answering Correctly

Lesson 1B: Detail Question Overview
Walk Through
Get It Right: Tips and Tasks for Answering Correctly

Progressive Practice

Lesson 2:   Purpose Questions and Inference Questions   24

Lesson 2A: Purpose Question Overview
Walk Through
Get It Right: Tips and Tasks for Answering Correctly

Lesson 2B: Inference Question Overview
Walk Through
Get It Right: Tips and Tasks for Answering Correctly

Progressive Practice

Lesson 3:   Function Questions and Attitude Questions   36

Lesson 3A: Function Question Overview
Walk Through
Get It Right: Tips and Tasks for Answering Correctly

Lesson 3B: Attitude Question Overview
Walk Through
Get It Right: Tips and Tasks for Answering Correctly

Progressive Practice

Lesson 4:   Organization Questions and Connecting Content Questions   48

Lesson 4A: Organization Question Overview
Walk Through
Get It Right: Tips and Tasks for Answering Correctly

Lesson 4B: Connecting Content Question Overview
Walk Through
Get It Right: Tips and Tasks for Answering Correctly

Progressive Practice

Listening Review Test   59

Guide to Speaking 73
Overview
Challenges and Solutions

Independent Questions

Lesson 1: Personal Experience Question Overview 86
Walk Through
Get It Right: Tips and Tasks for Answering Correctly

Progressive Practice

Lesson 2: Paired Choice Question Overview 96
Walk Through
Get It Right: Tips and Tasks for Answering Correctly

Progressive Practice

Integrated Questions

Lesson 3: Campus Matters Question Overview 106
Walk Through
Get It Right: Tips and Tasks for Answering Correctly

Progressive Practice

Lesson 4: Academic Reading and Lecture Question Overview 119
Walk Through
Get It Right: Tips and Tasks for Answering Correctly

Progressive Practice

Lesson 5: Campus Conversation Question Overview 132
Walk Through
Get It Right: Tips and Tasks for Answering Correctly

Progressive Practice

Lesson 6: Academic Summary Question Overview 144
Walk Through
Get It Right: Tips and Tasks for Answering Correctly

Progressive Practice

Speaking Review Test 155

Answer Key 168
Audio Scripts 184
Academic Word List 205

How to Use This Book

Skills for the TOEFL iBT® Test: Listening and Speaking and its companion edition, *Skills for the TOEFL iBT® Test: Reading and Writing* offer a comprehensive guide to the TOEFL test. If you use this series to prepare for the test, you can earn a top score on the TOEFL test and improve your chances at getting accepted by your university of choice.

No matter the level of your English, *Skills for the TOEFL iBT® Test: Listening and Speaking* provides you with all the tools you need to succeed on the test. Here's a glimpse of the learning tools included in this book:

» **Skill-specific *Challenges and Solutions* sections.** These sections offer strategy and skill reviews to help you learn how to overcome the most common challenges in each section of the test.

» ***Quick Guide* question overviews**. Each lesson provides a brief summary of the question type in an easy-to-read chart, making it simple for you to quickly understand what is important to know in order to answer the question correctly.

» ***Walk Through* samples.** Clear, visual examples show you the types of questions, passages, and responses you can expect to find on the test. Knowing what to expect is an important part of preparing for the test.

» ***Get It Right* presentations.** These presentations give an overview of the most important steps for doing well on each question. They include useful vocabulary and expressions that you can use when answering the questions and provide tips and tasks for noticing and understanding the important elements of each question type.

» ***Progressive Practice*.** For each question type, carefully designed activities gradually prepare you for the TOEFL test. This step-by-step practice builds the knowledge and skills you need for a high score and encourages independent learning while working up to TOEFL testing levels.

- *Get Ready* activities require you to look and listen for certain pieces of information, practice structured activities, and notice why answers are correct or incorrect.

- *Get Set* activities encourage even more practice working with the question types and answers and will help you gain the skills and confidence you need.

- *Go for the TOEFL Test* activities provide you with authentic test questions to practice what you have learned and further prepare you for the test.

» ***Answer Analysis* presentations.** The answer analyses will teach you how to eliminate incorrect answer options and select the best answers for various question types.

» **Skill-specific *Review Test* sections.** At the end of each section, you'll be able to put your skills to the test by taking a timed practice test. The review sections will help you identify your weaknesses so you can know what areas to focus on before the test.

» ***Test Tips.*** Throughout the book, you'll see *Test Tips* which offer best-practice strategies and useful advice on how to approach certain activity types.

» **Dictionary definitions.** *Collins COBUILD Advanced Dictionary* definitions and Web links are provided throughout the book to help you understand words and build your knowledge of academic vocabulary often found on the TOEFL test and in US university texts and lectures.

» **Academic Word List.** The Academic Word List, compiled by Averil Coxhead (2000), consists of 570 word families that occur frequently over a wide range of academic texts. Knowing and practicing these words will help you build your vocabulary base to understand and use more academic English words.

» **Audio Script and Answer Key.** Found at the back of this book, these tools will help you practice and check your answers as you prepare for the TOEFL test. The speaking section's answer key and audio script includes two sample responses and scores for each question type.

» **CDs.** The CDs included with this book provide you with all of the listening passages for the lessons and review tests. The speaking section's *Go for the TOEFL Test* and *Review Test* portions include authentic beeps so you can practice timing your responses. You will also find sample responses for the speaking section.

Tips for Success

Make a plan to succeed, and start by following these tips:

» **Register early for the test**. Check the application deadlines for the universities you are applying to. Make sure that you register to take the test well before the deadline to ensure that your scores arrive on time. For information on how to register, see page xi of this book.

» **Learn the score requirements for the universities you want to apply to**. Degree programs that have minimum score requirements typically post them on their admissions Web sites.

» **Start to study early.** The more you practice, the more you will improve your skills. Give yourself at least one month to review the materials and complete <u>all</u> of the practice activities in this book and in the companion edition, *Skills for the TOEFL iBT® Test: Reading and Writing*. Spend at least one hour a day studying, and don't give up. Remember, by using this book, you are on your way to high scores on the TOEFL test!

» **Time yourself** when you complete the exercises and practice tests in this book and in the companion book, *Skills for the TOEFL iBT® Test: Reading and Writing*

» **Listen to the scripts and model responses** as many times as you need to in order to understand the concepts taught in this book.

» **Complete the exercises** on the page. Also, don't be afraid to make your own notes on the page. For example, writing down the definitions of words you don't know will help you remember them later on.

» On the listening section, try not to go back to the questions once you've completed them. This will help you get used to the process on the actual test.

» On the speaking section, return to the prompts and try to come up with new responses. Practice until creating responses within the time limits becomes easy for you.

Overview of the TOEFL® Test

The TOEFL® iBT test (Test of English as a Foreign Language) measures your proficiency in English. The TOEFL test does not evaluate your knowledge of the English language. Rather, it measures your ability to <u>use</u> English in a variety of academic settings.

The test is divided into four timed parts: Reading, Listening, Speaking, and Writing. Each section tests key skills that you will need in order to succeed as a student at an English-speaking university.

Reading Section

The reading section is the first section on the test. It measures your reading comprehension abilities by presenting you with a series of academic passages. Then, you will answer a set of questions based on each reading. The questions in this section test your ability to:

» identify the main idea.

» understand the main details.

» make inferences.

» understand the organizational structure of the passage.

» use context clues to determine the definitions of key words.

There are three–five academic reading passages per reading section. Each passage is between 600 and 750 words long. After each reading passage, you will answer a set of questions. There are usually 12–14 questions per passage. In the reading section, you are allowed to go back to previously answered questions in the section to review or change your answers. For more information on the reading sections, see *Skills for the TOEFL iBT® Test, Reading and Writing.*

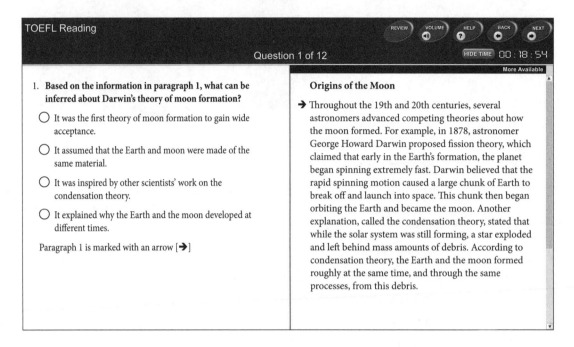

Listening Section

The listening section is the second section on the test. In order to evaluate your listening comprehension abilities, you will first listen to a lecture or conversation through your headphones. Then, you will answer a set of questions based on each listening. The questions in this section will test your ability to:

» identify the main idea or purpose of the listening.

» understand the main details.

» make inferences.

» identify the speaker's purpose.

There are six–nine listening passages per listening section. Each listening is between five and seven minutes long. After each listening passage, you will answer a set of questions. There are usually five–six questions per passage. In the listening section, you are <u>not</u> allowed to review questions that you have answered previously.

Speaking Section

The speaking section is the third section on the test. In this section, you will speak into the microphone your responses to a variety of tasks. The tasks test a number of speaking abilities, including:

» giving opinions.

» understanding and responding to questions in the classroom.

» participating in discussions on academic subjects.

» synthesizing (combining) information from two sources.

» reporting the opinions of others.

» interacting with university employees.

There are six speaking tasks in the speaking section: two independent tasks and four integrated tasks. Each item requires different skills, including reading, listening and speaking, and speaking only.

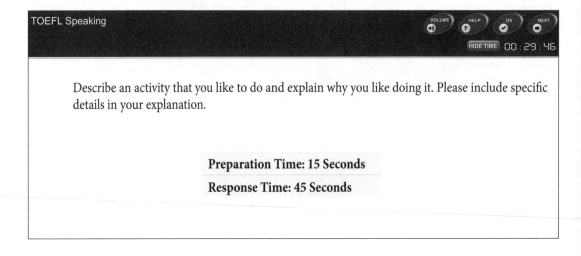

Writing Section

The writing section is the fourth section on the test. In this section, you will type on the computer your responses for each item. The tasks measure your ability to:

» plan and organize an essay.

» develop a written response by using examples or specific details.

» use a variety of grammatical structures and vocabulary.

» use correct spelling and punctuation.

There are two writing tasks in the writing section: one integrated writing task and one independent writing task. For more information on the writing section, see *Skills for the TOEFL iBT® Test, Reading and Writing*.

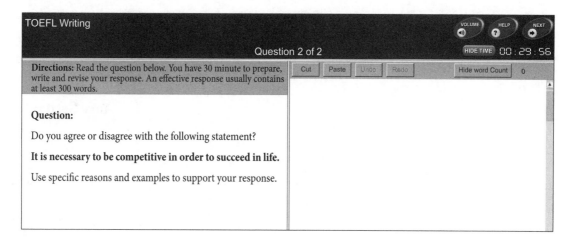

Experimental Sections

In order to field-test new materials, ETS always includes an experimental section in <u>either</u> the reading or listening section of each test. That means that on the day of the test, you will see extra passages and questions in either the reading section or the listening section. If the experimental section is part of the reading section, you will have to read an additional two passages and answer the accompanying questions for them. If the experimental section is part of the listening section, you will have to listen to an additional three listening passages (two lectures and one conversation) and answer questions that are based on them.

Please note that the experimental section is not graded. However, you will have no way of knowing which section is experimental, so it is very important that you try your best on <u>all</u> sections of the test.

QUICK GUIDE: TOEFL® Test

Section	Tasks	Timing	
Reading Section	Reading Passages: 3–5 Number of Questions: 39–70	Part 1 (1 Passage + Questions)	20 minutes
		Part 2 (2 Passages + Questions)	40 minutes
		Part 3* (2 Passages + Questions)	40 minutes
		Total Section Time: 60–100 minutes	
Listening Section	Listening Passages: 6–9 4–6 Lectures 2–3 Conversations Number of Questions: 34–51	Part 1 (2 Lectures, 1 Conversation + Questions)	
			30 minutes
		Part 2 (2 Lectures, 1 Conversation + Questions)	
			30 minutes
		Part 3* (2 Lectures, 1 Conversation + Questions)	
			30 minutes
		Total Section Time: 60–90 minutes	
	10-Minute Break		
Speaking Section	Number of Questions: 6 2 Independent 4 Integrated	**Total Section Time: 20 minutes**	
Writing Section	Number of Tasks: 2 1 Integrated 1 Independent	Integrated Task:	20 minutes
		Independent Task:	30 minutes
		Total Section Time: 50 minutes	

*These parts are experimental and will appear on either the reading or the listening section.

Scoring

You will receive a score for each section of the test. The score ranges per section are as follows:

Reading	0–30
Listening	0–30
Speaking	0–30
Writing	0–30

In order to calculate your total score, the individual scores for the four sections are added together. Thus, the highest score you can possibly achieve on the TOEFL test is 120.

The reading and listening sections are both scored by computer. However, in order to determine your scores for the speaking and writing sections, your responses are saved and sent to ETS, where they are scored by certified raters. Each of the six responses in the speaking section is assigned a score of 0–4. The scores for each task are added together and converted into a score on the 30-point scale described above. Similarly, the two tasks on the writing section are each given a score of 0–5. Again, the scores for both tasks are added together and then converted to a score between 0 and 30.

Score Reports

There are several ways to review your scores. First, you may view your scores online 15 business days after the test. All you have to do is visit the TOEFL Web site at *www.ets.org/toefl* and sign in to the "My TOEFL iBT account" with the username and password that you created when you registered for the test. Your online score report will show the following information:

» The date that you took the test

» Your scores for each section

» Your total score

» Performance evaluations for each section that describe whether your performance was low, medium, or high

You may access your scores online for tests that you have taken within the past two years. Please note that the universities and / or institutions that you have selected to receive your scores will also be able to view your scores online.

In addition to being able to access your scores online, you will receive a paper score report via mail two to three weeks after the test date.

TOEFL Test: What You'll See and Hear on the Day of the Test

Registration

There are a number of ways to register for the TOEFL iBT test.

» **Online Registration**: Visit the TOEFL Web site at *www.ets.org/toefl* and follow the instructions for registering. On the Web site, you will be able to find the nearest test center and dates for upcoming tests. Seats at test centers are limited, so be sure to register for the test early! You must register seven days before your desired test date. Late registration is also available up to three days before your desired test date, but you will be charged a late-registration fee.

» **By Phone**: Visit the TOEFL Web site and download the registration form. Then, call your regional registration center (check the Web site for phone numbers) and a representative will help you register. Late registration by phone is available until 5 p.m. the day before your desired test date.

» **By Mail:** Visit the TOEFL Web site and download, print, and complete the registration form. Send your completed form with payment to your regional registration center at least four weeks before the desired test date.

For payment information and other details about the registration process, visit the TOEFL Web site at *www.ets.org/toefl*.

Before the Test Starts

When you arrive at the test center, you will sign in and give your identification document, such as a passport, to a test-center employee (for information about accepted identification documents, see the ETS Web site at *www.ets.org*). Make sure that the name on your identification document matches the name under which you registered! If it does not match, you will not be allowed to take the test.

After you sign in, the employee at the test center will instruct you to put your personal belongings, such as your jacket, car keys, or cell phone, into a storage area. Review the TOEFL Web site for rules about personal items. You will also be given a document that outlines the rules of the test. At the end of the document, you will see a statement of confidentiality. You are required to write this statement at the bottom of the page. Then, you will sign and date the document and submit it to the employee.

Next, an employee at the test center will call your name. You will be asked to pose for a photograph in order to ensure that you are the person who signed up to take the test (this photo will appear on the paper copy of your score report). At this point, the employee will return your identification document. The employee will also give you two pencils and several sheets of blank paper for notes. You may be asked to show the employee the insides of your pockets to verify that you are not taking any unauthorized materials into the test room. Then, an employee will escort you to the computer on which you will be taking the test.

Screen-by-Screen Process

1. **Confirmation of Identity:** On the first screen, you will see your name and the photo taken of you before you entered the test room. Before you proceed, you must confirm that the information is correct.

2. **Copyright Screen:** The next screen contains copyright information about the TOEFL test materials. To proceed, click "Continue."

3. **Test Introduction:** You will see a screen that contains general information about the test, including:

   - a general description of the TOEFL test.
   - a short description of all four parts of the test.
   - timing guidelines.

   Once you have finished reading the introduction, click "Continue" to proceed to the next screen.

4. **Test Rules:** The next screen will describe the test policies. Be sure that you read the rules carefully and that you understand them, as breaking any of the rules may result in cancellation of your scores and the loss of your test fee. Click "Continue" when you've read and understood the rules.

5. **Confidentiality Statement:** You will see a confidentiality agreement on the next screen. The confidentiality agreement states that you will not share information about the test, such as passages or questions, with anyone. Read the statement carefully. By clicking "Continue" on this screen, you are agreeing to the terms of the confidentiality statement.

6. **Headset Instructions:** On the following screen, you will be instructed to put on your headset. The headset includes noise-canceling headphones and a microphone. You are allowed to wear the headset throughout the entire test.

xii

7. **Microphone Adjustment:** Next, you will see a screen that gives you instructions on how to adjust your microphone. You will be asked to speak a response to the following sentence: *Describe the city that you live in.* Please note that this portion is not graded and is used only to adjust your microphone. Just be sure to speak clearly and in your normal speaking voice.

You will continue to speak until a window appears that says the following: *Success: Your microphone is functioning properly.*

If your microphone adjustment is not successful, readjust the microphone so that it is closer to your mouth and try again. If you continue having problems adjusting your microphone, raise your hand to get help from an employee at the test center.

Section Screens

At the beginning of each section, you will see a screen that gives you directions about that particular section. Please note that the on-screen tools will vary according to the section. For more information about the screen-by-screen process for each section, see the *Overviews* and *Walk-throughs* for the different question types.

On-screen Tools

Throughout the test, you will have access to a number of on-screen tools. The tools vary slightly by section. For example, in the reading section, you will have a button that allows you to review your answers. In the listening section, you will have buttons that allow you to confirm your answers before you proceed. For more information about the specific on-screen tools, please see the *Overview* for each section.

"Help" Button

During the reading and listening sections, you will see a "Help" button on the toolbar at the top of the screen. By clicking on the "Help" button, you will be given:

» instructions for using the on-screen tools.

» instructions for marking your answers.

» section directions.

» test directions.

Please note that when you access the "Help" materials, the clock will keep running. If you must refer to these materials, be sure to do so quickly or you may waste precious time.

About the Break

After you've finished with the listening section, you are required to take a 10-minute break. The break screen will appear on the monitor. At this time, you may leave the test room. You will have to take your identification document with you. When you leave the test room, be sure to notify the test-center employee. You may be required to sign out during the break.

When you are ready to return to the test room, you will have to show the test-center employee the contents of your pockets once again. You may also have to sign back in. Then, the test-center employee will escort you back to your seat and unlock the screen so you can continue the test.

Please note that while you are allowed to use the bathroom at any point during the test, the clock will <u>not</u> stop unless it is your designated break time. Therefore, to ensure that you have enough time to finish each section, it is wise to leave the test room only during the break.

When You're Done

1. **Score Reporting:** After you've completed the final task of the writing section, you will see the score-reporting screen, which will give you the option of reporting or canceling your scores. If you choose to cancel the scores, you will not be able to see your scores. Furthermore, you will not receive a refund of the test fee.

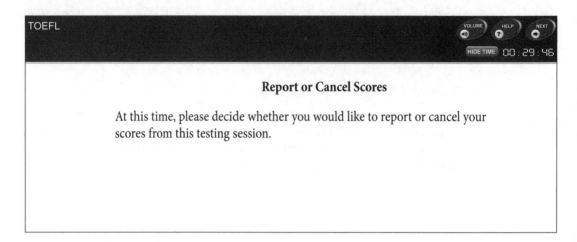

2. **Checking Out**: When you are finished, you may leave the test room. Be sure to bring your notepaper, pencils, and personal identification document. The test-center employee will take back the pencils and notepaper. You will sign out and indicate the time that you finished the test. Then, you can get your personal belongings from the storage area and leave the test center.

Overview of the Listening Section

The listening section is the second part of the TOEFL test. It tests your ability to understand spoken English by presenting you with a series of listening passages and then asking you a set of questions based on each listening passage.

QUICK GUIDE: TOEFL® Test Listening Section

Definition	The listening section tests your comprehension of English lectures and conversations. The section includes different types of listening passages spoken by native speakers. Some passages are about academic topics, while others are about experiences that a student may encounter on campus.
Targeted Skills	In order to do well on the listening section, you must be able to: • understand basic academic vocabulary. • identify a speaker's meaning based on intonation and tone. • take good notes. • answer questions within the given time (for more information about question types, see page 13).
The Listening Passages	The listening section includes between six and nine listening passages. A typical listening section consists of six listening passages, which you hear through your headset. (Please note that, on some occasions, the testing company ETS will include three additional pieces of sample material. This sample material is not scored. However, since you will not know which passages are sample materials, you should try your best on <u>all</u> of the passages.) There are three different types of passages in the listening section: academic lectures, office hours conversations, and service encounter conversations (for more information about passage types, see pages 4–5). Each passage is between three and seven minutes long, and you will hear each passage only once.
Questions	There are five or six questions per listening passage. After an academic lecture, you will answer six questions. After office hours and service conversations, you will answer five questions. The questions usually fall into the following categories: • Main Idea • Function • Detail • Attitude • Purpose • Organization • Inference • Connecting content
Timing	You will have **20 minutes** to answer the questions for a set of six listening passages; however, the clock will <u>not</u> run while you are listening to the passages. In other words, no time will be deducted while you are listening to the lectures / conversations. The entire section, including listening time, takes approximately **60–90 minutes** to complete.

Listening Section: What You'll See and Hear

On-Screen Tools

In the listening section, the information on the computer screen is slightly different than in other parts of the test. Study the sample screen below to familiarize yourself with the on-screen tools for the listening section.

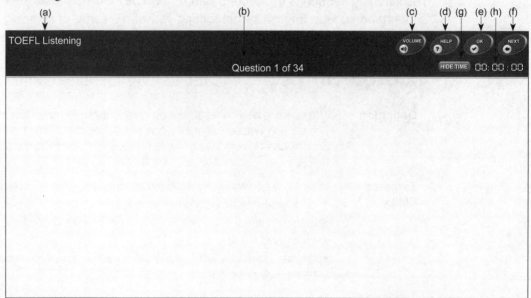

(a) indicates what **section of the test** you are currently working on

(b) shows how many of the **questions** you have **completed** in the section

(c) allows you to **adjust the volume** of the listening passages. When you click on this button, you will be able to move a slider up or down to increase or decrease the volume.

(d) allows you to **get important information** about the section. Keep in mind that the clock will continue to count down if you click on this button.

(e) is used to **confirm your answer**. You will make your answer choice on the screen and then click on this button to proceed to the next question (see *f*). Remember, once you go to the next question, you <u>cannot</u> go back to previous questions.

(f) is used to **move on to the next question**. You cannot proceed until you have confirmed your answer choice by clicking on the "OK" button (see *e*).

(g) allows you to hide / view the countdown clock

(h) shows how much time is left to answer the questions

Screen-by-Screen Process

In the listening section, you will see a number of screens. By familiarizing yourself with the screens and the instructions, you will know exactly what to do on the day of the test.

1. Instructions: First, you will see an instruction screen that gives you general information about the section, including the contents of the section, how much time is allotted for answering questions, instructions for marking your answers, etc. In addition to reading the information on the screen, the narrator will read the instructions. You must wait until the narrator has finished reading the instructions before you are allowed to move on to the next screen.

2. Preparation screen: Once the section begins, the narrator will tell you to prepare for the listening passage. The following message will appear on the screen: *Now get ready to listen.*

3. Listening: The lecture / conversation will start. As you listen, a picture of a university setting will appear on your screen (the picture will vary according to passage type). A blue bar on the bottom center part of the screen marks the progress of the passage. For example, if half of the bar is blue, the listening passage is half over. Use this bar to gauge how much time is left in the listening passage.

4. Transition to the questions: After the conversation is done, the narrator will instruct you to prepare to answer the questions. The following message will appear on the screen: *Now get ready to answer the questions. You may use your notes to help you answer.*

5. Questions: Then, the narrator will read the question. After the narrator has given the question, it will appear on your screen, along with the answer options. To mark the answer, click on the circle you want to choose. The circle will turn dark when it has been selected. To deselect a choice, click on the circle again. You must select an answer option to continue. After selecting an answer option, click on the "OK" button that appears at the top right part of the screen to confirm your answer. Then, click on the "Next" button to proceed to the next question. <u>Remember, you cannot go back to previous questions after you click "Next," so be careful when using it!</u>

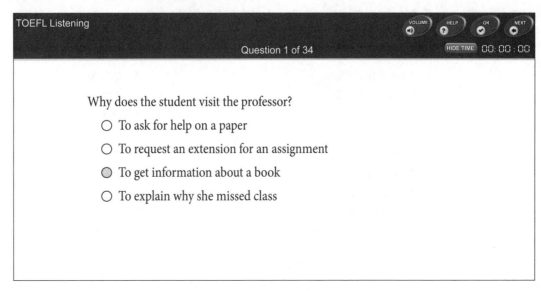

In the listening section, there are three types of listening passages: office hours conversations, service encounter conversations, and academic lectures. Each passage type differs in terms of content.

Office Hours Conversations   Office hours conversations typically focus on topics that may come up in a conversation between a student and a professor. In North American universities, office hours are a set time during which professors meet with students in order to answer questions or discuss school-related matters.

The office hours conversations on the TOEFL test last between five and seven minutes. There is <u>always</u> at least one office hours conversation per listening comprehension test. Topics vary and may include:

- discussions of paper topics or assignments.
- inquiries for more information on or clarification of a concept introduced in class.
- requests for letters of recommendation or career advice.

Service Encounters   Meanwhile, service encounter conversations deal with issues that a student at a North American university may experience in a number of on-campus situations. Service encounter passages are conversations that occur between a university student and an employee of the university. The employee may work in any of the following departments:

- housing
- student life
- registrar
- financial aid
- campus security
- career services
- library

The service encounter conversations on the TOEFL test last between five and seven minutes. There is <u>always</u> at least one service encounter conversation per TOEFL test. The topics of service encounter conversations are not academic; rather, they deal with issues that a student may experience while at a university. Sample topics of service encounter passages include:

- getting a new roommate
- joining a club
- adding or dropping a class
- learning about scholarships
- reporting a lost item
- advice for finding an on-campus job
- reserving a book at the library

Academic Lectures   Finally, academic lectures focus on academic topics that draw from a variety of academic subjects. These listening passages are similar to lectures given by professors that students might encounter in university classrooms. The topics for academic lectures are drawn from a wide range of academic subjects, including:

- anthropology
- archaeology
- art history
- astronomy
- botany
- biology
- education
- engineering
- environmental science
- history
- geology
- geography
- literature
- music
- paleontology
- photography
- psychology
- sociology
- urban studies

There are four to six academic lectures in the listening section. The academic lectures can be further classified into three types: professors' lectures, integrated lectures, and in-class discussions. The main distinction between each type is the amount of student interaction. See the table below for more information on each type of academic lecture.

Professors' Lectures	Integrated Lectures	In-class Discussions
Professor talks 100% of the time.	Professor talks 75% of the time. Students may ask questions or provide brief answers to the professor's questions, but the bulk of the content is spoken by the professor.	Professor and two students have roughly the same amount of talking time. In this type of discussion, students often address each other in addition to speaking to the professor.

Challenges and Solutions

» **CHALLENGE 1: "I don't know a lot of the words that I hear in the audio recordings or see in the questions."**

SOLUTION: Expand your vocabulary. The TOEFL test content focuses mainly on academic contexts. There are several word lists available that present the most common words found in academic settings. The Academic Word List (AWL), developed by Averil Coxhead, is a list of 570 words that are commonly included in introductory college texts. Getting to know these words will likely help you perform better on the test and prepare for entering English-language courses.

SOLUTION: Listen for definitions when you hear a word you don't know. When a specific term is introduced, the professor will <u>always</u> define the word in the lecture.

SOLUTION: Use the context, words, or phrases around unknown words in recording, questions, or answer options to help you figure out meaning. In the listening section, speakers will often provide a number of meaning clues for the definitions of key terms. See the table below for common ways that speakers give context clues for key terms. To practice, try listening to English-language news programs. Announcers often make the meaning of new terms clear by using these types of clues.

Ways of Giving Context Clues			
Repetition	**Rewording**	**Definition Signposts**	**Giving Examples**
The speaker will repeat a key term several times in the same paragraph.	The speaker will often reword a phrase so that the meaning of a term is clearer. A rewording often includes the following phrases: • *By that, I mean . . .* • *What I'm talking about here is . . .* • *In other words . . .*	Speakers use certain terms to introduce a definition, including: • *This refers to . . .* • *This means . . .* • *That's a . . .* • *I think a definition is in order here.*	In order to clarify a definition, speakers will give examples. Listen for the following phrases for examples: • *like* • *such as* • *you know*
Example	**Example**	**Example**	**Example**
Animals use <u>camouflage</u> to protect themselves from predators. An animal might blend in with the background, and that's <u>camouflage</u>.	*Why do companies <u>vet</u> new hires? I mean, why do they <u>perform background checks and check out the potential employee's history</u>?*	*It's a matter of agency. <u>I think a definition is in order here.</u> Agency is people's ability to make choices that will influence their futures.*	*Engaging in <u>recreational activities, such as jogging or playing an instrument</u>, has been shown to reduce stress levels.*

» **CHALLENGE 2: "I get lost as I listen to lecture portions of the listening test."**

SOLUTION: The lectures in the listening section of the TOEFL test are typically between five and seven minutes long. Sometimes it's difficult to stay focused throughout the test. One way to avoid problems with this is to learn the organizational structure of TOEFL listening passages. If you understand how each passage is generally structured, you will be able to better predict what type of information will be included in the lecture and where this information will appear in the lecture. If you lose concentration while listening, you just have to think about how the passage is structured in order to get back on track. Note that nearly all of the academic lectures in the TOEFL listening section follow one of the following common organizational structures:

- definition
- compare and contrast
- process
- classification
- theory / support
- pros and cons (advantages and disadvantages)
- cause and effect

For more information about the organizational structures of listening passages, see page 52. To practice, try listening to some of the lectures on the audio for this book. See if you can identify what types of structures they are.

SOLUTION: Listen for signposts. A signpost is a word or phrase that is used to signal a specific type of information in a listening passage. For example, some signposts signal the introduction of a new topic (e.g., *On another note . . .*), while others signal the definition of a key term (e.g., *By that, I mean . . .*). By listening for signposts, you can get a better sense of what is happening in the lecture, which will help you become focused again. For more information on specific types of signposts and for practice identifying them, see the Get It Right pages. To practice, listen to a recording of a lecture from this book and write down all the signpost words you hear. Then, check your notes against the script. How many did you notice?

SOLUTION: Recognize what information is important and what is not. During a listening passage, speakers often digress, or talk about information that is not directly related to the main topic of the lecture or conversation. If you get lost while you are listening, recognizing digressions will help you refocus on the important information. See the table below for words and expressions that are often used to introduce digressions.

Expressions that Signal Digressions
Now, this won't be on the test, but it's interesting to think about.
You don't have to write this down, but consider that . . .
Just as an aside, I want you all to know that . . .
This is only somewhat related, but . . .
It doesn't really make a difference to what we're discussing today, but don't you think that . . . ?
Don't let this confuse you, because it doesn't really apply to what we're talking about today.
This may be oversimplified, but for the purposes of today's lecture, it's really all you need to know about X.

» **CHALLENGE 3: "I don't always understand the conversations in the audio recordings—there's so much back and forth and corrections and other stuff."**

SOLUTION: Like written English, spoken English is vital to communication. However, unlike written language, spoken language is more informal and includes interruptions, mispronunciations, repetition, clarifications, pauses, intonation changes to make a point, etc. The listening passages on the TOEFL test are authentic-sounding lectures and conversations and include many common features of spoken language.

Try listening to the audio passages in this book and notice features like interruptions, misspeaks, and repetitions. These features are included in order to make the listening passages sound more natural. By noting and understanding how speakers use these features, you will become more accustomed to the flow of the listening passages on the TOEFL test.

	Common Features of Spoken English		
	Interruptions	**Misspeaks / Corrections**	**Repetition**
Examples	*Pardon me . . .*	*Now, their meaning is entirely explicit—or rather, entirely implicit.*	*OK, this is important.*
	Wait, but what about . . . ?		*Let me say that again.*
	A: So you're a junior and— *B: A senior, actually.*	*Another difference between the two animals is that salamanders—sorry, I mean lizards—can live in a much drier environment.*	*Did you get that?*

Common Features of Spoken English		
Interruptions	**Misspeaks / Corrections**	**Repetition**
Typically, if someone interrupts another person, the information is important. For example, a person might interrupt the other speaker to give correct or updated information.	When a speaker misspeaks, be sure to write down the correction, since answer options for detail questions are often based on these.	Repeated information is often tested on the TOEFL test. If you hear repeated information, write it down in your notes.

(Notes)

SOLUTION: Get used to the flow of native English by exposing yourself to as much natural English as possible. The more exposure you have to native English speech, the more you'll understand the native English used on the TOEFL test. Ways for increasing your exposure to spoken English include:

- watching TV shows or movies. The TV shows don't have to be educational—comedies and dramas include great examples of natural spoken English. While you watch, note how people often interrupt others, correct themselves after making a mistake, or quickly change topics. If you find this difficult, try renting movies with subtitles. Listening can be easier when you can read to check understanding.

- joining an English-language speaking club. You might find that your university, local library, or community center has one. By joining, you will not only be able to practice speaking English, you will also have the opportunity to hear native speakers and take part in natural conversations.

» **CHALLENGE 4: "There's too much information to remember!"**

SOLUTION: During the TOEFL test, you will listen to the passage first and then see the questions one at a time. The listening passages may include a lot of information, but remember that you are allowed to take notes during this portion of the test. Because of this, it's important to develop your note-taking skills. Taking notes during the lectures / conversations will force you to listen carefully and help you remember important information that you'll need to answer the questions. Of course, you won't be able to write down <u>all</u> that you hear, but using the following note-taking strategies will help you write down the most important information.

- Use abbreviations. You won't have enough time to write everything out, so be sure to use shorter forms whenever possible. Also, use abbreviations that make sense to you—it won't matter if you write something down if you don't remember what it means. See the table below for tips for abbreviations. Then, practice writing down things you hear using abbreviations, but remember to be sure you understand what they mean!

Abbreviation Tip	**Examples**
Use numerals instead of writing out numbers.	one, two, three, etc. → 1, 2, 3, etc.
Leave the vowels out of words.	conversation, forest, novel → cnvrstn, frst, nvl
Use symbols instead of words.	Jane and Jack → Jane + Jack Jane or Jack → Jane / Jack everyone except Jack → everyone -Jack the numbers increased → the #s ↑ eight-hundred dollars → $800 fifty percent → 50% at → @

Abbreviation Tip	Examples	
Use common abbreviations.	without → w/o	because → b/c
	within → w/in	before → b4
	approximately → approx.	example → ex.
	et cetera → etc.	regarding → re

- During the lectures, some key words might appear on whiteboards—just like the kind you see in classrooms—on your screen. Write down terms that appear on the whiteboard. While you usually won't be tested on the definition of these terms, they may be related to important ideas, so having them in your notes will be useful.

- Make note of information that is emphasized by the speaker. Be sure to mark in your notes which speaker made the comments. Speakers often emphasize information by changing their tone. In other cases, information may be emphasized by the amount of time that is spent talking about one subject. In either case, be sure to underline that information in your notes so you know that it was emphasized.

- Organize your notes as you write. It can be very helpful to write down the following words and use them as headings:

  - Main Idea
  - Detail 1
  - Support
  - Detail 2
  - Support

Then, if you leave room beneath each of the above points, you can write down supporting details under them later. By organizing your notes well, you will be able to look at them and understand how the lecture / conversation was organized. Furthermore, it might be helpful to keep a log of the notes you take while doing the activities in this book. Later, you can review them and look for ways to better organize your notes.

» **CHALLENGE 5: "I don't always understand the speakers. Sometimes they talk too fast."**

SOLUTION: The speakers in the listening passages on the TOEFL test are native speakers of English. Differences in pronunciation and speed reflect the way that native speakers of English actually talk. There are many common English reductions that you may hear on the TOEFL test. Reductions are shortened forms of certain word combinations that omit sounds or blend two or more words. Reductions are very common in the listening passages of the TOEFL test, so make sure you know how they are formed. Study the table below for common reductions. You can practice by listening to audio passages from this book and noticing the reductions. Are some harder than others to understand? Focus on them, and listen as many times as it takes for the meanings to become clear.

Common Reductions on the Listening Section	
Who did you go to the movies with?	→ _Whodja_ go to the movies with?
What did you do that for?	→ _Whatdja_ do that for?
When did you finish?	→ _Whendja_ finish?
Where did you get those shoes?	→ _Wheredja_ get those shoes?
How did you do on the test?	→ _Howdja_ do on the test?
How have you been doing?	→ _Howvya_ been doing?
Don't you like _him_?	→ _Doncha_ like _'im_?
Did you talk to _her_?	→ _Didja_ talk to _'er_?
What are you _going to_ do?	→ What are you _gonna_ do?
How _about_ this one?	→ How _'bout_ this one?
I'm _trying to_ finish my homework.	→ I'm _tryna_ finish my homework.
A lot of people were there.	→ _Alotta_ people were there.
I _don't know_.	→ I _dunno_.
I've _got to_ go now.	→ I've _gotta_ go now.
Could you help me with this?	→ _Couldja_ help me with this?

SOLUTION: Download some English-language podcasts or radio programs that you can store on your computer. At first, practice listening to only a minute or two of the program at a time. As your comprehension improves, increase the listening time to seven minutes, the maximum time limit for any one TOEFL listening passage. When you listen, focus on understanding the speakers' pronunciation throughout the entire program. Listen to the programs as many times as you need to until you understand the main ideas.

SOLUTION: If possible, purchase a digital recording device with variable-speed playback capabilities. Using a variable-speed digital recorder, you can record English-language radio broadcasts, television shows, and podcasts. At first, you can play back this media at a slow speed. As your comprehension level increases, you can increase the playback speed until you are listening to the broadcasts at their original speed.

» **CHALLENGE 6: "None of the answer options "feels" right. It's as if the lecture and the answer options are not related."**

SOLUTION: The writers of the TOEFL test are looking to see if you can understand and interpret what is said, how it is said, and what it may or may not mean. Therefore, it's important to understand how correct answer options are created so you will be able to identify the correct option more easily. One extremely common feature of correct answer options on the TOEFL test is the rewording of key information. Basically, a correct answer option will <u>always</u> contain key words that you've heard in the lecture / conversation. However, the correct answer option typically mixes up the information and doesn't contain the exact wording from the listening passage. In other words, the correct answer option will include paraphrased information from the listening passage. Information in answer options may be paraphrased by:

- changing out key content words (using synonyms).
- including general information about a concept that is described in detail in the listening.
- changing the voice of the information from passive to active (or vice versa) in the answer option (e.g., The boy <u>hit</u> the ball. vs. The ball <u>was hit</u> by the boy.). The passive voice is formed by using a form of the verb _be_ + past participle.

Study the table below for specific examples of how paraphrasing may be used on the TOEFL test. If you want to practice, after you complete an activity in this book, try to identify the paraphrase types used in some of the answer options. This may help you improve your ability to recognize correct and incorrect answers.

Paraphrase Type	You'll Hear This in the Lecture:	You'll See a Question Like This:	You'll See Answer Options Like This:
Changes to Content Words	*The bengal scampered swiftly.*	How did the tiger run?	Fast (✓) Slowly (✗)
Specific to General	*OK, you'll just need to tell me your mailing address, date of birth, and student ID number.*	What does the clerk ask for?	Some personal information (✓) A change of address form (✗)
Voice Changes	*The make up exam was given by the TA on Friday.*	What happened at the end of the week?	The students retook the test. (✓) The TA took the test again. (✗)

(✓) correct answer option
(✗) incorrect answer option

SOLUTION: Use a process of elimination. Read each answer option carefully and draw a line through those that contain:

- information that states the opposite of the facts and details presented in the passage.
- information that does <u>not</u> answer the question.
- the exact wording from the passage. Remember, the correct answer typically paraphrases information from the passage, so an answer option that includes the same wording is probably incorrect.

SOLUTION: Don't spend too much time answering any one question. Remember, you have only 20 minutes to answer all of the questions in the listening section. Therefore, if you aren't certain of an answer, select whatever answer option you feel is the most appealing and move on to the next question.

Overview of Question Types on the Listening Section

Question Type	Description	Frequency Per Listening Passage
Main Idea	Asks you to identify the main idea of the lecture.	1 (typically with academic lectures only)
Detail	Asks you about factual information presented in the lecture / conversation.	1–2
Purpose	Asks you about the purpose of the conversation as a whole.	1 (typically with conversations only)
Inference	Asks you to draw a conclusion based on information presented in the lecture / conversation.	0–1
Function	Asks you about why the speaker has said something in particular.	0–1
Attitude	Asks you about the speaker's opinion.	0–1
Organization	Asks you about how the lecture is organized.	0–1 (typically with academic lectures only)
Connecting Content	Asks you to complete a table with information from the lecture / conversation.	0–1

Main Idea Questions

A main idea question asks you to identify the general gist, or main idea, of a lecture or conversation. There is almost always one main idea question per academic lecture, so it's important that you know the keys to answering them.

Main idea questions may be worded as follows:

» *What is the main idea of the lecture / conversation?*

» *What is the professor mainly discussing?*

» *What was the lecture / conversation mostly about?*

» *What problem does the speaker have?*

» *What are the speakers mainly discussing?*

QUICK GUIDE: Main Idea Questions

Definition	Main idea questions ask you about the gist, or general theme, of a lecture / conversation. They are based on the main topic of an <u>entire</u> lecture / conversation, not just detailed parts or sections.
Targeted Skills	In order to correctly answer a main idea question, you must be able to: • listen for the most important ideas in the passage. • distinguish between main ideas and minor details. • generalize the information presented in the entire lecture / conversation.
The Correct Answer	The correct answer for a main idea question accurately reflects the most important idea of the lecture / conversation. The correct answer will <u>not</u> include minor details.
Wrong Answer Options	Watch out for answer options that include: • minor details from the passage. This information may be factual but does not represent the main idea of the entire passage. • information that contradicts the information given in the lecture / conversation. • exact wording from the audio script. The correct answer usually rewords the information found in the audio script. Remember, the testers are interested in checking your comprehension of the ideas, not your ability to recognize phrases that you've heard.

WALK THROUGH: Main Idea Questions

Below is a sample script and sample main idea question for a test item based on part of a lecture in a history class. While you listen, underline words in the script that you think might indicate what the main idea of the lecture is. 🎧 CD1, Track 2

SAMPLE SCRIPT ▶
for reference only, not available in test

Professor: OK, everybody . . . so last time, we talked about the Columbian Exchange. As I mentioned earlier, this term is named for Christopher Columbus, the explorer who sailed from Spain to the Americas. His contact with the Americas in . . . uh . . . 1492 marked the beginning of the European colonization of the Americas. Anyway, who can tell us what the Columbian Exchange was?

Student 1: Wasn't it . . . um . . . it was the exchanges between cultures that started taking place after Columbus reached the Americas?

Professor: Yes, that's right. OK . . . well, as you may remember, we also discussed the negative effects of the Columbian Exchange. But let's put those negative effects aside for today. See, there was something we didn't get to talk about in class last time: the advantages of the Columbian Exchange. That's what we'll be addressing today. One advantage that comes to mind is the exchange of animals. See, when Columbus arrived, most of the original inhabitants in the Americas didn't have beasts of burden.

Student 1: Like donkeys and horses?

Professor: Yes. These animals were important because they are able to do, um, hard work, like carry heavy materials. Their introduction made life easier for the peoples of the Americas. OK, and that's just one thing . . . now let's continue with some others.

History and the Columbian Exchange

Glossary:

€ POWERED BY COBUILD

colonize: to go and live in and take control of a place

exchange: to give something to each other

Now look at the sample main idea question below. Review the parts of the script that you underlined above to choose the best answer.

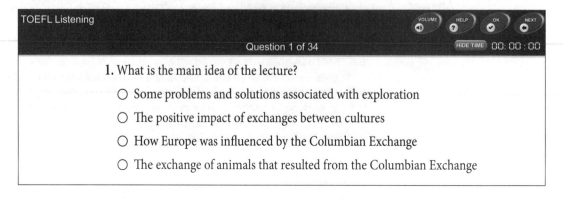

TOEFL Listening

Question 1 of 34

1. What is the main idea of the lecture?

○ Some problems and solutions associated with exploration

○ The positive impact of exchanges between cultures

○ How Europe was influenced by the Columbian Exchange

○ The exchange of animals that resulted from the Columbian Exchange

GET IT RIGHT: Tips and Tasks for Answering Correctly

» **TIP 1: Listen carefully to the beginning of the lecture / conversation.** The main idea of a lecture / conversation may appear anywhere, but it typically appears within the first minute of the audio track.

TASK 1: Underline the introduction of the main idea in the lecture on page 14.

» **TIP 2: Listen for lecture style markers.** The correct answer for main idea questions usually reflects the style of the lecture, e.g., advantages / disadvantages of something, steps in a process, etc. The table below shows several lecture styles and common key words and expressions you might hear in them.

Lecture Style	Common Key Words and Expressions
Pros / cons	the **advantages** / **disadvantages** of . . . the **positive** / **negative** influence of . . . ways that X **positively** / **negatively** impacted Y
Compare and Contrast	**similarities** / **differences** between X and Y a **comparison** of . . .
Process	the **development** / **formation** / **steps** / **ways to** . . . [do something] a **method** for . . . / a **process** of . . . [doing something]
Cause and Effect	the **cause** / **basis** / **purpose** / **source** of . . . the **effect** / **result** / **outcome** of . . . the **consequences** of . . .
Definition	a **theory** about . . . / **problems** with . . . / **solutions** for . . .
Classification	various **types** of . . . / the **kinds** of . . . / different **forms** of . . .

TASK 2: Circle three key words or expressions that indicate the style of the lecture on page 14. What lecture style is it?

» **TIP 3: Listen for main idea signpost words.** Listen for certain expressions that speakers use to introduce the main idea of a lecture, as noted in the table below.

Main Idea Signposts	
What I want to talk about today is . . .	What we really need to discuss today is . . .
Today, we'll be discussing . . .	The point we'll be addressing today is . . .
Today's lecture will focus on . . .	So today, we'll look into . . .

TASK 3: Double underline one signpost that indicates a main idea in the lecture on page 14.

» **TIP 4: Watch out for distracter topics!** Distracting information is often included in the beginning of the lecture / conversation. This may include the topics of previous lectures or explanations of terms.

TASK 4: Name one distracter topic mentioned in the first few lines of the lecture on page 14.

» **TIP 5: Eliminate answer options about minor points.** Correct answers are based on the <u>entire</u> lecture / conversation. Reject answer options that focus on secondary points or minor details.

TASK 5: Draw a line through one answer option on page 14 that focuses on a minor point.

» **TIP 6: Check the language in the answer options against your notes.** The correct answer is often reworded information. Carefully study any answer option that includes the exact same language before choosing it.

TASK 6: Which answer option on page 14 rewords the introduction of the main idea from the lecture?

Detail Questions

A detail question asks you about factual information presented in a conversation or lecture. There are typically no more than two detail questions per conversation / lecture. You'll find detail questions for both academic lectures and conversations.

Detail questions may be worded as *Wh-* questions like the following:

» *According to the professor, **what** is true about X?*

» ***Who** was responsible for . . . ?*

» ***Why** was X important?*

» ***How** does X affect Y?*

» ***Where** did X occur?*

QUICK GUIDE: Detail Questions

Definition	Detail questions ask about important facts presented in the lecture that support the main points of the lecture. You will <u>never</u> be asked about a trivial fact, such as the spelling of a name or the exact year that something occurred. You will, however, need to know the definitions of key terms and the order of events.
Targeted Skills	In order to correctly answer a detail question, you must be able to: • identify the main points of the lecture / conversation and the details used to support them. Often, detail questions relate directly to the main gist of the lecture / conversation. However, in some cases, you will be asked about details of secondary points as well. • understand the relationships between two events or concepts. Is one caused by the other? Did one occur after the other? Is one more important than the other?
The Correct Answer	The correct answer for a detail question contains factual information that was presented in the lecture / conversation. Correct answers typically contain reworded information from the lecture / conversation. For some questions, you may need to choose <u>two</u> correct answers. For questions with five answer options, you may need to choose <u>three</u> correct answers.
Wrong Answer Options	Watch out for answer options that include: • information that contradicts the information from the lecture / conversation. • the exact wording from the audio script but that don't answer the question. (The correct answer usually rewords the information. Sometimes distracters use exact wording but don't give the correct information.) • information that is <u>not</u> mentioned or supported by the lecture / conversation.

WALK THROUGH: Detail Questions

Below is a sample script and sample detail question for a test item based on part of a lecture in an art class. While you listen, underline words and phrases in the script that you think might be important details. 🎧 CD1, Track 3

SAMPLE SCRIPT ▶
for reference only, not available in test

Professor: Another type of art that emerged in the early twentieth century is kinetic art. "Kinetic" means "moving." So it makes sense that kinetic art is an art object with moving parts. Let me give you an example. All of you know what a mobile is, right? It's . . . um . . . a structure that often hangs from ceilings. And the components of the structure are meant to move freely in the air. A lot of people hang them . . . um . . . in nurseries to entertain their babies. Anyway, because the parts of the mobile are meant to move, it's an example of kinetic art. So this is important, now . . . basically, kinetic art is any type of art that depends on movement in order to achieve its full effect, right?

OK, so . . . a lot of people argue that the first piece of kinetic art was created by a French artist named Marcel Duchamp. In 1913, he created a sculpture called *Bicycle Wheel.* And this piece was basically a bicycle wheel mounted on a stool. What you would do is go up to it and spin the wheel. Duchamp described the experience of viewing the spinning wheel as an excellent distraction. In fact, he compared it to viewing a fire in a fireplace. You don't really have to know that much about that, but I found it interesting. So, uh, let's move on . . .

Glossary:

€ POWERED BY COBUILD

mount: to fix something firmly to something else

distraction: something intended to entertain and amuse

Now look at the sample detail question below. Review the parts of the script that you underlined above to choose the best answer.

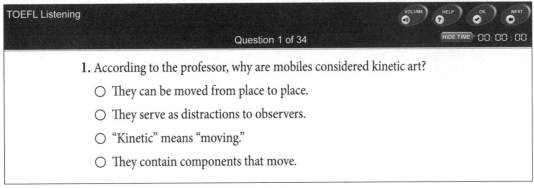

TOEFL Listening

Question 1 of 34

HIDE TIME 00:00:00

1. According to the professor, why are mobiles considered kinetic art?
   ○ They can be moved from place to place.
   ○ They serve as distractions to observers.
   ○ "Kinetic" means "moving."
   ○ They contain components that move.

17

GET IT RIGHT: Tips and Tasks for Answering Correctly

» **TIP 1: Listen for repeated information.** Many detail questions are based on information that the professor repeats several times. Pay attention to any repeated ideas or definitions, and make sure to write them down in your notes.

TASK 1: Underline one word or idea that is repeated more than once in the lecture on page 17. What word or idea is the most often repeated?

» **TIP 2: Listen for expressions that introduce details.** Certain expressions are used by speakers to introduce details. Some of these expressions are listed in the table below.

Expressions for Important Details	Expressions for Minor Details
This is important . . .	*Now, this isn't so important, but it's interesting.*
You might want to write this down.	*You won't be tested on this, but you might be interested to know that . . .*
It's really important that you understand . . .	*You don't really need to know about that.*

TASK 2: Circle three key words or expressions that introduce important or minor details in the lecture on page 17.

» **TIP 3: Watch out for exact word matches!** Correct answers for detail questions usually contain reworded information from the lecture / conversation. Be cautious about answer options that contain the exact wording from the lecture / conversation—they may not include the information that the question is asking for.

TASK 3: Which answer option on page 17 contains exact wording from the lecture but doesn't answer the question?

TEST TIP!

Be sure to take as many notes as possible while listening during the test. You won't see the questions until after you've heard the conversation / lecture, so you need to get as much information as you can for reference!

» **TIP 4: Make guesses related to the main idea if you're unsure.** Detail questions are often asked about supporting details for main points. If you are stuck, choosing the answer option that coincides with the main idea of the lecture / conversation might be a good guessing strategy. (See page 13 for more about finding main ideas.)

TASK 4: Which answer option on page 17 is most closely related to the main topic of the lecture, kinetic art?

PROGRESSIVE PRACTICE: Get Ready

A Listen to part of a discussion in a music class and check (✓) the points written in the notes below as you hear them. 🎧 CD1, Track 4

- History of the piano
    - ☐ Invented in early 1700s by B. Cristofori in Italy
    - ☐ At 1ˢᵗ, only royals had $ to buy them
    - ☐ 1800s > more common in wealthy and ↑ mid-class households b/c wider dist. of wealth throughout Eu.

- What did piano rep. in Eu cultures?
    - ☐ Status symbols: $ and education; parents paid for lessons
    - ☐ In-home entertainment: no radios, TV, comp., so families made music tog.; pop. of 4-hand piano

B Review the questions. What kinds of questions are they? Then, answer the questions. Note the correct answers and read why the answer options are correct or incorrect.

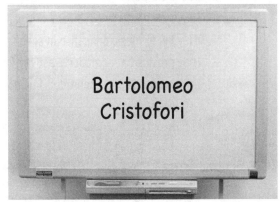

Bartolomeo Cristofori

1. What aspect of pianos does the professor mainly discuss in the lecture?
    - ○ The role of the piano in European society
    - ○ The importance of the piano in Western music
    - ○ Differences between early and modern pianos
    - ○ Reasons for the high cost of early pianos

ANSWER ANALYSIS ▶

Question Type: **Main Idea**
- ✓ **At the beginning of the lecture, the professor mentions that the assigned reading was about the history of the piano. The main points of the lecture show what the piano represented in European society.**
- ✗ The lecture focuses on events in the West (throughout Europe) but does not deal specifically with Western music.
- ✗ He says that early pianos were expensive but does not make comparisons between early pianos and modern pianos.
- ✗ The high cost of early pianos is mentioned briefly in the lecture, but it is not the main idea of the lecture.

2. According to the professor, what is true about early pianos?
    - ○ They did not have keyboards.
    - ○ They were extremely expensive.
    - ○ They replaced the harpsichord.
    - ○ They were meant to be played by royalty.

ANSWER ANALYSIS ▶

Question Type: **Detail**
- ✗ The professor says that <u>both</u> harpsichords and pianos had keyboards.
- ✓ **The professor states that only royalty could afford pianos because they were very expensive.**
- ✗ While it's true that the harpsichord is less common than the piano, there is no information given to support this.
- ✗ In the lecture, the professor says that only royalty could afford pianos when they were first invented. This does not mean that the piano was invented specifically for royalty.

19

3. According to the professor, what change led to the increased popularity of pianos in the 1800s?

- ○ The price of the materials used to make pianos decreased.
- ○ People stopped regarding pianos as luxury items.
- ○ Individuals in Europe were becoming wealthier.
- ○ Royals encouraged people to learn how to play the piano.

ANSWER ANALYSIS ▶

Question Type: Detail

- ✗ The professor does not indicate that the price of pianos or the materials used to make them decreased.
- ✗ In the lecture, the professor states that pianos were considered luxury items in the 1800s.
- ✓ **He explains that wealth was distributed more during the 1800s, meaning that more people were able to become wealthy.**
- ✗ The professor does not mention the royals' attitudes toward the piano in the lecture.

4. According to the professor, what role did pianos play in European society?

Choose 2 answers.

- ☐ They indicated a family's level of wealth.
- ☐ They led to music education in schools.
- ☐ They provided a recreational activity for families.
- ☐ They helped talented individuals gain wealth.

ANSWER ANALYSIS ▶   NOTE: This is a two-answer detail question. Be sure to choose <u>two</u> answers for this question type.

Question Type: Detail

- ✓ **The student says that the piano was a status symbol, and the professor agrees. He says that having a piano showed a family's wealth and access to education.**
- ✗ The professor says that parents paid instructors to teach children within the home. There is no mention of music education in schools in the lecture.
- ✓ **The professor says that music was a source of entertainment for families. They played the piano for fun.**
- ✗ The professor says that pianos were a symbol of a family's wealth. He does not mention that playing the piano helped individuals become rich.

5. What was an advantage of four-hands piano?

- ○ It allowed family members to play the piano together.
- ○ It let piano players perform complicated pieces.
- ○ It could be played by musicians with different skill levels.
- ○ It made playing the piano more affordable for families.

ANSWER ANALYSIS ▶

Question Type: Detail

- ✓ **The student states that four-hands piano involves two people playing the piano at once. The professor says that "the piano has the power to bring families together and provide in-home entertainment."**
- ✗ Neither the professor nor the students directly say that four-hands piano allows people to play more complicated pieces.
- ✗ The skill of the players when playing four-hands piano is not mentioned in the discussion.
- ✗ There is no information about the added affordability of four-hands piano in the discussion.

PROGRESSIVE PRACTICE: Get Set

A Listen to part of a discussion in a history class. Then, complete the notes below. 🎧 CD1, Track 5

❶ _____ BC - bronze in E. and M.E. for knives, cookware, swords (Bronze Age)

❷ _____ BC - Iron Age

Q: Why shift?

A: ❸ _____ devlp'd tech to make
❹ _____ better than ❺ _____
(stronger, durable, hold edge)

Techniques
1. Iron extraction (smelting) improved
        iron ore = iron + other stuff
        melting pt iron ore = 1500°C > invented hotter furnaces
        that could ❻ _____ iron
2. Pure iron is ❼ _____. Dissolve carbon into iron to create steel (harder than iron): carburization

iron ore
carburization

B Answer the questions. Then, write the letter of each answer option next to the reason why it is correct or incorrect in the *Answer Analysis* box.

1. **What is the discussion mainly about?**

   ○ A comparison of metal use in Europe and the Middle East [A]

   ○ The differences between bronze and iron [B]

   ○ The social history of Europe during the Bronze Age [C]

   ○ Reasons for the transition into the Iron Age [D]

ANSWER ANALYSIS ▶

_____ ✓ **The professor says she wants to focus on why the shift from the Bronze Age to the Iron Age occurred. The rest of the discussion is centered on the technologies that enabled the shift.**

_____ ✗ While the professor mentions aspects of European history, she does not refer to the social history of Europe during the Bronze Age.

_____ ✗ The professor and students talk about ways that bronze and iron are different, but this is a minor point and is not the main idea of the discussion.

_____ ✗ In the discussion, the students mention metal use in Europe and the Middle East but do not make comparisons between the two regions.

2. **According to the professor, what is true about the Iron Age?**

   ○ It occurred in Europe before reaching the Middle East. [A]

   ○ The exact date that it began is unclear. [B]

   ○ People started using bronze only for decorative items during this time. [C]

   ○ Many regions used iron extensively before it started. [D]

ANSWER ANALYSIS ▶

_____ ✗ A student describes some uses for bronze at the beginning of the discussion, but there is no further mention of its uses in the rest of the discussion.

_____ ✓ **After a student gives an approximate date for the start of the Iron Age, the professor says that there's not an exact date for when the Iron Age started.**

_____ ✗ The professor says that in the Iron Age, iron was the most commonly used metal in Europe and the Middle East.

_____ ✗ There is no information in the discussion to support the claim that any region used iron before the Iron Age.

3. According to the professor, why was bronze preferred to early types of iron?

Choose 2 answers.

☐ Tools made from bronze were more durable. [A]

☐ Bronze weapons held their edges better. [B]

☐ Bronze did not rust over time. [C]

☐ Bronze costs more to mine than iron ore. [D]

ANSWER ANALYSIS ▶

_____ ✗ During the discussion, nobody mentions the cost of mining bronze or iron ore.

_____ ✗ There is no mention in the discussion of whether or not bronze rusts.

_____ ✓ **The professor explains that swords made of bronze held a sharp edge longer than early types of iron.**

_____ ✓ **She states that bronze lasted a long time because it was harder than early forms of iron. Thus, it was more durable.**

4. According to the professor, what is true about most naturally occurring metals?

○ They are generally difficult to find. [A]

○ Separating metals from ores requires heat. [B]

○ They are combined with other materials. [C]

○ They have melting points over 1500 degrees Celsius. [D]

ANSWER ANALYSIS ▶

_____ ✗ The professor does not discuss separating ores or the melting point for metals other than iron.

_____ ✓ **The professor says that the majority of metals are typically mixed with other substances.**

_____ ✗ She does not mention that naturally occurring metals are rare or hard to find.

_____ ✗ The melting point of iron—not most naturally occurring metals—is said to be over 1500 degrees Celsius.

5. According to the professor, what limitation did early ironworkers face?

○ Their furnaces did not burn hot enough. [A]

○ They didn't have the tools to mine iron ore. [B]

○ They couldn't measure the melting points for different metals. [C]

○ They lacked the proper techniques for creating iron ore. [D]

ANSWER ANALYSIS ▶

_____ ✗ She does not mention the tools needed in order to mine iron ore.

_____ ✓ **The professor states that the furnaces of early metalworkers could not reach the melting point of iron. When hotter-burning furnaces were invented, ironworkers were able to smelt iron more easily.**

_____ ✗ The professor does not say that measuring melting points for metals presented a challenge for early ironworkers.

_____ ✗ The professor describes iron ore as a substance that occurs naturally. Ironworkers wouldn't need to create iron ore.

PROGRESSIVE PRACTICE: Go for the TOEFL Test

Listen to part of a lecture in a photography class and take notes. 🎧 CD1, Track 6

TOEFL Listening

NOTES:

_____

_____

_____

_____

_____

_____

_____

_____

Now answer the questions. You may use your notes.

1. What is the main topic of the lecture? 🎧 CD1, Track 7
   ○ The origins of the camera obscura
   ○ Different types of early cameras
   ○ The life of Joseph Nicéphore Niépce
   ○ The history of early photography

2. According to the professor, what is true about photography? 🎧 CD1, Track 8
   ○ It was developed to assist painters and sculptors.
   ○ It is a relatively recent art form.
   ○ It was not considered an art form in the past.
   ○ Its invention occurred as a result of an accident.

3. What role did the study of optics play in the development of modern photography? 🎧 CD1, Track 9
   ○ It led to the invention of the camera obscura.
   ○ It gave insight about the power of light.
   ○ It provided a scientific background for artists.
   ○ It helped develop photographic methods.

4. According to the professor, how was the camera obscura improved? 🎧 CD1, Track 10
   Choose 2 answers.
   ☐ It became more portable.
   ☐ It was able to produce color reproductions of scenes.
   ☐ It was modified to produce clearer images.
   ☐ Its walls were altered to prevent the entry of light.

5. According to the professor, what was the significance of Johann Schulze's discovery? 🎧 CD1, Track 11
   ○ It allowed the projection of images outside of a camera obscura.
   ○ It inspired other scientists to combine optics and chemistry.
   ○ It enabled photographers to capture images with light-sensitive material.
   ○ It demonstrated the ability to create light-sensitive images.

6. What was the problem with Wedgwood's photographs?
   🎧 CD1, Track 12
   ○ They were destroyed when exposed to light.
   ○ They took a long time to produce.
   ○ They required expensive materials.
   ○ They could not be reproduced.

Purpose Questions

A purpose question asks about the main purpose of an <u>entire</u> conversation / lecture. Purpose questions are typically asked only about conversations, though they do appear with a lecture on occasion. Expect to see at least one purpose question per conversation.

Purpose questions may be worded as follows:

» *Why does the speaker visit the XX office?*

» *Why does the student go to see the professor?*

» *What is the main purpose of the lecture?*

QUICK GUIDE: Purpose Questions

Definition	A purpose question asks you the reason that a speaker visits a professor or specific office on campus. The <u>entire</u> conversation / lecture will be about this reason and may involve: • solving a problem. • clarifying a process or concept. • explaining a concept from class. • discussing an assignment.
Targeted Skills	In order to correctly answer a purpose question, you must be able to: • understand <u>why</u> the conversation / lecture is taking place. • draw a conclusion about the main reason for the conversation.
The Correct Answer	The correct answer for a purpose question correctly identifies the reason that a conversation is taking place. Usually, the answer is stated directly by the speaker, although sometimes you will have to infer the purpose based on the conversation.
Wrong Answer Options	Watch out for answer options that include: • reasons that are stated early in the conversation. Several purposes may be stated or implied in the conversation. Be sure to choose the one that represents the speaker's real purpose. • the exact wording from the conversation. Usually, the correct answer will include reworded information from the conversation.

WALK THROUGH: Purpose Questions

Below is a sample script and sample purpose question for a test item based on part of a conversation between a student and an astronomy professor. While you listen, underline words in the script that you think might indicate why the student is visiting the professor. 🎧 CD1, Track 13

SAMPLE SCRIPT ▶
for reference only, not available in test

Student: Hi, Professor Stanley. Is this a good time?

Professor: Sure, Samantha. Let me guess . . . you want to know more about dwarf planets? I'm surprised how many people have asked me about it since that lecture.

Student: No . . . actually, I wanted to talk about the final paper.

Professor: Oh, how far along are you? You know, it's due this Friday.

Student: Well, I've already outlined it, but I haven't exactly started writing it yet. The thing is, I've had to write a lot of papers this semester. I had to write two research papers for other classes. So . . . I've been overloaded.

Professor: I know that has to be hard, but it says right on the syllabus what the requirements for the course are. When you signed up for the course, you should have taken a look at this and planned for it.

Student: I know . . . it's just I thought I could handle it. Anyway, what I'm hoping is . . . maybe I can get an extension. I would just need a few days.

Professor: Samantha, I'm afraid I can't do that. I have to turn in the grades a week after the due date. As you can imagine, it takes some time to read through them and grade them. So an extension for the final paper just isn't an option. But if you're really concerned, you might want to file for an incomplete.

Glossary:

ⓒ POWERED BY COBUILD

dwarf: species of plants and animals which are much smaller than the usual size for their kind

Now look at the sample purpose question below. Review the parts of the script that you underlined above to choose the best answer.

TOEFL Listening

Question 1 of 34

1. Why does the student go to see the professor?
   ○ To find out more about a topic discussed in class
   ○ To ask if she can change her paper topic
   ○ To discuss the process of filing for an incomplete
   ○ To ask the professor for extra time to write her paper

GET IT RIGHT: Tips and Tasks for Answering Correctly

» **TIP 1: Notice who the speakers are**. Before a conversation, the narrator will say who the speakers are. By knowing this, you can predict why the speakers are talking. For example, a student and a professor will probably have a very different reason for talking than a student and a university employee.

Conversation / Speakers	Setting	Focus
Office Hours Student and professor	Office hours conversations typically take place in a professor's office.	Topics may include: • questions about grades. • help with assignments. • requests for extensions. • clarification about topics discussed in class.
Service Encounter Student and university employee	Service encounter conversations typically take place in a university office. Settings may include the following: • Registrar's Office • Campus Police Office • Office of Student Life • Residence Hall Office	Topics are often about problems and may include: • finding volunteer positions or internships. • adding or dropping classes. • changing housing options. • requesting information about financial aid.

TASK 1: Who are the speakers in the conversation on page 25? Is it an office hours or a service encounter conversation?

» **TIP 2: Listen for key phrases that signal the speaker's purpose**. The speaker will often use certain expressions to state the purpose. By listening for these, you can identify the speaker's purpose.

Purpose Signposts	
I wanted to talk to you about . . .	*Maybe you can help me with . . .*
I'm wondering about . . .	*Professor X asked me to . . .*
What I'm hoping for is . . .	*Would you be able to . . . ?*

TASK 2: Underline two expressions in the conversation on page 25 that signal the speaker's purpose.

» **TIP 3: Pay attention to explanations of problems.** Speakers often describe the problem they're having <u>before</u> they say what they want. Listen carefully after an explanation for the speaker's purpose.

TASK 3: Circle the section of the conversation on page 25 in which the student describes the problem. Double underline the request that she makes to indicate her purpose after describing her problem.

» **TIP 4: Watch out for purposes that the other speaker suggests!** In many conversations, the second speaker may guess what the student hopes to accomplish. Unless the student says the guess is correct, be sure to eliminate any answer choices that refer to these guesses and predictions.

Expressions for Making Guesses and Predictions	
Let me guess . . .	*You must want to talk about . . .*
I bet you want to talk about . . .	*Are you here to ask about . . . ?*
Are you here about . . . ?	*A lot of students have asked about . . .*

TASK 4: Double underline one expression the professor uses to make a prediction in the conversation on page 25. Does the student confirm or reject the professor's guess?

TASK 5: Draw a line through one answer option on page 25 that refers to the professor's incorrect guess.

Inference Questions

An inference question asks you to draw a conclusion based on the information presented in a lecture or conversation. The answer for an inference question will <u>never</u> be stated outright. Rather, you will have to connect the given information in order to make an inference. There is typically no more than one inference question per lecture / conversation.

Inference questions may be worded as follows:

» *What does the professor imply about . . . ?*

» *What can be inferred about . . . ?*

» *What will the speaker probably do next?*

» *What is probably true about . . . ?*

QUICK GUIDE: Inference Questions

Definition	Inference questions ask you to make a judgment based on information that is strongly implied in the lecture / conversation. While the answer is not stated in the lecture / conversation, you should be able to make a strong inference about a person, an event, or a situation based on the information provided.
Targeted Skills	In order to correctly answer an inference question, you must be able to: • make an assumption based on the context of the lecture / conversation. • interpret meaning based on the speaker's tone. • reference several details to understand a speaker's implied meaning.
The Correct Answer	The correct answer for an inference question correctly draws a conclusion. The inference will be supported by information in the passage but will not be stated directly in the lecture / conversation. The information needed to answer an inference question is often repeated or reworded once, twice, or sometimes three times in the lecture / conversation.
Wrong Answer Options	Watch out for answer options that include: • a conclusion that is true but is not supported by the information in the lecture / conversation. On the test, the correct answer to an inference question is <u>always</u> supported by the given information. You do not have to rely on previous or outside knowledge to answer a question. • information that contradicts the main idea or details of the lecture / conversation. • exact wording from the lecture / conversation. The correct answer will usually reword information.

WALK THROUGH: Inference Questions

Below is a sample script and sample inference question for a test item based on part of a lecture in a geology class. While you listen, underline words in the script that you think might be important details that could be used to make inferences.   🎧 CD1, Track 14

SAMPLE SCRIPT ▶
for reference only, not available in test

Professor: OK, so . . . we all know how devastating earthquakes can be. So, uh, it would be a great thing if we could predict earthquakes. But scientists haven't really found out any accurate methods for doing so. However, there are some theories about, um, I guess, events that can serve as precursors for earthquakes.

Take animal behavior. I bet a lot of you have probably heard about this. Um, some people think that animals—well, *some* animals—might be able to predict earthquakes. In 1996, there was a major earthquake in Southern California. Obviously, it's not that uncommon there. But anyway, shortly after the earthquake, scientists conducted a phone survey. Basically, researchers asked people whether they had seen animals behaving strangely before the event. Fifteen percent of the people they talked to said, um, they reported observing their pets acting frightened or disoriented—just strange behavior. Of course, 15 percent isn't a huge number. And there's no really good explanation for why some animals act strangely before an earthquake.

Earthquake Precursors

So . . . scientists are trying to find other precursors. There's a theory about radon emissions. Um, radon is a type of gas. Based on the current research, this idea about radon emissions seems promising. It could be really useful in the future. But at this point, we still don't know of any good ways to predict an earthquake.

Glossary:

◐ POWERED BY COBUILD

devastating: something that is shocking, upsetting, or terrible

precursor: a similar thing that happened or existed before that led to the existence or development of something

Now look at the sample inference question below. Review the parts of the script that you underlined above to choose the best answer.

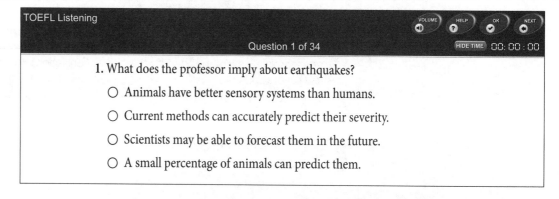

TOEFL Listening

Question 1 of 34

1. What does the professor imply about earthquakes?

  ○ Animals have better sensory systems than humans.

  ○ Current methods can accurately predict their severity.

  ○ Scientists may be able to forecast them in the future.

  ○ A small percentage of animals can predict them.

GET IT RIGHT: Tips and Tasks for Answering Correctly

» **TIP 1: Identify the speaker's tone when speaking about the topic that is being asked about.** Because the answer for an inference question won't be stated outright, you have to pay attention to hints about the speaker's meaning. Tone may indicate whether the speaker is skeptical, serious, or hopeful about something.

TASK 1: Listen again to track 14. What is the professor's tone when she talks about radon emissions? Does she sound like she's making a joke, or is she speaking seriously?

» **TIP 2: Pay attention to the main idea and organization of the lecture / conversation.** If you are having difficulty choosing an answer, you can eliminate any answers that contradict the main ideas of the lecture / conversation.

TASK 2: The main idea of the lecture on page 28 is that scientists are investigating several methods for predicting earthquakes. Draw a line through one incorrect answer option on page 32 that contradicts the main idea.

» **TIP 3: Eliminate answer options that aren't supported by the information in the lecture / conversation.** You might see an answer option that seems like it could be true. However, unless it is supported by the information in the lecture / conversation, it cannot be the correct answer.

TASK 3: Draw a line through one incorrect answer option on page 28 that presents an inference that may be true but is not supported by the lecture.

» **TIP 4: Watch out for answers that contain the exact language from the listening!** Remember, correct answers won't be stated outright in the lecture / conversation. Furthermore, the correct answer will usually reword any key ideas.

TASK 4: Draw a line through one incorrect answer option on page 28 that contains exact or similar wording from the lecture.

TEST TIP!

Compare key words from the inference question to your notes. This will help you identify what part of the lecture / conversation the inference question is based on. Then you can use your notes to help you eliminate inferences that aren't supported by the lecture / conversation.

PROGRESSIVE PRACTICE: Get Ready

A Listen to part of a conversation between a student and a clerk at the registrar's office. Check (✓) the points written in the notes below as you hear them.
🎧 CD1, Track 15

☐ Student and registrar's clerk
☐ Student has special situation—taking 3 classes but is interested in a 4th in the physics department
☐ Students can take up to 4 classes, so he can sign up if:
  ☐ he's taken the prerequisites.
  ☐ the class isn't full.
☐ Student's 3 classes are hard & are for his major (wants to do well).
  ☐ He just wants to sit in on the physics class.
Option: audit a class—attend lectures, no tests or grade
☐ 1. Fill out class registration slip (incl. name, ID #, course #, prof's name, and mark "audit").
☐ 2. Take slip to Prof. Yang and get her signature.
☐ 3. Bring signed slip to the registrar's office and they'll take care of it.
☐ Student says he thinks he'll do it (it's easy).

B Review the questions. What kinds of questions are they? Then, answer the questions. Note the correct answers and read why the answer options are correct or incorrect.

1. **Why does the student visit the registrar's office?**
   ○ To ask about the maximum course load
   ○ To find out about enrollment options
   ○ To drop a class from his schedule
   ○ To get advice on which courses to take

> ANSWER ANALYSIS ▶
>
> *Question Type:* **Purpose**
> ✗ The clerk mentions that the maximum student course load is four classes. The student does <u>not</u> visit the registrar's office to ask about this.
> ✓ **The student states that he has a special situation. He explains that the situation deals with enrollment, because he doesn't officially want to enroll in the class. He wants to know about his options for sitting in on the class.**
> ✗ The clerk mentions adding or dropping a class at the beginning of the conversation. The student dismisses this and responds by saying he has a special situation.
> ✗ The student already knows what classes he wants to take.

2. **What is implied about the student?**
   ○ He is currently taking the maximum course load.
   ○ He audited a course in the past.
   ○ He is not a physics major.
   ○ He probably can't pass the physics class.

ANSWER ANALYSIS ▶

***Question Type:* Inference**

✗ This option contradicts the facts stated in the passage. The clerk says that the maximum course load is four. The student is signed up for only three classes.

✗ The student is not familiar with auditing when the clerk mentions it. It is unlikely that he's audited a course if he doesn't know about the process.

✓ **When referring to the physics class, the student says he doesn't want to put too much pressure on himself for a class that doesn't count toward his major. Based on this information, you can make the inference that he is not majoring in physics.**

✗ The student says he does not want to put too much pressure on himself by taking a fourth course, because his other courses are pretty difficult. There is no information to suggest that the physics class is too difficult for him to pass.

3. **What can be inferred about the student's grade-point average?**

○ It would not be affected by auditing the physics class.

○ It has not remained constant throughout the semester.

○ It is not high enough to enroll in the class he wants to take.

○ It is a subject that the student is uncomfortable talking about.

ANSWER ANALYSIS ▶

***Question Type:* Inference**

✓ **The clerk mentions that the student will not be given a grade if he audits the physics class. It can therefore be inferred that his grade-point average will not be affected.**

✗ The student states that he has an A average but does not mention any changes in his grade-point average.

✗ The grade-point average that is required to enroll in the physics class is not mentioned. Furthermore, it can be inferred that with an A average overall, the student's grades would be high enough to take the class.

✗ The student tells the clerk what his grade-point average is and does not seem reluctant to discuss it.

4. **What will the student probably do after he fills in a form?**

○ Sit in on a physics class

○ Go and see Professor Yang

○ Talk with his advisor about the problem

○ Purchase the physics textbook

ANSWER ANALYSIS ▶

***Question Type:* Inference**

✗ The student must complete some required paperwork before actually sitting in on the class.

✓ **Today is the last day that the student can sign up to audit a class, and the registration office closes in an hour. Because he needs to bring back a form with the professor's signature on it today, it can be inferred that the student will visit the professor next.**

✗ The student mentions that the advisor warned him not to overload his schedule. But there's no reason to believe that the student will go and see his advisor now.

✗ The clerk does mention the physics textbook but states that its purchase is optional. The student has more important things to do now, and so it can be inferred that he will not go and purchase the textbook next.

PROGRESSIVE PRACTICE: Get Set

A Listen to part of a conversation between a student and a chemistry professor. Then, complete the notes below.

🎧 CD1, Track 16

Speakers: Student and ❶ _____
Situation: Office hours

Student is 20 minutes early to ❷ _____.
Professor asks if student has questions about ❸ _____.
  (A lot of other students asked about it.)
Student wants to know about grading policy—absences.
One point off of final grade for each ❹ _____
  absence (no more than 3 excused absences)
Student has 2 excused absences so far (sick with
  ❺ _____ 2 weeks ago).
Student will miss 3 more days to go to an out-of-town conference
  about biotech. Student studies ❻ _____.
  Conference relates to student's thesis.
Professor decides to allow student to miss classes but says he will give her a lower
  grade if she misses more classes.
Student will write a note and get it signed by her thesis advisor. The professor will
  put the ❼ _____ in his file.
Student says she'll bring the justification to the next class.

B Answer the questions. Then, write the letter of each answer option next to the reason why it is correct or incorrect in the *Answer Analysis* box.

1. Why does the student visit the professor?

   ○ To ask a question about the midterm [A]

   ○ To discuss the professor's attendance policy [B]

   ○ To talk to the professor about her thesis [C]

   ○ To complain about the professor's grading policy [D]

ANSWER ANALYSIS ▶

_____ ✓ **The student is concerned that her grade will suffer because she will have more than the allowed excused absences. She wants to discuss the professor's attendance policy.**

_____ ✗ The student asks about the grading policy as it relates to attendance. She does not make any complaints about the professor's policy.

_____ ✗ The student says she needs to attend the conference because it will help her write her thesis. She does <u>not</u> see the professor to speak about her thesis.

_____ ✗ The professor guesses that the student is there to talk about the midterm. But the student says she wants to talk about something else entirely.

2. What can be inferred about the student's visit?

   ○ It is at the same time as one of her other classes. [A]

   ○ It is not the first time that she has visited the professor during office hours. [B]

   ○ She confirmed the meeting time earlier with the professor. [C]

   ○ It is not during the professor's normal office hours. [D]

ANSWER ANALYSIS ▶

_____ ✗ Because the student is surprised to see the professor, it can be inferred that the meeting time was not agreed upon earlier.

_____ ✗ The student doesn't say anything about the visit occurring at the same time as any of her other classes.

_____ ✗ The student doesn't seem sure of when the professor's office hours actually are, so we can assume that she has not visited him in his office in the past.

_____ ✓ **There are several clues that suggest that this is not the professor's normal office hours. First, the student is surprised to find him in his office. She then confirms the time of normal office hours, but the professor tells her to come in anyway, saying, "I'm available anytime I happen to be in my office—regular hours or not."**

3. What can be inferred about the student?

○ Her thesis is about a chemistry topic. [A]

○ She made plans to attend the conference before she got sick. [B]

○ Her grade in the class will suffer because of her absences. [C]

○ She was sick with the flu for two weeks. [D]

ANSWER ANALYSIS ▶

_____ ✗ The professor tells the student that her grade will suffer only if she has more absences than those she discussed with him. The student doesn't imply that she will miss more classes, so her grade will probably not suffer.

_____ ✓ **The student says that she signed up for the conference earlier in the semester and that she wasn't planning on getting sick with the flu. From this, you can infer that she made plans before she got ill.**

_____ ✗ The professor teaches chemistry, but the student says that the conference is about biotechnology.

_____ ✗ The student says that she missed two classes two weeks ago because she had the flu. She doesn't suggest that she was sick for two weeks.

4. What can be inferred about the conference?

○ It will be held in a different city. [A]

○ The student is worried she'll be sick during it. [B]

○ The professor already knew about it. [C]

○ The student will make a presentation there. [D]

ANSWER ANALYSIS ▶

_____ ✗ The student says that Professor Montgomery will make a presentation at the conference. She does not say that she will make one there.

_____ ✗ Nothing in the conversation suggests that the professor already knew about the conference.

_____ ✓ **The student gives two clues suggesting that the conference will be held in another city. First, she implies that it is not local. Second, she states that she will be flying to it.**

_____ ✗ The student had the flu earlier, but she's not worried about being sick for the conference.

5. What will the student probably do the next time the class meets?

○ Introduce Professor Montgomery to the professor [A]

○ Talk about the conference with the professor [B]

○ Discuss her thesis topic with the class [C]

○ Give the professor a written explanation for her absences [D]

ANSWER ANALYSIS ▶

_____ ✗ The student and professor mention that the conference might be relevant to the class, but neither of them says that they will discuss her thesis in class.

_____ ✗ The student doesn't say anything about introducing the two professors to each other.

_____ ✓ **The student says she will bring the justification explaining her absences to the next class.**

_____ ✗ The student says that she will tell the professor about the conference when she returns.

PROGRESSIVE PRACTICE: Go for the TOEFL Test

Listen to part of a conversation between a student and a librarian and take notes. 🎧 CD1, Track 17

NOTES:

_____

_____

_____

_____

_____

_____

_____

_____

_____

Now answer the questions. You may use your notes.

1. Why does the student visit the library? 🎧 CD1, Track 18
   ○ To find out the name of a movie
   ○ To check out library materials
   ○ To get information about the borrowing policy
   ○ To ask about the availability of a video

2. Listen again to part of the conversation. Then, answer the question. 🎧 CD1, Track 19
   What does the librarian imply when he says this?
   ○ The student is mistaken.
   ○ The library's system is not functioning.
   ○ The professor can check out movies for only three days.
   ○ The librarian is unsure what the student is asking.

3. What can be inferred about Professor Harmon?
   🎧 CD1, Track 20
   ○ She has already left town.
   ○ She is not sure about the name of the video.
   ○ She teaches an astronomy class.
   ○ She doesn't expect the movie to be available.

4. What can be inferred about *Planets and Their Paths*?
   🎧 CD1, Track 21
   ○ It will not be available for viewing on Wednesday.
   ○ The student has seen it once before.
   ○ The professor will not watch it with her students.
   ○ The librarian will order it from another university.

5. What can be inferred about the reservation process?
   🎧 CD1, Track 22
   ○ The professor will not fill in a reservation form.
   ○ The student must tell the professor to reserve the movie.
   ○ The process has not changed for several years.
   ○ The school will eliminate the current system soon.

Function Questions

A function question asks you the purpose of a specific section from a lecture or conversation. For this question type, you will usually hear a 10- to 30-second audio clip from a lecture / conversation. The question is based on the information from the audio clip. Usually, the answer options for function questions begin with *to* infinitives (for example, To make a point about . . . or To give an example of . . .). There is typically no more than one function question per lecture / conversation.

Function questions will typically be followed by an audio clip containing a sentence or two from the lecture / conversation and may be worded as follows:

» *Why does the speaker say this?* 🎧

» *What does the professor imply when he says this?* 🎧

» *What does the professor mean when she says this?* 🎧

» *Why does the student mention . . . ?*

» *Why does the professor ask this?* 🎧

QUICK GUIDE: Function Questions

Definition	For most function questions, you listen to a short audio clip from a lecture / conversation, called an excerpt. Then, you are asked to determine the purpose of the excerpt in the context of the entire lecture / conversation.
Targeted Skills	In order to correctly answer a function question, you must be able to: • determine a speaker's motivations for saying or asking something. • interpret the speaker's meaning based on tone and context clues. • tell the difference between literal and figurative language. • understand how the information in the brief audio clip is related to the entire passage.
The Correct Answer	The correct answer for a function question correctly identifies the speaker's motivations for saying something. The speaker will <u>not</u> say the function outright in the lecture / conversation or in the audio clip. You will have to determine the function based on the speaker's tone and your understanding of the lecture / conversation.
Wrong Answer Options	Watch out for answer options that include: • possible interpretations of a spoken segment that don't explain the speaker's motivation or intention in the excerpt. • information that is mentioned in the excerpt but does not relate directly to the speaker's purpose.

WALK THROUGH: Function Questions

Below is a sample script and sample function question for a test item based on part of a lecture in an archaeology class. While you listen, underline words or phrases in the script that indicate changes in the speaker's tone.   🎧 CD1, Track 23

SAMPLE SCRIPT ▶
for reference only, not available in test

Professor: When we talk about underwater archaeology, we mean, uh, learning about the past through maritime discoveries . . . such as shipwrecks or ports. All around the world, there are well-preserved shipwrecks that we still haven't explored. And who knows how much we can learn from those wrecks. It's an exciting field. But, of course, underwater archaeologists have to deal with problems that archaeologists on land rarely face. I'm going to talk about one example.

OK, so one problem that marine archaeologists have to deal with is that the artifacts they collect are just saturated with water—they're soaked. This includes important samples like pieces of leather or wood. This is a problem because . . . well, letting these samples dry through evaporation can destroy them. That's why underwater archaeologists use a technique called lyophilization.

Lyophilization is a way to dry wood or leather without ruining it. Let me go through the steps. First, you freeze the sample. Then, instead of melting the ice, you use extremely low air pressure to turn the ice directly into gas. The important thing is, um, is that by using this technique you skip the liquid state of water entirely. This is very important, since the evaporation of water can destroy a sample.

Glossary:

⊂ POWERED BY COBUILD

archaeology: the study of the societies and people of the past

evaporation: the process of changing from a liquid into a gas

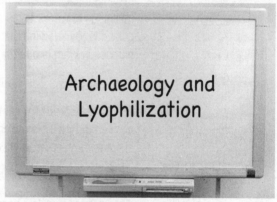

Archaeology and Lyophilization

Now look at the sample function question below. Review the parts of the script that you underlined above to choose the best answer.   🎧 CD1, Track 24

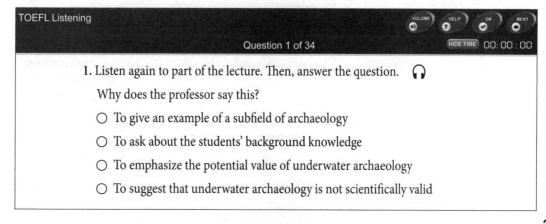

TOEFL Listening

Question 1 of 34

HIDE TIME 00:00:00

1. Listen again to part of the lecture. Then, answer the question. 🎧

Why does the professor say this?

○ To give an example of a subfield of archaeology

○ To ask about the students' background knowledge

○ To emphasize the potential value of underwater archaeology

○ To suggest that underwater archaeology is not scientifically valid

GET IT RIGHT: Tips and Tasks for Answering Correctly

» **TIP 1: Listen carefully to the speaker's intonation and stress during the recording.** Does the speaker's voice go up at the end of the sentence? Does the speaker emphasize a certain word or words? This information can provide clues about the speaker's motivations and help you eliminate answer options that can be interpreted in different ways.

Type of Intonation / Stress	Purpose
Pitch falls at the end of a sentence	Speaker is making commentary or asking a rhetorical question
Pitch rises at the end of a sentence	Speaker is asking a yes or no question and doesn't know the answer
Speaker stresses certain words or says them louder	Speaker wants to put emphasis on a certain word or wants to clarify a point

TASK 1: Look at the script on page 37 and listen to track 23 again. Circle one sentence in which the professor's intonation drops at the end. Underline stressed words or phrases. Then, draw a line through one incorrect answer option based on what you heard.

» **TIP 2: Know the difference between literal and figurative language.** When people speak literally, they mean exactly what they say. On the other hand, when people speak figuratively, they use symbolic meanings of words to get a point across. In other words, the meaning might not be obvious or exactly as it sounds. By knowing the difference between literal and figurative language, you can tell if the speaker's purpose is what is directly stated or not.

TASK 2: Draw a box around one piece of figurative language in the lecture on page 37.

» **TIP 3: Watch out for rhetorical questions!** A rhetorical question is a question that is <u>not</u> meant to be answered. Rather, speakers often use rhetorical questions with the purpose of persuading the audience about something or to encourage further consideration of an issue.

TASK 3: Double underline one rhetorical question in the lecture on page 37.

» **TIP 4: Pay attention to repeated or reworded information in the lecture / conversation.** Speakers often repeat or reword things to make a definition or key concept clear. If the audio clip includes a repetition of a concept that was introduced in another part of the lecture, the professor's purpose is likely to clarify or provide further explanation of a concept. Speakers will also sometimes repeat or reword information to correct a mistake or make something clearer.

Language	Function	Common Wording of Answer Options
Rhetorical Questions	To persuade an audience or to encourage further consideration of a subject	To emphasize . . . To remind students of . . . To suggest . . .
Definitions	To make a key point clear	To illustrate / demonstrate . . . To give an example of . . . To describe / explain . . .
Clarifications and Errors	To correct a speech error or explain something further	To correct the wording of a previous statement To avoid confusion among the students To clear up a possible misunderstanding

TASK 4: Triple underline the one instance in which the professor rewords key information in the lecture on page 37.

Attitude Questions

An attitude question asks you about a speaker's opinion or certainty about something. There is typically no more than one attitude question per conversation / lecture. You'll find attitude questions for both academic lectures and conversations.

Attitude questions may be worded as follows:

» *What is the professor's opinion of . . . ?*

» *What is the professor's point of view concerning . . . ?*

» *What is the man's / woman's attitude toward . . . ?*

» *What does the student mean when he / she says this:*

QUICK GUIDE: Attitude Questions

Definition	Attitude questions ask you to determine a speaker's opinion of a subject, such as a theory. For example, professors may give clues to indicate that they think that a theory is unfavorable or unrealistic. Attitude questions also ask about how sure a speaker is that something will happen or how certain a speaker is about the validity of a theory or idea.
Targeted Skills	In order to correctly answer an attitude question, you must be able to: • interpret the speaker's feelings based on tone and choice of words. • understand how certain a speaker is about what he or she is saying.
The Correct Answer	The correct answer for an attitude question correctly identifies the speaker's feelings or certainty about something. The speaker's attitude will never be stated outright in the lecture / conversation. Rather, you will have to infer the speaker's attitude based on his or her tone and choice of words.
Wrong Answer Options	Watch out for answer options that include: • possible interpretations of a phrase that do not show the speaker's attitude. • the speaker's attitude about a different topic. • descriptions of the attitude of the wrong speaker.

WALK THROUGH: Attitude Questions

Below is a sample script and sample attitude question for a test item based on part of a lecture in a psychology class. While you listen, underline words in the script that you think might relate to the speaker's attitude about Henry Murray's theory of psychogenic needs.   🎧 CD1, Track 25

SAMPLE SCRIPT ▶
*for reference only,
not available in test*

Professor: Personally, one of my favorite theorists is Henry Murray, who studied personality. In 1938, he came up with the theory of psychogenic needs. Now, according to this theory, each of us has a personality. And that personality, it's, um, determined by how we respond to needs, or, um, presses. By the way, "presses" is a word that Murray used to describe pressures. See, people have both primary needs and secondary needs. Primary needs are biological pressures, like food and oxygen—things that we absolutely couldn't live without, right? On the other hand, secondary needs are psychological presses, like . . . the need for independence or the, um, the need for achievement or success. Murray created a list of about 25 different secondary psychological needs. All of our primary and secondary needs combined help determine our individual personalities. Is everyone following so far? OK, to review, Murray thought that personality was determined by our responses to our needs and presses. Yes, Liz, do you have a question?

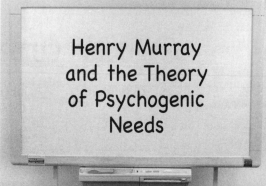

Henry Murray
and the Theory
of Psychogenic
Needs

Student: Yeah. What I don't understand is how these needs make our personalities different. Doesn't each person have all of these needs?

Professor: Good point. And, yes, each of us experiences all of these needs. But the beauty of the theory, if you ask me, is that Murray's theory accounts for difference. See, he said that different personalities arise because people have different levels of each need. For example, maybe Liz has a greater need for order than Stephanie. Order is, um, one of the secondary needs. If Liz needs more order than Stephanie, she will be more organized, which makes their personalities distinct.

Glossary:

ⓒ POWERED BY COBUILD

psychological: concerned with a person's mind and thoughts

distinct: different or separate from something

Now look at the sample attitude question below. Review the parts of the script that you underlined above to choose the best answer.

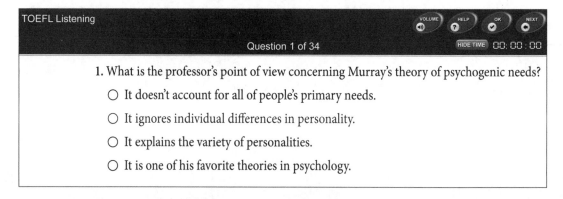

TOEFL Listening   VOLUME 🔊 HELP ❓ OK ✓ NEXT →

Question 1 of 34   HIDE TIME 00:00:00

1. What is the professor's point of view concerning Murray's theory of psychogenic needs?

○ It doesn't account for all of people's primary needs.

○ It ignores individual differences in personality.

○ It explains the variety of personalities.

○ It is one of his favorite theories in psychology.

GET IT RIGHT: Tips and Tasks for Answering Correctly

» **TIP 1: Notice key expressions that help you determine attitude.** Write down any information that helps you determine the speaker's attitude. To pinpoint such information, listen for the key expressions listed below.

Key Expressions	
Giving Opinions	**Expressing Certainty**
I think / I don't think . . .	*I'm sure / not sure that . . .*
The way I see it . . .	*It's hard to say whether . . .*
Personally, I . . .	*One thing we can be sure of is . . .*
Don't you think that . . . ?	*I don't know if . . .*
If you ask me . . .	*XX is only true to a certain extent.*
As far as I'm concerned . . .	*What I don't understand is . . .*

TASK 1: Find and underline one key expression in the first paragraph of the lecture on page 40 that gives a clue about the professor's opinion and one that gives a clue about his certainty.

» **TIP 2: Listen carefully to the speaker's tone throughout the conversation / lecture.** Does the speaker sound sympathetic, doubtful, or apologetic? The speaker's tone can help you interpret his or her opinion toward something.

Speaker's Tone	Key Expressions in Answer Options
Sympathetic	The speaker understands . . . The speaker wants to help . . .
Worried	The speaker is anxious about . . . The speaker is having a problem with . . .
Doubtful	The speaker is unsure / uncertain about . . . The speaker doubts . . .
Apologetic	The speaker is sorry about . . . The speaker wants to apologize for . . .

TASK 2: Listen again to track 25. What is the professor's tone when he speaks about Murray's theory of psychogenic needs at the beginning of the lecture? Is it doubtful or sympathetic?

» **TIP 3: Pay close attention to the conclusion of the lecture.** While hints about the professor's attitude appear in the <u>entire</u> lecture, professors often give their opinion of the issue or theory being discussed near the end.

TASK 3: Circle one expression in the last paragraph of the lecture on page 40 that gives a clue about the professor's attitude regarding Murray's theory of psychogenic needs.

» **TIP 4: Eliminate answers that describe the speaker's attitude toward something that is not being asked about.** The speaker may give opinions about a number of subjects. Make sure you choose the answer that's about the opinion in the question.

TASK 4: Draw a line through one incorrect answer option that describes an opinion on an unrelated subject.

» **TIP 5: Watch out for answer options that describe the wrong speaker's opinion!** In a lecture / conversation with more than one speaker, more than one opinion may be presented. Be sure to read the question carefully to see <u>whose</u> opinion you are being asked about.

TASK 5: Draw a line through one incorrect answer option that gives the opinion of the wrong speaker.

TEST TIP!

Be careful with answer options that involve cause and effect relationships. Incorrect answer options on the listening comprehension section of the TOEFL test often <u>reverse</u> the relationships heard in the listening passage. This makes a wrong answer look correct!

PROGRESSIVE PRACTICE: Get Ready

A Listen to part of a discussion in a sociology class and check (✓) the points that are written in the notes below as you hear them.   🎧 CD1, Track 26

- **Broken Windows Theory**
  - ☐ By James Wilson & George Kelling
  - ☐ Predicts that a neighborhood that looks bad will become bad
  - ☐ Broken window was the famous ex.
    - ☐ People see brok. window, they think auth. don't care, they start committing crimes, too
    - ☐ Other examples: graffiti, litter
- **New York City - lots of crime (1980s), esp. in subway**
  - ☐ Kelling hired as consultant in 1985
  - ☐ Kelling advised NYC to clean up graffiti
  - ☐ By 2001, crime in subways decreased - led to acceptance of theory
- **Student suggests that areas with broken windows have more crime to begin with**
  - ☐ Professor says "it's hard to argue with" NYC results

B Review the questions. What kinds of questions are they? Then, answer the questions. Note the correct answers and read why the answer options are correct or incorrect.

1. What is the professor's attitude toward the classical school of criminology?

   ○ He does not agree with it completely.

   ○ He thinks it is a modern approach.

   ○ He feels it influenced the broken windows theory.

   ○ He suggests other theories have disproved it.

ANSWER ANALYSIS ▶

***Question Type:* Attitude**

    ✓ **The professor mentions that many people—including him—might question the classical school's validity. Therefore, we can assume that he does not completely agree with it.**

    ✗ He mentions that the classical school is "very dated," which means that it is not a modern approach.

    ✗ While the professor talks about both the classical school and the broken windows theory, he does not suggest that one led to the other. In fact, he does not link them in any way.

    ✗ Although he disagrees with the classical school of criminology, he does not mention other theories that disprove it.

2. Listen again to part of the discussion. Then, answer the question.

   Why does the professor say this?   🎧 CD1, Track 27

   ○ To check which students completed the assignment

   ○ To encourage other students to participate

   ○ To indicate that the student's answer was incorrect

   ○ To suggest that the class needs to review more

ANSWER ANALYSIS ▶

***Question Type:* Function**

    ✗ He says that the class had an assignment, but he checks who did it at the beginning of the lecture.

    ✓ **The professor wants a different student to participate in the discussion.**

✗ After the student's response, the professor says the answer was correct.

✗ He says he wants to review the theory with them. He does not mean the class needs to review more.

3. Listen again to part of the discussion. Then, answer the question.

   Why does the professor say this? 🎧 CD1, Track 28

   ○ To suggest a possible result of neighborhood crime

   ○ To describe a way in which criminals can enter a building

   ○ To introduce a new theory of crime prevention

   ○ To propose a reason that serious crimes occur

   ANSWER ANALYSIS ▶

   Question Type: **Function**

       ✗ The professor states that a broken window is the cause of crime, not the result of existing crime.

       ✗ The professor says nothing about criminals entering a building through a broken window.

       ✗ The professor has already introduced the broken windows theory and is not introducing a new theory at this point in the discussion.

       ✓ **The professor says that a broken window can actually be the cause of major crime within an area. He suggests that a single broken window can make people think that the authorities do not care about an area, leading people to commit crimes.**

4. Listen again to part of the discussion. Then, answer the question.

   Why does the student say this? 🎧 CD1, Track 29

   ○ To give her opinion on the effects of crime in urban areas

   ○ To suggest that broken windows are not causes of crime

   ○ To confirm that she agrees with the professor's opinion

   ○ To describe a situation that she has personally witnessed

   ANSWER ANALYSIS ▶

   Question Type: **Attitude**

       ✗ The student is giving her opinion on the causes of crime, not its effects.

       ✓ **The student thinks that neighborhoods with problems like broken windows are probably just more likely to be crime-ridden areas. She doesn't see a direct cause / effect relationship between broken windows and the crime rate.**

       ✗ The student is disagreeing with the professor's opinion. She's not agreeing with it.

       ✗ The student has said nothing about witnessing these problems herself.

5. What is the professor's point of view with regards to the broken windows theory?

   ○ He thinks there is sufficient evidence to support it.

   ○ He is concerned that it ignores important variables.

   ○ He doubts that it could be applied to different cities.

   ○ He believes that it improves upon previous theories.

   ANSWER ANALYSIS ▶

   Question Type: **Attitude**

       ✓ **The professor responds to the student by saying that the results in New York City are hard to argue with. The phrase "hard to argue with those results" implies that he thinks there is evidence to support the theory.**

       ✗ During the discussion, a student proposes that the theory ignores other "factors," which is another word for "variables." Thus, this is the opinion of a different speaker, <u>not</u> the professor.

       ✗ He implies that he supports the theory, which means that he thinks it could be applied elsewhere.

       ✗ The professor doesn't mention any other theories in the discussion.

PROGRESSIVE PRACTICE: Get Set

A Listen to part of a conversation between a student and a sociology professor. Then, complete the notes below.

🎧 CD1, Track 30

Speakers: Student and ❶ _____
Student is busy, can't think of ❷ _____
Professor wants to ❸ _____
Student interested in ❹ _____ - when cultural traits
  spread from the culture region
Tone change (professor): joking / laughing / impressed, likes the student's
  ❺ _____
Professor suggests looking at theories that explain cultural diffusion
  ex. NYC
Suggestion: how ❻ _____ experience cultural diffusion;
  both direct and indirect cultural diffusion (prof. didn't talk about this
  in class)
Dir: when cultures are close to each other
Indir: when exchange happens thru a mid.man like ❼ _____

B Answer the questions. Then, write the letter of each answer option next to the reason why it is correct or incorrect in the *Answer Analysis* box.

1. Listen again to part of the conversation. Then, answer the question. Why does the professor say this? 🎧 CD1, Track 31

  ○ To acknowledge his willingness to help [A]
  ○ To ask the student the meaning of her joke [B]
  ○ To suggest that the student should be more serious [C]
  ○ To show surprise that the student has not begun her assignment [D]

ANSWER ANALYSIS ▶
_____ ✗ The student is being serious and has a problem—she doesn't know what to write her paper on.
_____ ✗ The professor is not asking for an explanation of a joke. He knows that the student is not trying to be funny.
_____ ✓ **"Are you kidding?" is a common exclamation of surprise. The professor is happy to help her.**
_____ ✗ The professor is surprised but not at the fact that the student has not yet begun her assignment.

2. What is the professor's attitude toward the student's definition of cultural diffusion?

  ○ He is impressed by the student's knowledge. [A]
  ○ He thinks her definition is incomplete. [B]
  ○ He can tell she is not really interested in it. [C]
  ○ He thinks she doesn't understand the concept. [D]

ANSWER ANALYSIS ▶
_____ ✗ Nothing is said to suggest that the professor thinks the student is not interested in the topic.
_____ ✗ The professor's tone indicates that he's happy with the student's definition. Also, there are no other clues in the conversation to show that he thinks she doesn't understand.
_____ ✓ **The professor expresses amazement by saying, "Wow!" Also, his tone is humorous when he says, "So you didn't do the reading, huh?" This means the opposite of what he said.**
_____ ✗ He's pleased with the definition, so we can judge that he thinks it fully explains the concept.

3. Listen again to part of the conversation. Then, answer the question.
   Why does the professor say this? 🎧 CD1, Track 32

   ○ To give his opinion about cultural diffusion [A]

   ○ To make a suggestion to the student [B]

   ○ To offer advice about research methods [C]

   ○ To provide background information about a topic [D]

ANSWER ANALYSIS ▶

_____ ✗ The professor is giving the student advice about possible topics, not research methods.

_____ ✗ The professor is not sharing his personal perspective about cultural diffusion. "Here's a thought" is function language that is often stated before giving advice.

_____ ✗ The professor and the student have already discussed the background information, and now the professor is helping the student select a topic.

_____ ✓ **The professor is making a recommendation about which aspect of cultural diffusion to write about.**

4. Listen again to part of the conversation. Then, answer the question.
   Why does the student say this? 🎧 CD1, Track 33

   ○ To politely change the subject [A]

   ○ To apologize for missing a recent lecture [B]

   ○ To explain why she hasn't heard of cultural diffusion [C]

   ○ To ask for clarification of some terms [D]

ANSWER ANALYSIS ▶

_____ ✓ **The student does not remember hearing about direct and indirect cultural diffusion in class. She thinks that she might have been absent on the day of that lecture. Therefore, she is indirectly asking for the meaning of the terms.**

_____ ✗ The student uses the word "sorry" to ask for clarification, not to apologize.

_____ ✗ The student knows about cultural diffusion—she just doesn't know about direct and indirect cultural diffusion.

_____ ✗ The student is not trying to change the subject.

5. Listen again to part of the conversation. Then, answer the question.
   What can we infer about the professor when he says this? 🎧 CD1, Track 34

   ○ He wants to extend the class's meeting time. [A]

   ○ He finds the topic of indirect cultural diffusion interesting. [B]

   ○ He thinks that the Internet can speed up cultural diffusion. [C]

   ○ He hopes the students pay better attention in class. [D]

ANSWER ANALYSIS ▶

_____ ✗ The professor would like to have more time to discuss the topic, but he says nothing about actually extending the class times.

_____ ✗ The professor says nothing about students not paying attention in class.

_____ ✗ The professor and the student do agree that the Internet can speed up cultural diffusion. However, this fact has nothing to do with the professor's remark.

_____ ✓ **The professor thinks that the students would be interested in the topic of indirect cultural diffusion. We can assume, then, that he finds the topic interesting as well.**

PROGRESSIVE PRACTICE: Go for the TOEFL Test

Listen to part of a lecture in an anthropology class and take notes.   🎧 CD1, Track 35

NOTES:

_____

_____

_____

_____

_____

_____

_____

_____

TOEFL Listening

HIDE TIME 00:29:46

Chola Dynasty
Rajaraja

Now answer the questions. You may use your notes.

1. Listen again to part of the lecture. Then, answer the question.
   Why does the professor say this?   🎧 CD1, Track 36
   - ○ To compliment the student for his knowledge
   - ○ To give her opinion of Rajaraja
   - ○ To urge the student to continue
   - ○ To emphasize the Chola empire's power

2. **According to the lecture, what is the professor's opinion of video games?**   🎧 CD1, Track 37
   - ○ They should not be played by adults.
   - ○ They teach students in a fun way.
   - ○ They can't be used for learning in most cases.
   - ○ They are usually historically accurate.

3. Listen again to part of the lecture. Then, answer the question.
   Why does the professor say this?   🎧 CD1, Track 38
   - ○ To suggest that the Chola empire was larger than people think
   - ○ To emphasize that Java is a large island
   - ○ To indicate where the Chola empire originated
   - ○ To clarify the location of a part of the Chola empire

4. Listen again to part of the lecture. Then, answer the question.
   Why does the professor say this?   🎧 CD1, Track 39
   - ○ To ask the personal opinions of the students
   - ○ To question the need for the Cholas' use of power

   - ○ To offer a reason for the Cholas' literary success
   - ○ To suggest that the Cholas were skilled warriors

5. Listen again to part of the lecture. Then, answer the question.
   What can be inferred about the professor's opinion of Chola literature?   🎧 CD1, Track 40
   - ○ She is hopeful that the students will enjoy reading it.
   - ○ She is hesitant to offer a firm opinion on it.
   - ○ She thinks that its quality varies considerably.
   - ○ She is certain of its continued significance.

6. **What is the professor's attitude toward the Chola stonecutters?**   🎧 CD1, Track 41
   - ○ She admires their high level of skillfulness.
   - ○ She suggests they were influenced by another culture.
   - ○ She wishes she could visit their work in person.
   - ○ She doubts that they used metal tools.

Organization Questions

An organization question asks you about the organizational structure of a lecture or class discussion. In lectures, information may be organized in a number of ways. For example, a professor may compare and contrast two things, classify something into types, or use some other method to develop the organization of a lecture.

Usually, the answer options for organization questions begin with *to* infinitives (for example, "To give an example of..." or "To illustrate...") or *by* statements (for example, *by emphasizing . . .* or *by showing . . .*). There is typically no more than one organization question per lecture, and this question type doesn't usually appear with conversations.

Organization questions may be worded as follows:

» *How does the professor introduce . . . ?*

» *Why does the professor mention . . . ?*

» *What point does the professor make about . . . ?*

» *Why does the professor talk about / discuss . . . ?*

» *How does the professor organize the information about . . . ?*

» *How is the discussion organized?*

QUICK GUIDE: Organization Questions

Definition	An organization question tests your understanding of how a lecture is structured. You may be tested on the overall organization of a lecture or on the relationship between two different parts of a lecture.
Targeted Skills	In order to correctly answer an organization question, you must be able to: • understand how information in a lecture is presented / organized and understand the language associated with those organizational structures. • recognize how part of a lecture relates to the rest of a lecture. • listen for points that signal how the details of a lecture are related. • identify the role that examples, comparisons, and rhetorical questions play in a lecture.
The Correct Answer	The correct answer for an organization question accurately states the organizational structure of a lecture or how one part of a lecture relates to the rest of a lecture. A professor will not state the organizational structure of a lecture directly. Instead, a professor will use key words that suggest the overall organizational structures.
Wrong Answer Options	Watch out for answer options that include: • information that contradicts the facts stated in the lecture. • relationships that are not supported by the lecture.

WALK THROUGH: Organization Questions

Below is a sample script and organization question for a test item based on part of a lecture in a chemistry class. In this part of the lecture, the professor is contrasting (showing the difference between) two different definitions. While you listen, underline words or phrases in the script that might indicate the organizational structure of the lecture. 🎧 CD1, Track 42

SAMPLE SCRIPT ▶
for reference only, not available in test

Professor: Um, OK, so there are a couple of ways to treat water, so it's, um, well, safe to drink. For example, we can treat water using chemical methods. And one method we should . . . we should probably talk about is adsorption. Don't confuse "adsorption" with "absorption," since they are different. To "absorb" something—with a "b"—it means to incorporate a substance into another one. Let me . . . let me give you an example. Like, um, say there's a puddle of water on the floor, and you place a sponge on it. The sponge's pores fill up with the water—the water is soaked up by the sponge. The sponge absorbs the water. Meanwhile, "adsorption"—with a "d"—means to attract and capture molecules or particles. Imagine, um, imagine the dust clinging to a computer screen. The surface of the screen adsorbs the dust. So . . . that's a good example of the underlying principles of adsorption.

Glossary:
⊜ POWERED BY COBUILD

particle: a very small amount of something: a piece of matter

underlie: the cause or basis of something

So now that we know how adsorption works, let's talk about how it's used to treat unclean water. First, you add a chemical to the water. The substance most commonly used is activated carbon. And that's because activated carbon is specially formulated to capture contaminants, the pollutants—the things that make water unfit to drink. I'm simplifying the process a bit, but the point is that the activated carbon adsorbs these impurities so the water itself is safe to drink.

Now look at the sample organization question below. Review the parts of the script that you underlined above to choose the best answer.

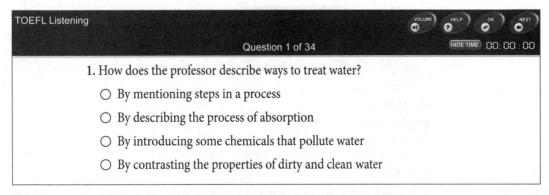

1. How does the professor describe ways to treat water?
   - ○ By mentioning steps in a process
   - ○ By describing the process of absorption
   - ○ By introducing some chemicals that pollute water
   - ○ By contrasting the properties of dirty and clean water

GET IT RIGHT: Tips and Tasks for Answering Correctly

» **TIP 1: Notice the organizational structures of the lecture.** The organization of a lecture will vary based on how specific points of a lecture are presented. Once you identify the structure, take notes that help you easily understand the organization of the lecture.

Organizational Structure	Tips for Note-taking	Common Key Words and Expressions
Definition	Write down the main definition and any examples or main supporting points.	X is . . . X serves as . . . X is used for . . .
Compare and Contrast	Write the two points being compared and contrasted. Make note of any examples used to make the comparisons.	While X is . . . , Y is . . . A key difference between X and Y is . . .
Process	Write down each step of a process. Use numbers to show the order in which each step occurs.	First . . . Second . . . To begin . . . Next . . . Finally . . .
Classification	Create two columns, and write at the top of the columns the things that are being classified. Then, write the key points of each in the appropriate column.	One type of X is . . . Y falls under the category of . . .
Theory / Support	In many lectures, disproven theories are presented. Listen closely for the professor's real opinion of any theory presented.	The first theory states that . . . In support of this theory . . .
Pros and Cons (Advantages and Disadvantages)	Create two columns, and write the pros under one and cons under the other.	An advantage of X is . . . Another problem with Y is . . . A drawback of X is . . .
Cause and Effect	Listen carefully to chains of causes and effects. Quite often, one thing causes another, which then causes another, and so on.	X causes . . . Y leads to . . . As a result of X . . . This has a number of effects, including . . .

TASK 1: Underline one phrase in the lecture on page 49 that signals the organizational structure for a definition. In addition, underline one phrase that gives a direct definition of a word.

» **TIP 2: Identify what part of the lecture the question is based on.** Check your notes to help you understand what the focus of the lecture is when the question topic is mentioned. Use this to think of the relationship between the topic the question is asking about and the part of the lecture you've identified.

TASK 2: Circle the part of the lecture on page 49 that is being asked about in the question on page 49.

» **TIP 3: Listen carefully for examples, comparisons, and rhetorical questions.** Organization questions are often based on these types of speech.

Speech Type / Definition	Example	Possible Answer Options
Rhetorical Question: A question that is not meant to be answered	*Now, what am I talking about here?*	To emphasize . . . To make a point about . . . To draw attention to . . .
Example: Something that serves to illustrate a point	*Let me give you an example of what I mean.*	To demonstrate / exemplify . . . To show / give an example . . .
Comparison: An examination of the ways that two things are similar and different	*While X is found only here, Y can be found worldwide.*	By comparing X to Y . . . By showing the differences / similarities between X and Y . . .

TASK 3: Underline two phrases in the lecture on page 49 that indicate the professor is giving examples.

Connecting Content Questions

A connecting content question asks you to complete a table based on the relationship between ideas presented in a lecture or conversation. There is typically no more than one connecting content question per lecture / conversation. Connecting content questions appear more commonly with lectures, though they occasionally appear with conversations as well. You can recognize connecting content questions because they are accompanied by tables.

The instructions for completing the table for connecting content questions may be worded as follows:

» *What type of X do the Y have? Place a check mark (✓) in the correct boxes.*

» *For each phrase / description / activity below, place a check mark (✓) in the "yes" or "no" column.*

» *Based on the information from the lecture, indicate whether the statements reflect . . .*

QUICK GUIDE: Connecting Content Questions

Definition	Connecting content questions ask you to apply your understanding of a lecture / conversation to complete a table. Depending on the instructions, you will need to: • classify the given information. • identify causes and effects. • put events or steps of a process in order. • indicate whether something was or was not included in a lecture. To complete a table, you will move your mouse over each correct box. When you click your mouse, a check mark (✓) will appear in the box.
Targeted Skills	In order to correctly answer a connecting content question, you must be able to: • understand the main concepts presented in a lecture / conversation. • listen for main supporting points. • listen for details that a speaker mentions. • understand how information in a lecture / conversation could be categorized.
The Correct Answer	The correct answer for a connecting content question correctly classifies the given information according to the directions. There is no partial credit for this question type, so you must fill in the <u>entire</u> table correctly in order to get credit.
Wrong Answer Options	Watch out for answer options that include: • incorrect characteristics, or traits, for a category. For example, in a classification lecture, an incorrect answer option might give a fact for the wrong overall category.

WALK THROUGH: Connecting Content Questions

Below is a sample script and sample connecting content question for a test item based on part of a lecture in a botany class. While you listen, underline words in the script that you think might indicate the general categories presented in the lecture.   🎧 CD1, Track 43

SAMPLE SCRIPT ▶
for reference only, not available in test

Professor: Obviously, plants can't move around and spread, or, um, disperse, their seeds themselves. No . . . instead, they rely on factors like water, wind, and . . . well, animals to do it for them. And this process, um, the process of spreading seeds, it's called seed dispersal. Let's talk about this. Jenna, it looks like you had a question.

Student: Yes, in my backyard, there's a plant that has these weird kinds of seeds . . . they have sort of hooks on them. I think they're called burrs. And they're always getting stuck on my dog's fur. He ends up leaving them all over the place, so now these plants are growing all over the yard. Um, so my question is, is that an example of seed dispersal?

Professor: Definitely! That's a great example of how animals help disperse seeds. Here's another example you're probably familiar with: the dandelion. You know, those yellow flowers that seem to grow everywhere. And their seeds are attached to these fluffy white "feathers." They help the seeds get carried in air currents and float away.

Before we run out of time, let me just give you one more example. Everyone has seen a coconut, right? Well, believe it or not, coconuts can float. There are reports of coconuts growing on uninhabited islands. They floated across oceans and grew somewhere new! So that shows how water can help with seed dispersal.

Glossary:

▣ POWERED BY COBUILD

disperse: to spread over a wide area

uninhabited: a place where nobody lives

Seed Dispersal Methods

Now look at the sample connecting content question below. Review the parts of the script that you underlined above to choose the best answer.

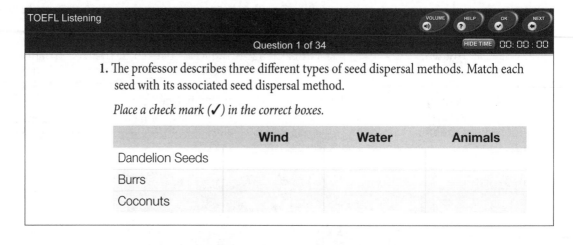

TOEFL Listening   VOLUME   HELP   OK   NEXT

Question 1 of 34   HIDE TIME 00:00:00

1. The professor describes three different types of seed dispersal methods. Match each seed with its associated seed dispersal method.

Place a check mark (✓) in the correct boxes.

	Wind	Water	Animals
Dandelion Seeds			
Burrs			
Coconuts			

GET IT RIGHT: Tips and Tasks for Answering Correctly

» **TIP 1: Identify the organizational structure of the lecture.** Connecting content questions often accompany lectures that provide definitions of a concept, show causes and effects, or present a process or historical event. By identifying the structure, you can take notes that help you classify information more easily.

TASK 1: What is the organizational structure of the lecture on page 52? (See page 50 for more about organizational structures.)

» **TIP 2: Listen carefully for categories presented by the professor.** These categories may include types of something, steps in a process, or the parts of a theory. The categories may be summarized at the beginning of the lecture when the professor introduces the main topic of the lecture.

TASK 2: Underline the words at the beginning of the lecture on page 52 that indicate what the lecture will be about.

» **TIP 3: Write the supporting ideas for each main point in the lecture while you listen.** The supporting ideas for main points are often the basis for connecting content questions. Supporting ideas might include explanations of steps, clarification of definitions, or examples.

TASK 3: Double underline the three examples that the professor gives in the lecture on page 52.

TEST TIP!

If you aren't sure how to categorize an item in a connecting content question, think of the main idea of the passage. Remember that the answers should support the main idea.

» **TIP 4: Read all the information given in the table.** This can include category titles and items that you are supposed to classify. Check your notes to determine the particular details assigned to each category. By understanding these details, you can avoid marking the wrong answers for a category.

TASK 4: What three items do you have to categorize for the question on page 52?

PROGRESSIVE PRACTICE: Get Ready

A Listen to part of a lecture in a geology class and check (✓) the points that are written in the notes below as you hear them. 🎧 CD1, Track 44

- **Mass wasting (mass movement)**
  - ☐ Definition: when rock or soil shifts to lower elevation due to gravity
  - ☐ 2 types: flow and creep

- **Flow - happens fast**
  - ☐ Landslides - slop and large amount of earth move downward
  - ☐ Mudslides - similar to landslides but mud moves
  - ☐ Rockfalls - rock(s) falling from a high place

- **Creep - happens slowly**
  - ☐ Caused by freezing and thawing of soil, animals grazing on the land
  - ☐ Creep is responsible for gentle sloping of hills

B Review the questions. What kinds of questions are they? Then, answer the questions. Note the correct answers and read why the answer options are correct or incorrect.

1. How is the lecture organized?
   ○ By presenting types of a geological event
   ○ By presenting a new theory and supporting it
   ○ By comparing two types of flow
   ○ By describing the causes of mass wasting

Mass Wasting

ANSWER ANALYSIS ▶

Question Type: Organization

  ✓ **The professor first gives a definition of mass wasting, then talks about the two main types, flow and creep.**

  ✗ The professor is not presenting and supporting a theory in her lecture. The information that she presents is all factual and is part of an extended definition of mass wasting.

  ✗ The professor discusses different types of flow, but she also discusses creep. When an answer option mentions "two types" of something, always read the option carefully before choosing it.

  ✗ The professor says that creep (a type of mass wasting) results from freezing and thawing of soil and from animal grazing. However, this is not the main organization of the lecture.

2. Why does the professor mention mass movement?
   ○ To compare it with mass wasting
   ○ To give an example of flow
   ○ To give an alternate term for mass wasting
   ○ To clarify the definition of mass wasting

ANSWER ANALYSIS ▶

Question Type: **Organization**

✗ By understanding the definition of mass wasting, you know that mass wasting and mass movement are the same thing. Therefore, they cannot be compared to each other.

✗ She doesn't discuss flow until later, so it's unlikely that mass movement is an example of flow. Look at your notes and see what part of the lecture the term comes from, and you will be able to eliminate this option.

✓ **The professor says that some people call mass wasting "mass movement." She is giving a different way of saying the term "mass wasting."**

✗ The professor says she will use the term "mass wasting" only for the sake of clarity. She is not defining it. Notice that wrong answers will often include similar language from the lecture to trick you.

3. Why does the professor discuss the difference between landslides and rockfalls?

○ To show the main difference between flow and creep

○ To make the point that there are many types of flow

○ To remind students of the dangers of mass wasting

○ To clarify a defining characteristic of flow

ANSWER ANALYSIS ▶

Question Type: **Organization**

✗ Both landslides and rockfalls are types of flow, so discussing them doesn't involve creep at all.

✗ She doesn't say anything to suggest that it's important for students to know that there are a lot of types of flow.

✗ While both landslides and rockfalls can be dangerous, she doesn't mention this at all.

✓ **After describing the difference, she says that both landslides and rockfalls occur quickly — a key feature of flow.**

4. The professor describes two types of mass wasting. Indicate what type of mass wasting each description is associated with.

Place a check mark (✓) in the correct boxes.

	Flow	Creep	Both
Examples include landslides and rockfalls			
Occurs as a result of gravity			
Creates the gentle slopes of some hills			
Happens very quickly			

ANSWER ANALYSIS ▶

Question Type: **Connecting Content**

	Flow	Creep	Both
Examples include landslides and rockfalls	✓		
Occurs as a result of gravity			✓
Creates the gentle slopes of some hills		✓	
Happens very quickly	✓		

Flow: After defining flow, the professor says that landslides, mudslides, and rockfalls are examples.

Both: When defining mass wasting, the professor says that it involves the downward movement of earth due to gravity. This applies to both flow and creep.

Creep: The professor says that creep causes the gentle slopes of hills.

Flow: The professor says that flow happens really fast.

PROGRESSIVE PRACTICE: Get Set

A Listen to part of a lecture in an engineering class. Then, complete the notes below. 🎧 CD1, Track 45

5 students ❶ _____ about what nanotechnology (NT) is used for: ❷ _____ - field of sci. that deals with manipulating matter on small scale (nanoscale)

Nanoscale expl.: measure meters, centimeters, ❸ _____ (we usually don't deal with smaller stuff than that)

NT deals with ❹ _____ - tiny units of matter, need special microscope to see them

One molecule is one-billionth of a ❺ _____

Ex. because students are confused:

1. Sunscreen uses ❻ _____ (tiny chemical compounds created by scientists) - makes it easier to rub sunscreen into skin, avoiding white tinge like before

2. Some clothing uses layers of nanoparticles to protect from UV rays (harmful rays from the ❼ _____) - scientists might be able to use nanoparticles to make clothes waterproof or stain-resistant

Ex. show that field is expanding

B Answer the questions. Then, write the letter of each answer option next to the reason why it is correct or incorrect in the *Answer Analysis* box.

1. How does the professor organize the information about nanotechnology that she presents to the class?

○ By comparing nanotechnology to large-scale technology [A]

○ By explaining the nanoscale and how scientists use it [B]

○ By discussing different applications of nanotechnology [C]

○ By talking about the history of the field of nanotechnology [D]

ANSWER ANALYSIS ▶

_____ ✗ The professor discusses the nanoscale in order to define nanotechnology. However, the entire lecture is not organized according to the explanation of the nanoscale.

_____ ✗ The professor refers to the future of nanotechnology when he says that the field is expanding. He does not discuss the history of nanotechnology.

_____ ✓ **When the professor sees that students are confused after he defines nanotechnology and the nanoscale, he says he will give examples of how it is used so the students will understand.**

_____ ✗ He describes the nanoscale, but she does not talk about large-scale technology during the lecture.

2. What point does the professor make when she refers to the e-mails she received?

○ He thinks students are not very interested in learning about nanotechnology. [A]

○ The students would benefit if he returned to a topic she discussed previously. [B]

○ Students should feel free to send him questions by e-mail. [C]

○ He doesn't use the e-mail system very often. [D]

TOEFL Listening

Nanotechnology Microparticles

ANSWER ANALYSIS ▶

_____ ✗ The large number of e-mails that the professor received suggests that the students are interested in learning about nanotechnology.

_____ ✓ **He says that he received e-mails from five students asking for clarification about the uses of nanotechnology. He also says that he thinks that students weren't clear on the topic. He thinks the concept will be clearer, if he talks about nanotechnology again.**

_____ ✗ The professor says he received e-mails but does not suggest that he doesn't use the e-mail system very often.

_____ ✗ He says he received e-mails that contained questions. However, he doesn't encourage students to e-mail him with questions.

3. How does the professor highlight the relative size of a molecule?

○ By describing how many of them would fit on a pinhead [A]

○ By comparing meters to centimeters and millimeters [B]

○ By mentioning the number of molecules that make up everyday items [C]

○ By describing units of matter that are smaller than nanoparticles [D]

ANSWER ANALYSIS ▶

_____ ✓ **To highlight the very small size of a molecule, he says that one million can fit on the head of just one pin.**

_____ ✗ The professor mentions all of these units of measurement. However, he does not compare them to one another—she says only that nanoparticles are much smaller than any of them.

_____ ✗ The professor talks about several everyday items, including a pin, sunscreen, and clothing. However, he does not mention how many molecules make up any of these items.

_____ ✗ The professor makes no reference in the lecture to anything smaller than a nanoparticle.

4. Based on the information in the lecture, indicate whether the statements below about nanotechnology are correct or incorrect.

Place a check mark (✓) in the correct boxes.

	Correct	Incorrect
It involves manipulation of molecules. [A]		
It is exclusively for medical uses. [B]		
It is a subfield of nanoscale manufacturing. [C]		
It has been used to develop nanoparticles. [D]		

ANSWER ANALYSIS ▶

	Correct	Incorrect
It involves manipulation of molecules. [A]	✓	
It is exclusively for medical uses. [B]		✓
It is a subfield of nanoscale manufacturing. [C]		✓
It has been used to develop nanoparticles. [D]	✓	

_____ Correct: If nanotechnology is the field of using and changing molecules, then we know that nanotechnology was used to create nanoparticles.

_____ Incorrect: He discusses the nanoscale to clarify what nanotechnology is. He does not discuss subfields of nanotechnology.

_____ Incorrect: The professor says that it is common to hear about the medical and industrial uses of nanotechnology, but he gives two examples of applications that aren't related to medicine.

_____ Correct: The definition of nanotechnology describes it as the field of using and changing molecules.

PROGRESSIVE PRACTICE: Go for the TOEFL Test

Listen to part of a discussion in a biology class and take notes. 🎧 CD1, Track 46

NOTES:

_____

_____

_____

_____

_____

_____

_____

_____

Now answer the questions. You may use your notes.

1. **Why does the professor mention laying eggs?**
   🎧 CD1, Track 47
   ○ To describe one of the features that all birds possess
   ○ To point out a difference between flying and non-flying birds
   ○ To give an example of a behavior that helps birds fly
   ○ To illustrate a biological problem that birds have

2. **Listen again to part of the lecture. Then, answer the question. Why does the professor say this?** 🎧 CD1, Track 48
   ○ He wants to relate a previously mentioned detail to the main topic.
   ○ He can't remember what he wants to talk about next.
   ○ He thinks the students can provide examples of non-flying birds.
   ○ He is unsure if the students understand the point he just made.

3. **How does the professor explain the concept of lift?**
   🎧 CD1, Track 49
   ○ By comparing it to bird flight
   ○ By describing the way in which a kite flies
   ○ By classifying different kinds of bird feathers
   ○ By explaining the role of wing rigidity in flight

4. **The professor discusses features of birds that are designed to help them fly. Match each statement with the bird feature with which it is associated.**

   Place a check mark (✓) in the correct boxes. 🎧 CD1, Track 50

	Feathers	Skeleton	Neither
Lets the bird fly without using a lot of energy			
Allows the bird to move upward and off the ground			
Permits the bird to travel over long distances without getting lost			
Helps the bird control the direction it is flying in			

Listening Review Test

The following section will test the skills that you've learned so far. In the *Listening Review Test*, you will listen to six listening passages. You will not be able to see the scripts for the passages. After each passage, you will answer a set of five or six questions. The difficulty of these listening passages and questions is the same as those that appear on the TOEFL test.

Note that the listening section in the review test is divided into two subparts, just as it is on the real test. For each subpart, you will listen to three listening passages. You will have 30 minutes to answer 17 questions in each subpart. See the timing guide below for details on how much time you will have to answer the questions.

Listening Section Timing Guide	
Passage	**Time to Answer Questions**
1. Office Hours Conversation	Questions 1–17 30 minutes
2. Academic Lecture	
3. Academic Discussion	
4. Service Encounter Conversation	Questions 18–34 30 minutes
5. Academic Discussion	
6. Academic Lecture	

When you start the review test, be sure to follow the directions exactly as they appear on the page. Use a clock to time yourself while you answer the questions, and make sure that you don't take more than 30 minutes for each subpart. Just remember to stop your clock when you are listening to the audio passages!

Furthermore, because you are <u>not</u> allowed to review previously answered questions on the TOEFL test, we advise you to avoid looking at previous questions when you take the practice test. You might use a sheet of blank paper to cover the questions you have already answered. This will keep you from returning to them.

After you complete the review test, use the answer key to check if your answers are correct. Look at the questions you got wrong and determine what type of questions they are. Did you have trouble with a particular question type? If so, make sure to review that question type before you take the TOEFL test.

PART 1: LISTENING 1

Listen to a conversation between a student and her international business professor. Take notes. 🎧 CD2, Track 2

NOTES:

Now answer the questions. You may use your notes.

1. **Why does the student visit the professor?**   CD2, Track 3
   ○ To ask for research tips for her final project
   ○ To explain her poor performance in the class
   ○ To discuss the best project format for her
   ○ To change the topic of her final project

2. **What is the student's attitude toward the people in her group?**   CD2, Track 4
   ○ She has enjoyed working with them.
   ○ She thinks that they are unreliable.
   ○ She fears they don't have the same academic interests.
   ○ She thinks that they are too busy.

3. **What did the professor ask the student to do for her group?**   CD2, Track 5
   ○ Ask them for a list of sources
   ○ Discuss changing the topic
   ○ E-mail them to change the meeting time
   ○ Share her research with them

4. **Listen again to part of the conversation. Then, answer the question.**   CD2, Track 6

   What is the professor trying to find out from the student?
   ○ How much time she has spent researching her topic
   ○ Whether she has found a specific topic for her paper
   ○ Where she found sources that discuss the topic
   ○ Whether she has had any problems writing the paper

5. **What will the student probably do next?**   CD2, Track 7
   ○ Meet with her group
   ○ Visit the library
   ○ Check her e-mail
   ○ Begin writing her paper

LISTENING 2

Listen to part of a lecture in a management class and take notes. 🎧 CD2, Track 8

NOTES:

Now answer the questions. You may use your notes.

6. What is the lecture mainly about?　CD2, Track 9
   ○ The common types of scheduling systems used by managers
   ○ The problems with conventional workday schedules
   ○ The advantages and disadvantages of a flextime scheduling system
   ○ The kinds of companies that benefit from flextime schedules

7. Listen again to part of the lecture. Then, answer the question.

   What does the professor imply when he says this?　CD2, Track 10
   ○ Most of the students in the class have part-time jobs.
   ○ The university limits how many hours students can work per week.
   ○ Flextime is fairly common amongst people with full-time jobs.
   ○ Almost all employers allow employees to use flextime scheduling.

8. Why does the professor mention school schedules?　CD2, Track 11
   ○ To show other places that use flextime schedules
   ○ To liken a condensed schedule to a typical school day
   ○ To explain why flextime schedules were originally created
   ○ To describe how flextime can be useful for working parents

9. According to the professor, how do companies benefit from offering flextime?　CD2, Track 12
   ○ It gives managers flexibility when creating schedules.
   ○ It makes it easier to plan staff meetings.
   ○ It builds loyalty among workers.
   ○ It encourages employees to work harder.

10. What can be inferred about flextime?　CD2, Track 13
   ○ It is probably not offered at jobs where managers must closely observe employees.
   ○ It is not popular among employees who have no family obligations.
   ○ Altered schedules are the most common type of flextime schedule.
   ○ Most people prefer conventional work schedules to flextime schedules.

11. The professor discusses two types of flextime schedules. Match each statement with the flextime schedule with which it is associated.　CD2, Track 14

   Place a check mark (✓) in the correct boxes.

	Condensed Schedule	Altered Schedule	Neither
Helps working parents			
Allows employees to work fewer than 40 hours a week			
Permits employees to work full-time in fewer than five days			
Good for people who are able to work more than eight hours a day			

LISTENING 3

Listen to part of a discussion in an oceanography class and take notes.
CD2, Track 15

diel vertical migration

NOTES:

Now answer the questions. You may use your notes.

12. **What is the main topic of the discussion?** 🎧 CD2, Track 16

○ A comparison of diel vertical migration and reverse migration

○ Why some organisms use diel vertical migration

○ The relationship between size and hunting behavior in ocean animals

○ How scientists discovered diel vertical migration

13. **Listen again to part of the discussion. Then, answer the question.**

Why does the student say this? 🎧 CD2, Track 17

○ To ask about the origins of the word "diel"

○ To show that she understands the concept

○ To suggest that the professor's definition was incomplete

○ To find out the correct pronunciation of a word

14. **Why does the professor mention squid?** 🎧 CD2, Track 18

○ To name a predator that typically hunts during the day

○ To describe an animal that lives in shallow waters

○ To give an example of an organism that uses diel vertical migration

○ To suggest that few animals use diel vertical migration

15. **What does the professor say about reverse migration?** 🎧 CD2, Track 19

○ It doesn't occur as often as diel vertical migration.

○ It is more common in lakes than it is in the ocean.

○ Some animals use both reverse migration and diel vertical migration.

○ Many scientists don't think it exists.

16. **Based on the information in the discussion, what can be inferred about aquatic predators?**
🎧 CD2, Track 20

○ They hunt primarily by using their sense of sight.

○ They don't follow their prey's migration patterns.

○ They are less vulnerable to sunlight than their prey is.

○ They often prey on creatures that use reverse migration.

17. **Based on the information in the discussion, indicate whether the statements below about diel vertical migration are correct or incorrect.** 🎧 CD2, Track 21

Place a check mark (✓) in the correct boxes.

	Correct	Incorrect
Provides security for animals		
Helps animals find new sources of food		
Protects animals from damaging sunlight		
Occurs in oceans and lakes		

PART 2: LISTENING 4

Listen to part of a conversation between a student and an employee at the housing office. Take notes. 🎧 CD2, Track 22

NOTES:

Now answer the questions. You may use your notes.

18. **Why does the student visit the housing office?** ⌾ CD2, Track 23
    - ○ To complain about the residents in her dorm
    - ○ To request to live off campus
    - ○ To apply to live in a special dormitory
    - ○ To find out about the quiet hours in her dorm

19. **What problem is the student having?** ⌾ CD2, Track 24
    - ○ She can't study in her room.
    - ○ She doesn't get along with her roommate.
    - ○ She lives too far from her classes.
    - ○ She can't afford to pay the dorm fees.

20. **According to the conversation, what are the benefits of living on campus?** ⌾ CD2, Track 25
    Choose two answers.
    - ☐ It is relatively inexpensive.
    - ☐ It provides students with social support.
    - ☐ It gives students access to important services.
    - ☐ It is quieter than off-campus housing.

21. **What is the student's attitude about the Quiet Dorm?** ⌾ CD2, Track 26
    - ○ She fears that its rules are too strict.
    - ○ She thinks it's a good option for her.
    - ○ She feels that it's too far away from the library.
    - ○ She thinks it will give her a way to meet new people.

22. **What will the student probably do next?** ⌾ CD2, Track 27
    - ○ Report her neighbors to campus authorities
    - ○ Change her schedule so she can study in the library
    - ○ Start searching for housing off campus
    - ○ Apply to live in the Quiet Dorm

LISTENING 5

Listen to part of a discussion in a biology class and take notes. 🎧 CD2, Track 28

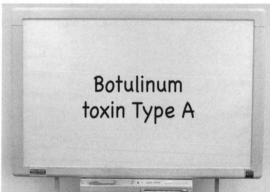

Botulinum toxin Type A

NOTES:

Now answer the questions. You may use your notes.

23. What is the discussion mostly about?　🎧 CD2, Track 29
   ○ How animals produce biotoxins
   ○ Ways for treating biotoxin poisoning
   ○ Common types of biotoxins
   ○ The medicinal uses of biotoxins

24. Listen again to part of the discussion. Then, answer the question.

   Why does the professor say this?　🎧 CD2, Track 30
   ○ To help the students understand the definition of a key term
   ○ To encourage students to think about a familiar topic in a new way
   ○ To suggest that the topic will appear on a test
   ○ To demonstrate how biotoxins can be useful

25. Why does the professor mention bees?　🎧 CD2, Track 31
   ○ To explain how animals use biotoxins
   ○ To give an example of a nonpoisonous animal
   ○ To illustrate the danger of biotoxins
   ○ To emphasize how common biotoxins are

26. What does the professor imply about bacteria?　🎧 CD2, Track 32
   ○ Most people don't consider them living organisms.
   ○ They are commonly added to many medications.
   ○ Most types of bacteria are not harmful to humans.
   ○ They should not be considered biotoxins.

27. According to the discussion, what is true about painkillers?　🎧 CD2, Track 33
   ○ There are many types currently available.
   ○ They are all made from biotoxins.
   ○ They are inexpensive compared to other medications.
   ○ They are dangerous even in small doses.

28. Based on the information in the discussion, indicate whether the statements below describe botulinum type A, conotoxin, or both.　🎧 CD2, Track 34

Place a check mark (✓) in the correct boxes.

	Botulinum Type A	Conotoxin	Both
Produced by a living organism			
Must be purified before it can be used as medication			
Can be used as a painkiller			
Can be used to cure migraines			

LISTENING 6

Listen to part of a lecture in an astronomy
class and take notes. 🎧 CD2, Track 35

NOTES:

Now answer the questions. You may use your notes.

29. What aspect of Mars does the professor mainly discuss? ☊ CD2, Track 36
    ○ Its seasonal similarities to Earth
    ○ How its weather patterns are changing
    ○ The basic characteristics of its climate
    ○ Its suitability for supporting life

30. Listen again to part of the lecture. Then, answer the question.

    Why does the professor mention life on Mars? ☊ CD2, Track 37
    ○ To prove that Mars's climate is unrelated to its ability to support life
    ○ To illustrate why scientists are interested in studying the Martian climate
    ○ To challenge the idea that the climate on Mars is similar to Earth's climate
    ○ To propose that Mars will be able to support life in the future

31. Why does the professor tell the students that Mars takes twice as long as Earth to go around the sun? ☊ CD2, Track 38
    ○ To explain the length of Martian seasons
    ○ To demonstrate the differences between Earth and Mars
    ○ To argue that Mars has more than four seasons
    ○ To suggest that distance from the sun doesn't affect temperatures

32. According to the lecture, what is true about temperatures on Mars? ☊ CD2, Track 39
    ○ They vary less than temperatures on Earth.
    ○ They are below freezing at all times.
    ○ They change according to location and time.
    ○ They were probably colder in the past.

33. Based on the information in the lecture, what can be inferred about Mars? ☊ CD2, Track 40
    ○ The position of its poles changes often.
    ○ It has higher wind speeds than Earth does.
    ○ It may influence weather patterns on Earth.
    ○ It will be less windy there in the future.

34. According to the professor, what do scientists believe about dust storms on Mars?
    ☊ CD2, Track 41
    ○ They're responsible for the long seasons.
    ○ They are affecting larger parts of the planet than in the past.
    ○ They're related to extremely high wind speeds.
    ○ They're occurring less frequently because of colder weather.

Overview of the Speaking Section

The speaking section is the third part of the TOEFL test. It tests your ability to speak English by presenting you with a variety of tasks. During this section, you will wear a headset. The headphones of the headset are noise-canceling, which means that you will not be able to hear the other test-takers give their responses while you are working on the section. The headset is also equipped with a microphone that you can adjust so that your spoken responses can be digitally recorded.

QUICK GUIDE: TOEFL® Test Speaking Section

Definition	The speaking section tests your ability to understand written and spoken English and respond to questions appropriately. For each question, you will be presented with a specific task that may test the following skills: reading, listening and speaking, and speaking only.
Targeted Skills	In order to do well on the speaking section, you must be able to: • understand and respond to questions. • express your opinion about a subject. • report the ideas and / or opinions of other people. • summarize the main idea of a listening passage. • combine information from different sources. • answer questions within the given time.
The Questions	The speaking section includes six distinct questions. The first two questions are independent questions, and the remaining four are integrated exercises (for more information about question types, see page 85).
Timing	The time that you have to prepare and respond to each question varies by question type. See the list below for the order in which the questions appear on the test and the preparation and response times for each question type.

Question Type	Preparation	Response
1. Personal Experience	15 seconds	45 seconds
2. Paired Choice	15 seconds	45 seconds
3. Campus Matters	30 seconds	60 seconds
4. Academic Reading and Lecture	30 seconds	60 seconds
5. Campus Conversation	20 seconds	60 seconds
6. Academic Summary	20 seconds	60 seconds

The entire section takes approximately **20 minutes** to complete.

Speaking Section: What You'll See and Hear

On-screen Tools

You will see a number of on-screen tools during the speaking section. Study the sample screen below to familiarize yourself with the on-screen tools for the speaking section.

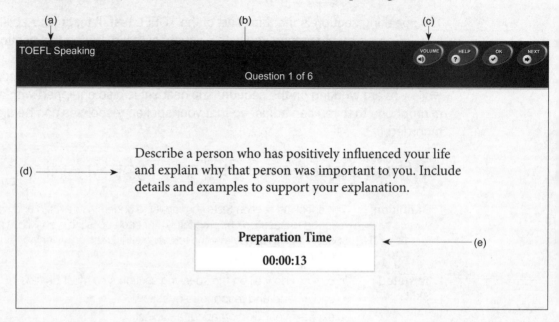

(a) indicates what **section of the test** you are currently working on

(b) shows how many of the **questions** you have **completed** in the section

(c) allows you to **adjust the volume** of the listening passages. When you click on this button, you will be able to move a slider up or down in order to increase or decrease the volume.

(d) shows you the prompt on the screen. You will also hear the narrator reading the prompt through the headphones.

(e) shows how much time you have left to prepare. During your response time, the on-screen clock will show how much time you have left to respond.

Screen-by-Screen Process

There are a total of six questions on the speaking section. The screens that you will see during the test will vary by question type. Familiarize yourself with the screens on this section so that you will know what to expect on the day of the test.

Section Introduction

1. Instructions: First, you will see an instruction screen that directs you to put on your headphones. You will be instructed to click "Next" on the toolbar to proceed.

2. Volume Adjustment: On the next screen, you will be reminded how to adjust the volume using the on-screen tools. At this time, you can adjust the volume or click "Next" on the toolbar to go to the next screen.

3. Microphone Adjustment: You will see a screen that gives you instructions on how to adjust your microphone to make sure that it is functioning properly. When you are ready to start the adjustment, you will click "Next."

On the next screen, you will be instructed to speak a response to the following sentence: *Describe the city that you live in.* Please note that this portion is not graded and is used only to adjust your microphone. Just be sure to speak clearly and in your normal speaking voice.

You will continue to speak until a screen appears that says the following: *Stop speaking.* At this point, you will be notified whether your microphone is ready or not. If you have problems adjusting your microphone, you will need to raise your hand and get help from an employee at the test center.

If your microphone is functioning properly, you will continue to the next screen.

4. **Section Instructions:** You will see an instruction screen that gives you general information about the section, including the number of tasks in the section, how much time is allotted for preparing and answering each question, comments on scoring, etc. In addition to being able to read the instructions on the screen, you will hear the narrator read the instructions through your headphones. You must wait until the narrator has finished reading the instructions before you are allowed to move on to the next screen. When you click "Next," you will continue to the six tasks.

Questions 1 and 2: Independent Speaking Tasks

1. **Preparation Screen:** You will briefly see a picture of a person with headphones. The narrator will instruct you to prepare for the question.

2. **Question Screen:** Then, you will see a screen with the question. In addition to being able to read the question on the screen, you will hear the narrator read the question through your headphones. After the narrator finishes reading the question, the preparation and response time will appear on the screen. At this time, a clock will appear on the screen and will begin to count down your preparation time. When the preparation time is done, the narrator will say the following: *Please begin speaking after the beep.* After the beep, a clock on the screen will count down how much time you have left. After your time is up, you will hear another beep and the screen will change automatically.

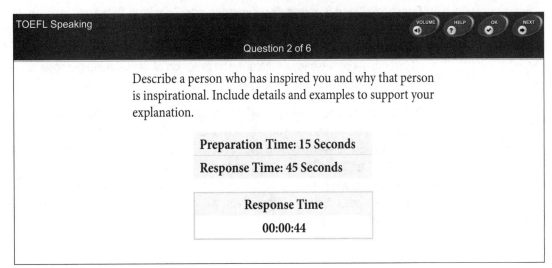

Questions 3 and 4: Integrated Reading, Listening, and Speaking Tasks

1. **Reading Screen:** You will see a reading passage on the screen. The narrator will describe the general topic of the reading and tell you how much time you have to read the passage. The amount of time you have to read the passage will also be on the screen.

Reading Time : 45 seconds

Animal Adaptations in the Desert

In the desert, the heat and lack of water have led animals to take on two specific adaptations that encourage survival. Some animals adapt to the limited food supply by expanding the types of food they ingest. Unlike animals that only eat plants or hunt to survive, some desert animals eat any plant or animal they can. By doing so, these animals increase the likelihood of ingesting enough water and nutrients to survive.

Others maximize their opportunities to locate food by hunting at peak hours of prey activity throughout the day, like the early evening and early morning. This provides opportunities to hunt creatures that are active at night as well as those that are active during the day.

2. Listening Screen: On the next screen, you will see a picture of a university setting (the picture will vary according to passage type). The narrator will describe the setting and topic of the listening, and you will listen to a passage. The progress of the listening passage is marked by a blue bar on the bottom center of the screen.

3. Question Screen: Then, you will see a screen with the question. In addition to being able to read the question on the screen, you will hear the narrator read the question through your headphones. After the narrator finishes reading the question, the preparation and response time will appear on the screen. At this time, a clock will appear on the screen and will begin to count down your preparation time. When the preparation time is done, the narrator will say the following: *Please begin speaking after the beep.* After the beep, a clock on the screen will count down how much time you have left. After your time is up, you will hear another beep and the screen will change automatically.

Questions 5 and 6: Integrated Listening and Speaking Tasks

1. Listening Screen: On the first screen, you will see a picture of a university setting (the picture will vary according to passage type). The narrator will describe the setting and topic of the listening, and you will listen to a conversation or lecture. The progress of the listening passage is marked by a blue bar on the bottom center of the screen.

2. Question Screen: Then, you will see a screen with the question. In addition to being able to read the question on the screen, you will also hear the narrator read the question through your headphones. After the narrator finishes reading the question, the preparation and response time will appear on the screen. At this time, a clock will appear on the screen and will begin to count down your preparation time. When the preparation time is done, the narrator will say the following: *Please begin speaking after the beep.* After the beep, a clock on the screen will count down how much time you have left. After your time is up, you will hear another beep and the screen will change automatically.

Speaking Section: Item Types

In the speaking section, there are two types of items: independent questions and integrated questions. The main difference between the item types is the skills involved in answering them. Some involve speaking only, others involve listening and speaking, while others still involve a combination of listening, reading, and speaking.

Independent Tasks: The first and second questions (Personal Experience and Paired Choice questions) are independent tasks. For these questions, you will be asked a short question about general topics.

Independent Tasks	
Question 1	**Question 2**
Skill: Speaking Only	**Skill: Speaking Only**
You will be presented with a question on a general topic. You will be able to respond to this question based on your personal experiences and do not need any knowledge in a specific academic subject to respond.	You will be presented with 2 options. You will state the option that you prefer and provide support based on your personal experiences. Again, you do not need any specific academic knowledge.

Integrated Tasks: The remaining four questions in the speaking section are integrated tasks. These tasks require you to use a combination of skills in order to answer the questions.

Integrated Tasks	
Questions 3 and 4	**Questions 5 and 6**
Skills: Reading / Listening / Speaking	**Skills: Listening / Speaking**
First, you will read a text. Then, you will hear a listening on the same topic of the text. The question will involve combining information from the text and the listening.	First, you will hear a listening. Then, you will answer a question that is based on the listening. In your response, you will have to summarize the information from the listening.

Speaking Section: Scoring: The responses that you give on the speaking section are digitally recorded and sent to ETS, where they are scored by human raters. Three raters will review each response and give it a rating of 1–4, with 4 being the highest score possible. The 3 ratings are added together, and the sum is converted to a score that falls on the 0–30 score range.

When scoring your responses, the raters will listen to the entire response and assign you a rating based on your overall skill. This means that it's possible to make a few mistakes and still receive a top score as long as your overall response fulfills the general scoring criteria described below.

Scoring Category	What Raters Will Be Looking For
Delivery	• You don't speak too fast or too slowly. • You make use of all of the allowed time when you give your response. • Your language is easy to understand.
Language Usage	• You use proper grammar in your response. • You use varied vocabulary. • You are able to produce complex sentence structures in English.
Topic Development	• You stay on topic for the duration of your response. • Your response is well organized and easy to understand. • You provide sufficient support for your response. • You clearly show the relationships between your ideas.

Please note that raters don't expect your response to be perfect. For example, some pronunciation and / or intonation mistakes are OK as long as you can still be understood.

Challenges and Solutions

» **CHALLENGE 1: "I don't know what to say when I give my answers."**

SOLUTION: Learn exactly what ETS is looking for in an answer. While the scoring criteria vary slightly according to the question, there are some general features that every response on the speaking section should include. Look at the scoring guide on page 155 for a general overview of how your responses will be scored. The explanations for each question (page 85) also provide a more detailed guide as to what you should include in your responses. Knowing ahead of time exactly what information you will be expected to give for each question will give you a general idea of what to say on the day of the test.

SOLUTION: Quickly write a bare-bones outline of your response. Depending on the question, you will have between 15 and 30 seconds to prepare your response. You should use this time to quickly prepare an outline of your response. Don't bother writing out the entire response; rather, you should focus on writing down a few words to help you remember and organize the key parts of your response. This will serve as a guide for you when you start speaking and help keep you from freezing during the response time.

Also, remember that the preparation time won't start until after the narrator has finished reading the question. Since the question also appears on your screen, you can earn some extra time to prepare by reading the question yourself and starting to write your outline as soon as you have read and understood the question. Finally, remember that people tend to lose focus when they feel nervous. By preparing an outline, you will feel more confident when you give your response, which will keep you from rambling.

SOLUTION: Use the templates found in the *Get Set* sections of this book to organize your answers. For each question type, there is specific information that you must include in your response. By understanding what information you need to include for each question type, you will have a better idea of what you need to say during the response time.

Templates by Question Type		

Question 1
Restatement of the Prompt
Topic Sentence
    Key Point 1
        Personal Details
    Key Point 2
        Personal Details
	Question 2
	Restatement of the Prompt
	Topic Sentence
	    Key Point 1
	        Personal Details
	    Key Point 2
	        Personal Details
		Question 3
		Proposed Change
		    Reason 1 for Change
		    Reason 2 for Change
		Student's Opinion
		    Reason 1 for Opinion
		        Supporting Details
		    Reason 2 for Opinion
		        Supporting Details

Question 4
Reading and Lecture Topic
    Relationship Between Sources
Key Point 1 from Reading
    Support from Lecture
Key Point 2 from Reading
    Support from Lecture
	Question 5
	Summary of Problem
	    Description of Possible Solutions
	    Recommendation
	Reason 1
	    Supporting Details
	Reason 2
	    Supporting Details
		Question 6
		Main Topic of Lecture
		    Key Point 1
		        Supporting Details
		    Key Point 2
		        Supporting Details

» **CHALLENGE 2: "I always run out of time and end up getting cut off before presenting all my information."**

SOLUTION: Time yourself when you practice for questions in the speaking section. There are many practice speaking items provided in this book. A good strategy for preparing for the speaking section is to use a clock to time yourself when you complete the practice sections. The following chart shows how much time to give yourself for each question.

Response Times by Question		
Question 1 Personal Experience **45 seconds**	**Question 2** Paired Choice **45 seconds**	**Question 3** Campus Matters **60 seconds**
Question 4 Academic Reading and Lecture **60 seconds**	**Question 5** Campus Conversation **60 seconds**	**Question 6** Academic Summary **60 seconds**

By timing yourself while you practice, you will learn how to pace yourself when giving your responses. That way, you won't speak too fast (or too slowly) and you will be able to give a complete response during the allotted time.

SOLUTION: Use the on-screen tools to help you determine how much time you have left. When you give a response on the speaking section, you will see a clock on your computer screen that will count down how much time you have left to respond. While you are speaking your answer into the microphone, check the clock to determine whether you will have enough time to finish your response. If you see that you have only a little time left, try to speed up, but not so much that your speech is difficult to understand.

SOLUTION: Focus on quality and <u>not</u> quantity. The raters are not concerned with how much information you can provide in the given time. Rather, they want to know if you can give a response that adequately answers the question. If you organize your response using the templates provided in this book, you are sure to provide all of the information that raters are looking for in a top-scoring response—and none of the extra information that will waste your given response time.

An added advantage of using the templates to organize your responses is that they will help you reduce the number of fillers you use while you give your response. Fillers are words or sounds that speakers use to get extra time while they think of what to say next. In English, common fillers include *um*, *uh*, and *like*. When you organize your response before you start speaking, you won't need to use fillers to think of what you will say next. This will help you save time when you give your response.

SOLUTION: Know which questions in the speaking section require you to express opinions. Some questions require you to give your opinion, while others ask you to describe the opinions of other people. Knowing this information will help you prepare before you take the test. Use the table below to help you know when and how to use opinion language.

Question	Whose Opinion Will You Give?	Expressions You Can Use in Your Response
Question 2: Paired Choice	Give <u>your own opinion</u> about which of the two provided options is best.	• *While some people think that X, I personally believe that . . .* • *I know that some people feel differently, but it's my opinion that . . .* • *I realize that not everybody will agree, but I think that . . .* • *Of the two choices given, I strongly believe that . . .* • *Other people might disagree, but my view is that . . .*
Question 3: Campus Matters	Give the opinion of <u>one student in the conversation</u>. One student in the conversation will either strongly agree or disagree with the campus matter. Do <u>not</u> give your own opinion for this task!	• *The woman feels that . . .* • *The man in the conversation thinks X is a good / bad idea.* • *The woman says she supports / opposes . . .* • *In the man's opinion, X is a good / bad plan . . .* • *The woman's view is that X is positive / negative . . .*
Question 5: Campus Conversation	Give <u>your own opinion</u> about what the speaker in the conversation should do. Your recommendation should be based on the options provided in the conversation.	• *If you ask me, the man's best option is to . . .* • *My recommendation for the woman is . . .* • *I think that the man should . . .* • *My suggestion is that the woman . . .* • *If I were in the man's position, I would . . .*

Each question type in the speaking section is addressed in detail and includes more opinion language for specific question types.

SOLUTION: Be aware that there are no right or wrong opinions on the TOEFL test. In other words, you are <u>not</u> being graded based on your opinions themselves. What's really important is how well you support your opinion in your response. For questions that require you to give your own opinion, try to determine which opinion would be easiest to support. If you think of it this way, you will feel more confident about speaking your opinions because you will know that you can support them. Also, remember that giving an opinion on the TOEFL test is just part of a task—it's not an activity that exposes you or your personal feelings.

» CHALLENGE 4: "I forget most of the information given in the reading passages and audio recordings as I'm giving my response."

Solution: Know what to expect. Four of the six tasks in the speaking section are integrated tasks. This means that they require listening / speaking skills or a combination of reading / listening / speaking skills. Although you can't know exactly which topics will appear on the test, by studying in this book the descriptions of each question type, you will understand how the reading and listening passages are organized and what type of information is typically included in them. This knowledge might help you fill in the gaps or guess the general ideas of the information you've forgotten.

For example, imagine that you are on question 5 (Campus Conversation) on the test and you can't remember what the conversation was about. If you know that the speakers in Campus Conversation questions <u>always</u> talk about a problem that one of the speakers is having, it might help you remember other details, too.

SOLUTION: Take notes! While you read or listen, you should be sure to write down important information that you can use in your response. How do you know what information is important? If you're familiar with all of the question types, you'll know what information you'll be expected to include in your responses. Study the table below for the basic information you should be writing down for each question type.

Question	Skills	What You Should Write Down
Question 3: Campus Matters	Reading / Listening	<u>Reading</u> • Proposed change • Two reasons for change <u>Listening (Conversation)</u> • Student's opinion of change • Two reasons for that opinion
Question 4: Academic Reading and Lecture	Reading / Listening	<u>Reading</u> • Main idea • Two key points <u>Listening (Lecture)</u> • Two supporting details for topic from reading
Question 5: Campus Conversation	Listening	• Student's problem • Two possible solutions • Advantages and disadvantages of each possible solution
Question 6: Academic Lecture	Listening	• Main topic of lecture • Two key points

CHALLENGE 5: "On the integrated tasks, I never have enough time to finish reading the reading passage before the audio recording begins."

SOLUTION: Be prepared to begin reading the passages for Questions 3 and 4 as soon as they appear on the screen. On the day of the test, the reading passage will appear on the screen while the narrator introduces the passage. Don't wait until the narrator finishes speaking to begin reading. By beginning to read while the narrator is still speaking, you will gain a few extra seconds to read the passage.

SOLUTION: Use the on-screen tools to help you keep track of how much time you have. Remember, when the narrator finishes introducing the reading topic, the clock on the screen will begin counting down the time. As you read, look at the clock to see how much time you have left. You may need to read faster or scan for details (see below) if you are running out of time.

SOLUTION: Time yourself while you read excerpts from textbooks and on-campus notices. The practice readings should be about 100 words each, and you should give yourself 45 seconds to read each one. If you practice reading the same types of texts that appear on the test, you're more likely to improve your reading speed.

To find texts like those that appear on Campus Matters questions, try visiting student-life sections of university Web sites. These sites are likely to have announcements about campus events or notices that are similar to those that appear on the test.

To find texts like those on Academic Reading and Lecture questions, look through introductory textbooks. Be sure to look for subjects that commonly appear on the TOEFL test, including biology, botany, marketing, sociology, and psychology.

SOLUTION: Practice scanning texts for major details. In some cases, you will not have time to read all of the text that is provided on the test. If you don't think you will be able to finish reading in the time you have left, you will need to scan the rest of the reading for important details. This means quickly looking for important details that will help you create a strong response. Look for the signposts below to help you quickly find the key points and supporting details while you scan.

Key Points Signposts	Supporting Details Signposts
The first / second reason . . .	For example . . .
Another example of . . .	According to . . .
Furthermore . . .	A recent survey shows . . .
In addition . . .	To illustrate . . .
Other ways that . . .	For instance . . .

» **CHALLENGE 6: "I'm worried that the raters won't understand me. My pronunciation is bad."**

SOLUTION: Record yourself speaking English. Start by recording yourself while you speak the model responses found in this book. When you are done, compare your recording with that of the native speaker. How is your pronunciation different from the native speaker? Keep recording your voice until you sound more like the native speaker.

For extra practice, download an English-language news program or podcast. Write down a section of the program. Then, record yourself while you read the transcription. Compare the recording of your voice with the original newscaster. Can you match the pronunciation and intonation of the native speaker? Keep practicing until you do.

SOLUTION: Ask your friends to listen to a recording of you speaking English. Sometimes it is hard to judge whether or not your language is easy to understand. By listening to your speech, your friends might be able to point out pronunciation problems that you didn't notice on your own. In particular, ask your friends if it is easy to understand what you are saying. What parts do they have difficulty understanding? Using the feedback from your friends, practice speaking the words that you had the most trouble with until it is easy for others to understand your speech.

SOLUTION: Listen to as much English as possible. When you listen to native English speakers talk, make sure to notice important pronunciation and intonation patterns. You might want to try listening to English-language radio programs while you work or watching English-language television in your free time. Then, start using the pronunciation and intonation patterns you hear to sound more like a native speaker. This will greatly improve the clearness of your English.

SOLUTION: Find opportunities to practice speaking English with native English speakers. To find native English speakers in your area, try going to tourist attractions in your city, like museums or landmarks. You may also want to join an English-language speaking club at your school. If your school doesn't have an English-language speaking club, check for one at the local library.

SOLUTION: Don't forget that the stress of many words may depend on whether you use the word as a noun or a verb. For the words listed below, the first syllable is stressed if you use the word as a noun. Conversely, the second syllable is stressed if you use the word as a verb. If you choose to use these words in your responses on the speaking section, make sure to use the correct pronunciation.

address	combat	conduct	confine
conflict	construct	contest	contract
contrast	converse	convert	decrease
detail	discount	frequent	impact
incline	increase	insert	invite
object	perfect	permit	present
proceed	produce	protest	record
refuse	reject	research	rewrite
survey	transfer	update	upgrade

Overview of Question Types on the Speaking Section

	Question Type	Skills	Description
Independent Tasks	1. Personal Experience	Speaking	• The question will ask you about a familiar topic. **Preparation Time**: 15 seconds **Response Time**: 45 seconds
	2. Paired Choice	Speaking	• The question will ask for your preference between two choices. You must state your preference and explain why you chose that option. **Preparation Time**: 15 seconds **Response Time**: 45 seconds
Integrated Tasks	3. Campus Matters	Reading Listening Speaking	• First, you will read a short text about a campus matter. • Then, you will listen to a conversation between two students. The students will discuss the campus matter addressed in the reading. • The question will ask you to summarize the text and the student's opinion of the campus matter. **Preparation Time**: 30 seconds **Response Time**: 60 seconds
	4. Academic Reading and Lecture	Reading Listening Speaking	• First, you will read a passage about an academic subject. • Then, you will listen to a professor's lecture on the same topic. • The question will ask you to connect information from both the reading and the lecture. **Preparation Time**: 30 seconds **Response Time**: 60 seconds
	5. Campus Conversation	Listening Speaking	• You will listen to a conversation between two students. In the conversation, one student has a problem, and the two students discuss possible solutions to the problem. • The question will ask you which possible solution you think is best and to explain your choice. **Preparation Time**: 20 seconds **Response Time**: 60 seconds
	6. Academic Summary	Listening Speaking	• You will listen to a short academic lecture. • The question will ask you to summarize the main points in the lecture. **Preparation Time**: 20 seconds **Response Time**: 60 seconds

Personal Experience Questions

For speaking task 1, you will be asked to give your opinion based on your personal experiences and preferences. The subject matter includes familiar topics, such as school, family, etc. You will then speak about these topics. You will have to provide personal examples to support your answers.

Sample prompts may be worded as follows:

» *Describe a type of movie that you don't typically enjoy and explain why.*

» *Describe somewhere that you would like to travel to in the future. Why?*

» *Describe the best class that you've ever taken and explain why you liked that class.*

QUICK GUIDE: Personal Experience Questions

Definition	Personal experience questions ask you to talk about something that is familiar to you, such as a person, place, or thing you know. You will <u>not</u> need to have any in-depth knowledge of specific academic subject matter in order to answer the questions.
The Question	• First, you will hear the narrator speaking the prompt. The prompt will also appear on the screen and will remain there until you have finished responding. • You will then have 15 seconds after the beep to prepare your response. A clock will count down the time for you. • You will have 45 seconds to speak your response into the headset.
Targeted Skills	In order to achieve a high score for the personal experience question, you must: • analyze the prompt. • create an outline for your response. • state your opinion based on the prompt. • support your opinions with personal details. • organize your response so it is clear and easy to understand.
A Great Response	A top-scoring response will accurately and fluently address all of the points asked about in the prompt within the time provided. Furthermore, a top-scoring response will have good organization and be supported with personal details.
Things to Remember	1. First, analyze the prompt. What information do you need in your response? 2. Next, write a very quick outline. What do you want to talk about, and what do you want to say? You have only 15 seconds to do this, so just write key words that will help you remember what to say. 3. You will hear a beep signaling the time to start. Begin your answer by stating a topic sentence. Do this by restating the prompt and adding your opinion. 4. Explain the first main reason for your preference and then provide personal details to support this reason. 5. Explain the second main reason for your preference and then provide personal details to support this reason.

WALK THROUGH: Personal Experience Questions

A Below is a sample prompt for a personal experience question. Underline two pieces of information that must be included in the response.

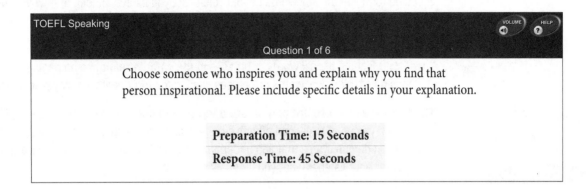

TOEFL Speaking

VOLUME HELP

Question 1 of 6

Choose someone who inspires you and explain why you find that person inspirational. Please include specific details in your explanation.

Preparation Time: 15 Seconds

Response Time: 45 Seconds

B Now review the sample outline that the test taker made to prepare her response. Notice the types of things she wants to talk about.

TEST TIP!

When you restate the prompt, be sure to use the same verb and many of the same words that appear in the prompt.

```
SAMPLE OUTLINE
Sister:
■ Works hard
   - work & school — 11:00!
   - effect on me
■ Reliable
   - helped with project tho busy
   - fulfills commitments
```

C Below is a sample response for a personal experience question. While you listen, notice how the speaker turns her outline from Part B into a full response. 🎧 CD2, Track 42

SAMPLE RESPONSE ►

Glossary:

ⓒ POWERED BY COBUILD

dedication: giving a lot of me and effort to something

reliable: someone or something that can be trusted work well or behave in the ay that you want

My older sister, Helen, is someone who inspires me in a number of ways. For one, my sister is a very hard worker. For example, she often stays late at work, even though she has to go to school early in the morning. In fact, last week she worked until 11 o'clock one night to finish a project! Seeing her dedication makes me want to work hard, too. Another reason I am inspired by my sister is that she is reliable. One time, she promised me she would help me with a school project. That week, she was very busy, but she made time to help me anyway. No matter how busy or tired she is, she always fulfills her commitments.

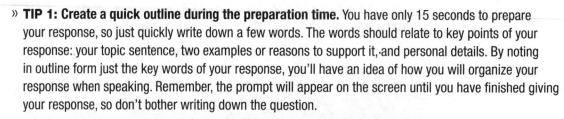

GET IT RIGHT: Tips and Tasks for Answering Correctly

» **TIP 1: Create a quick outline during the preparation time.** You have only 15 seconds to prepare your response, so just quickly write down a few words. The words should relate to key points of your response: your topic sentence, two examples or reasons to support it, and personal details. By noting in outline form just the key words of your response, you'll have an idea of how you will organize your response when speaking. Remember, the prompt will appear on the screen until you have finished giving your response, so don't bother writing down the question.

TASK 1: Underline the six words or phrases in **the sample response** on page 87 that are included in the student's notes. Mark key words or phrases used in the topic sentence, key points, and supporting details.

» **TIP 2: Analyze the prompt and create a topic sentence.** By analyzing the prompt, you'll know what information you need to give an effective response. In your response, rephrasing the prompt and stating your opinion demonstrates that you understand the basic topic. Use signposts like the ones in the table below to tell your listener what you'll be talking about.

Signposts: Giving Opinions
Two reasons that I believe XX are . . .
XX inspires me in several ways, including . . .
I feel this way for a couple of different reasons.
I enjoy / don't enjoy XX for a couple of reasons.
There are a couple reasons that I think X.

TASK 2: Double underline the restatement of the prompt in **the sample response** on page 87.

» **TIP 3: Provide at least two key points to support your topic sentence.** In order to strongly support your topic sentence, you must discuss at least two key points that explain and reinforce your topic sentence. Make sure your two key points are <u>very</u> different from each other. Include any of the following signposts to introduce your key points.

Signposts: Offering Key Supporting Points	
For one thing, . . .	*Another reason that I think that this is true is . . .*
My first / second reason for thinking this way is . . .	*Additionally, . . .*
First, . . . / Second, . . . / Next, . . .	*Furthermore, . . .*
To begin with, . . .	*First of all, . . .*

TASK 3: On page 87, circle two key points that the speaker uses in his **sample response** to support his opinion. Note the phrases that use the typical key-point language.

» **TIP 4: Use specific details and examples to support each of your key points.** After you state a key point, you should give a personal detail to provide further explanation. A good way to add personal details is to offer examples, but make sure your examples and details are relevant to the prompt!

Signposts: Giving Examples

For example . . . / Here's one example.
Take XX, for example.
Let me give you an example of what I'm talking about.
I can illustrate this point with an example.
And here's another example of what I'm talking about.

TASK 4: On page 87, draw a box around two personal details that the speaker uses in **the sample response** to support the key point.

» **TIP 5: Practice your pronunciation.** A part of your score is based on how well you are able to pronounce English. The best way to improve your pronunciation is by practicing often.

TASK 5: Read **the sample response** on page 87 aloud. Then, play the sample response (Track 42). Did your pronunciation sound like the native speaker's? Did you stress the same information as the native speaker?

PROGRESSIVE PRACTICE: Get Ready

A Look at the prompt and circle two pieces of information that must be included in the response.

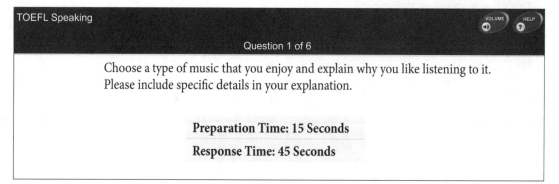

TOEFL Speaking

VOLUME HELP

Question 1 of 6

Choose a type of music that you enjoy and explain why you like listening to it. Please include specific details in your explanation.

Preparation Time: 15 Seconds

Response Time: 45 Seconds

B Why did the test taker write down the information below? Answer the questions about the person's outline.

Jazz: ❶
- Helps me relax ❷
  – exam week
- Bond ❸
  – brother ❹
  – We saw live jazz. ❺

1. What does item 1 in the notes tell us?

○ The first key point to support the speaker's topic

○ The topic of the speaker's response

2. What does item 2 in the notes tell us?

○ The personal details for the speaker's first reason

○ The first key point to support the speaker's topic

3. What does item 3 in the notes tell us?
- ○ A restatement of the prompt
- ○ The second key point to support the topic

4. What do items 4 and 5 in the notes tell us?
- ○ The main idea of the speaker's response
- ○ The personal details for the speaker's second reason

C Listen to a sample response to the above prompt. Notice the words and expressions the speaker uses to introduce her topic, introduce and talk about key points, and introduce and talk about personal details. Then, listen again. Identify the purpose of each section in the sample response. Write the numbers of the phrases from the box below in front of the correct sentences. 🎧 CD2, Track 43

1. Key Point 1	2. Key Point 2	3. Personal Detail 1
4. Personal Detail 2	5. ~~Topic Sentence~~	

SAMPLE RESPONSE ▶

[5] One type of music that I really enjoy listening to is jazz. I like jazz music for a number of reasons.

[ ] First of all, it helps me relax.

[ ] For instance, during exam week, I'm usually really tense and stressed out. But I always put on jazz when I come home from the tests. As I listen, I can actually feel my body and mind relaxing!

[ ] Additionally, I like jazz because it helps me bond with other people.

[ ] Take my older brother, who introduced me to jazz when I was only eight years old. Last month, we went to see a jazz show live. Not only was it a great show, but I got to spend some time with my brother. Enjoying the show together helped me feel closer to him!

D Now fill in the template below with your own experiences and opinions. Use your own ideas or the ideas below. Then, practice saying your response aloud. Record your response if you can.

Types of Music	Describing Music
Rock and roll	*It's so relaxing.*
Hip-hop	*It makes me feel happy.*
Classical	*It's fun to dance to.*
Jazz	*It's cool.*
Folk / Traditional	*It has a great beat.*
Disco	

TEST TIP!

Refer to the countdown clock from time to time while you're giving your response. Make sure you're not spending too much time on any one part of your response.

[*Topic sentence*] A genre of music that I like listening to is _____. I like _____ for two reasons.
[*Key point 1*] First of all, _____ is _____.
[*Personal detail 1*] For example, _____
_____.
[*Key point 2*] The next reason that I like listening to _____ is that _____
_____.
[*Personal detail 2*] For me, _____
_____
_____.

E Now think about your response or listen to it again if it was recorded. Then, read the statements below. Did your response meet the scoring requirements for personal experience questions? Check (✓) *Yes* or *No*. Keep practicing until you can check *Yes* for all of the statements.

Response Checklist: Personal Experience Questions	Yes	No
1. My response was thorough and complete. I answered the prompt directly and did not include unnecessary information.	☐	☐
2. My response was well-paced. It was neither too fast nor too slow, and I spoke for the full amount of time.	☐	☐
3. I used correct grammar, vocabulary, and pronunciation.	☐	☐
4. I gave a clear topic sentence.	☐	☐
5. I supported my topic sentence with two key points that were supported by personal details and examples.	☐	☐
6. I used signposts and transition words to effectively show the relationships between my ideas.	☐	☐

TEST TIP!

Try to speak with native speakers of English as much as possible. The more you practice speaking with native speakers, the more you will feel comfortable producing English independently. When you talk to native speakers, you may want to ask them if your pronunciation is clear. They might be able to tell you about pronunciation problems that a non-native speaker wouldn't notice.

PROGRESSIVE PRACTICE: Get Set

A Look at the prompt below and write the three pieces of information that must be included in the response.

1. _____

2. _____

3. _____

TOEFL Speaking   VOLUME   HELP

Question 1 of 6

Describe an activity that you like to do and explain why you like doing it. Please include specific details in your explanation.

Preparation Time: 15 Seconds

Response Time: 45 Seconds

B Read the notes below and write the number of the words in the box to label the main points that the speaker has outlined.

1. Key Point 1	2. Key Point 2	3. Personal Detail 1
4. Personal Detail 2	5. Topic Sentence	

```
[   ] Bike-riding
   [   ] – Inexpensive
       [   ] – spent $300/sem on bus
   [   ] – Exercise
       [   ] – wouldn't exercise otherwise
```

C The information in the sample response below is out of order. Write the numbers 1–5 to put the sentences in the order they should appear. Then, listen to the sample response and check your answers.   🎧 CD2, Track 44

SAMPLE RESPONSE ▶ _____ First of all, it's a really inexpensive way of getting around compared to other types of transportation.

_____ Before I began riding my bike, I was really out of shape. In fact, when I first started riding, it really made me exhausted. But as I rode more and more, I got in better and better shape. And best of all, since I started riding my bike, I've lost 10 pounds!

_____ For example, in order to ride the bus, I'd have to pay one dollar for every trip that I make. Some days, I take several trips by bus. Off the top of my head, it would probably cost me about $300 to ride the bus to and from school each semester! But this isn't a problem if I ride my bike, since it's always free.

_____ An activity that I like to do is ride my bike. I enjoy riding my bike for two reasons.

_____ The next reason I like riding my bike is because it's a good way to get exercise.

D Now fill in the template with your own experiences and opinions. Use your own ideas or the ideas below. Then, practice your response aloud. Record it if you can.

Types of Activities	Giving Reasons
Walking	*It keeps me in shape.*
Riding a bike	*It's fun to do with friends.*
Reading a book	*It doesn't cost much at all.*
Playing tennis	*It's a highly competitive sport.*
Going bowling	*It's very relaxing.*

An activity that I enjoy doing is _____.

I enjoy _____ for a number of reasons.

First, _____.

_____

_____.

Next, _____.

_____

_____.

E Now think about your response or listen to it again if it was recorded. Then, read the statements below. Did your response meet the scoring requirements for personal experience questions? Check (✓) *Yes* or *No*. Keep practicing until you can check *Yes* for all of the statements.

Response Checklist: Personal Experience Questions	Yes	No
1. My response was thorough and complete. I answered the prompt directly and did not include unnecessary information.	☐	☐
2. My response was well-paced. It was neither too fast nor too slow, and I spoke for the full amount of time.	☐	☐
3. I used correct grammar, vocabulary, and pronunciation.	☐	☐
4. I gave a clear topic sentence.	☐	☐
5. I supported my topic sentence with two key points that were supported by personal details and examples.	☐	☐
6. I used signposts and transition words to effectively show the relationships between my ideas.	☐	☐

PROGRESSIVE PRACTICE: Go for the TOEFL Test

Listen to a statement about a familiar subject. After you hear the statement, you will have 15 seconds to prepare and 45 seconds to give your spoken response. 🎧 CD2, Track 45

TOEFL Speaking	VOLUME 🔊	HELP ❓

Question 1 of 6

Describe two places you have traveled to and the ways in which they were different.

Preparation Time: 15 Seconds

Response Time: 45 Seconds

NOTES:

Preparation time used: _____ seconds
Response time used: _____ seconds

To see and hear sample responses and possible scores, see page 196 and listen to CD2, Track 46.

Paired Choice Questions

For speaking task 2, you will be presented with two choices and be asked to choose one. As in the personal experience question, the choices will relate to everyday life and you will <u>not</u> need any background information in order to answer. To give an effective response, you will have to give your preference between the two choices given in the prompt. Then, you will have to provide support for your position using examples or details.

Sample prompts may be worded as follows:

» *Some people prefer to spend money on objects, like clothes. Others like to spend money on experiences, like traveling. Which do you prefer and why?*

» *Some people think that people's personalities change over the course of their lives. Others think that personalities stay the same. Which do you think is true and why?*

» *Some people prefer to work in the morning. Others would rather work in the evening. When do you prefer to work and why*

QUICK GUIDE: Paired Choice Questions

Definition	Paired choice questions require you to choose between two options and justify your reasons for selecting that option. The paired choices will <u>always</u> relate to familiar topics, and you will not need specialized knowledge in order to give an effective response.
The Question	• First, you will hear the narrator speaking the prompt. The prompt will also appear on the screen and will remain there until you have finished responding. • Next, you will have 15 seconds after the beep to prepare your response. A clock will count down the time for you. • You will have 45 seconds to speak your response into the headset.
Targeted Skills	In order to achieve a high score for the paired choice question, you must do well on the following: • Overall delivery: You will be graded on pace, fluency, and intonation. • Use of language: You will be graded on vocabulary and grammar usage. • Development of topic: You will be graded on your ability to support opinions with personal details and to organize your response so it is clear and easy to understand.
A Great Response	A top-scoring response will accurately and fluently address all of the points asked about in the prompt within the time provided. Furthermore, a top-scoring response will have good organization and be supported with personal details.
Things to Remember	1. First, analyze the prompt. Which of the two options do you prefer? 2. Next, write a very quick outline. How will you support your preference? You have only 15 seconds to do this, so just write key words that will help you remember what to say. 3. You will hear a beep signaling the time to start. Begin your answer by restating the prompt and stating your preference. 4. Explain the first main reason for your preference. Add personal details to support this reason. 5. Explain the second main reason for your preference. Add personal details to support this reason as well.

WALK THROUGH: Paired Choice Questions

A Below is a sample prompt for a paired choice question. Underline two pieces of information that must be included in the response.

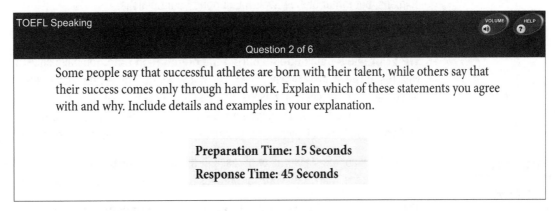

TOEFL Speaking

VOLUME   HELP

Question 2 of 6

Some people say that successful athletes are born with their talent, while others say that their success comes only through hard work. Explain which of these statements you agree with and why. Include details and examples in your explanation.

Preparation Time: 15 Seconds

Response Time: 45 Seconds

TEST TIP!

To practice for the speaking test, try retelling stories that you know well until you are able to speak quickly and with few mistakes. Telling a familiar story again and again will help you improve the speed of your speech and make you more comfortable speaking aloud.

B Now review the sample outline that the test taker made to prepare his response. Notice the types of things he wants to talk about.

SAMPLE OUTLINE
Hard work, not natural ability
■ Basketball:
  – NOT natural
    – tall but beat by shorter players
  – Hard work
    – practiced and got better

C Below is a sample response for a personal experience question. While you listen, notice how the speaker turns his outline from Part B into a full response. 🎧 CD2, Track 47

SAMPLE RESPONSE ▶

Glossary:

⋐ POWERED BY COBUILD

opponent: in sports, the person you are playing against

improvement: changing for the better; the act of becoming better at something

In my opinion, successful athletes gain their skills through hard work rather than through natural ability. I hold this opinion for several reasons. First of all, in some cases, natural advantages can work against you. Take me, for example. I play basketball, so it's good that I'm very tall. However, because of my height, I thought that I didn't have to work as hard as shorter people. Imagine my surprise when I played basketball against shorter kids and I lost! It was because I thought my height was all I needed to win, while my shorter opponents worked harder to gain skills. My next reason is because improvement comes through practice. For instance, when I lost against those shorter kids at basketball, it made me want to win. So I started practicing every day, and sure enough, I got better. The next time I played them, I won!

GET IT RIGHT: Tips and Tasks for Answering Correctly

» **TIP 1: Choose your position wisely.** When you hear the choices for a paired choice question, think about which option you can support easily in the given time—even though it might <u>not</u> be the one that corresponds with your personal beliefs. Remember, the graders aren't scoring you based on your opinions, but rather on how well you support your opinions.

TASK 1: Underline the option in **the prompt** on page 97 that the speaker chose.

» **TIP 2: Create a quick outline during the preparation time.** You have only 15 seconds to prepare your response, so just quickly write down a few words. The words should relate to key points of your response: your choice, two reasons, and personal details. That way, you'll have an idea of what you want to talk about and how you will organize your response. Remember, the prompt will appear on the screen until you have finished giving your response, so don't bother writing it down during your preparation time.

TASK 2: Underline six words or phrases in **the sample response** on page 97 that are included in the student's notes. Mark key words or phrases used in the topic sentence, key points, and supporting details.

» **TIP 3: Start by restating the prompt and saying your choice.** For paired choice questions, your topic sentence <u>must</u> include the option you've chosen. You can also combine in the same sentence the restatement of the prompt and your topic sentence. Use the suggested signposts below to state your preference between the two choices presented in the prompt.

Signposts: Stating Preferences	
I realize that a lot of people may think differently, but in my opinion . . .	*Though some people believe X, I am of the opinion that Y is best.*
I know that some people like X, but personally, it's my belief that . . .	*While some people may think that X, I believe Y.*

TASK 3: Circle two sentences in **the sample response** on page 97 that contain the restatement of the prompt and the topic sentence.

» **TIP 4: Provide two key points to support your topic sentence.** Your key points serve to justify, or give clear reasons for, the choice you made. A strong response will include two key points that explain your opinion. Use the same typical key-point language that you used for speaking task 1 (page 88).

TASK 4: Double underline two key points that the speaker of **the sample response** on page 97 uses to support the topic sentence.

» **TIP 5: Use specific details and examples to support each of your key points.** After you state a key point, you should give a personal detail to provide further explanation. Try to use your personal experiences as much as possible to support your key points. Just make sure your personal details relate to the prompt and help support your position!

TASK 5: Draw a box around two personal details in **the sample response** on page 97 that the speaker uses to support the key point.

PROGRESSIVE PRACTICE: Get Ready

A Look at the prompt and circle two pieces of information that must be included in the response.

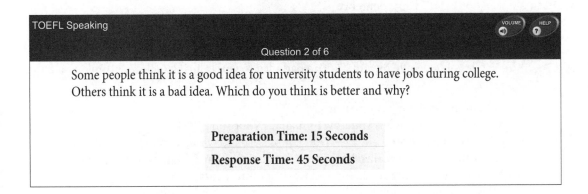

TOEFL Speaking

VOLUME   HELP

Question 2 of 6

Some people think it is a good idea for university students to have jobs during college. Others think it is a bad idea. Which do you think is better and why?

Preparation Time: 15 Seconds

Response Time: 45 Seconds

B Listen to a recording of a sample response and look at the sample notes. Check (✓) each section of the notes as you hear it in the response.   🎧 CD2, Track 48

SAMPLE NOTES
□ Good to work ❶
  □ Time management ❷
    – schedule ❸
  □ Independence
    – earn own $ ❹

C Why did the test taker write down the information in the notes above? Answer the questions about the person's notes.

1. What does item 1 in the notes tell us?

○ The first key point of the response

○ The position of the response

2. What does item 2 in the notes tell us?

○ The personal details for the first key point

○ The first key point of the response

3. What does item 3 in the notes tell us?

○ The personal details for the first key point

○ The second key point of the response

4. What does item 4 in the notes tell us?

○ The personal details for the first key point

○ The personal details for the second key point

D Listen to a sample response to the prompt from Part A. Notice the words and expressions the speaker uses to introduce her topic, introduce and talk about key points, and introduce and talk about personal details. Then, listen again. Identify the purpose of each section in the sample response. Write the numbers of the phrases from the box below in front of the correct sentences. ∩ CD2, Track 48

1. Key Point 1	2. Key Point 2	3. Personal Detail 1
4. Personal Detail 2	5. ~~Topic Sentence~~	

SAMPLE RESPONSE ▶   [5] While some people may think it's a bad idea to work during college, I think it's a good idea.

[   ] I hold this belief for two reasons.

[   ] First, I think it teaches you how to manage your time.

[   ] For example, before I got a part-time job, I used to waste a lot of time watching television. Now that I work, I realize how precious my time is, and I follow a strict schedule. That way, I can fulfill my academic and work commitments.

[   ] Next, I think working in college is a great way to be independent.

[   ] A lot of people I know depend on their parents for money, but not me. By working, I am able to earn my own money and determine exactly how I spend it.

E Now fill in the template on the next page with your own experiences and opinions. Use your own ideas or the ideas given below. Then, practice your response aloud. Record your response if you can.

Problems with Working While in College	Advantages to Working While in College
Can interfere with class schedule	Can teach students to manage their time
Can prevent student from studying as much as possible	Can promote independence
Can make student too tired for school	Can allow students to earn money for school and leisure
Can earn limited money working part-time	Can provide valuable work experience
Can cause unnecessary stress	Can offer a break from academic life

[*Topic Sentence*] I know that some people may think differently, but in my opinion, it is a
_____ idea to work during college. I have this opinion for several reasons.

[*Key Point 1*] First of all, working during college is _____ .
[*Personal Detail 1*] For example, _____
_____
_____
_____

[*Key Point 2*] The next reason that I think that it's _____ to work during college is
_____
[*Personal Detail 2*] In my case, _____
_____
_____
_____ .

F Now think about your response or listen to it again if it was recorded. Then, read the statements below. Did your response meet the scoring requirements for paired choice questions? Check (✓) *Yes* or *No*. Keep practicing until you can check *Yes* for all of the statements.

Response Checklist: Paired Choice Questions	Yes	No
1. My response was thorough and complete. I answered the prompt directly and did not include unnecessary information.	☐	☐
2. My response was well-paced. It was neither too fast nor too slow, and I spoke for the full amount of time.	☐	☐
3. I used correct grammar, vocabulary, and pronunciation.	☐	☐
4. I clearly stated my opinion about which option was best.	☐	☐
5. I supported my opinion with two key points, personal details, and examples.	☐	☐
6. I used signposts and transition words to effectively show the relationships between my ideas.	☐	☐

PROGRESSIVE PRACTICE: Get Set

A Look at the prompt and write the three pieces of information that must be included in the response.

1. _____

2. _____

3. _____

TOEFL Speaking

Question 2 of 6

Some people think that it is necessary to make your own mistakes in order to learn important lessons. Others think that it is best to learn from the mistakes of others. Which do you think is best and why?

Preparation Time: 15 Seconds

Response Time: 45 Seconds

B Read the notes below and write the numbers of the words in the box to label the main points that the speaker has outlined.

1. Key Point 1	2. Key Point 2	3. Personal Detail 1
4. Personal Detail 2	5. Topic Sentence	

```
[    ] – Learn from mistakes
  [    ] – Faster
      [    ] – older bro
  [    ] – Less stressful
      [    ] – Randy was upset.
```

C The information in the sample response below is out of order. Write the numbers 1–5 to put the sentences in the order they should appear. Then, listen to the sample response and check your answers.

🎧 CD2, Track 49

SAMPLE RESPONSE ▶ _____ For example, my older brother, Randy, recently made the mistake of procrastinating on a school project. The problem was that he waited too long to start writing an important term paper. He ended up missing the deadline as a result. Since he told me about this, I now know never to procrastinate. I don't have to waste my time learning this lesson on my own.

_____ I know when my brother missed his deadline, he was really upset. By learning from his mistakes, I avoided all the stress that would have come if I had made the mistake myself.

_____ I know that some people think it's good to learn by making your own mistakes, but it's my belief that it's best to learn from the mistakes of others. I feel this way for a couple of reasons.

_____ In addition, learning from the mistakes of others is less stressful.

_____ First of all, it saves time.

D Now fill in the template below with your own experiences and opinions. Use your own ideas. Then, practice your response aloud. Record it if you can.

> [*Topic Sentence*] I realize that some people think it's _____ to learn from the
>
> mistakes of others, but I am of the opinion that it's better to _____
>
> _____. I think this for several reasons.
>
> [*Key Point 1*] To start with, _____ .
>
> [*Personal Detail 1*] For instance, _____
>
> _____
>
> _____ .
>
> [*Key Point 2*] Furthermore, _____
>
> _____ .
>
> [*Personal Detail 2*] Once, _____
>
> _____
>
> _____

E Now think about your response or listen to it again if it was recorded. Then, read the statements on the next page. Did your response meet the scoring requirements for paired choice questions? Check (✓) *Yes* or *No*. Keep practicing until you can check *Yes* for all of the statements.

SKILLS FOR THE TOEFL IBT TEST   LISTENING AND SPEAKING

Response Checklist: Paired Choice Questions	Yes	No
1. My response was thorough and complete. I answered the prompt directly and did not include unnecessary information.	☐	☐
2. My response was well-paced. It was neither too fast nor too slow, and I spoke for the full amount of time.	☐	☐
3. I used correct grammar, vocabulary, and pronunciation.	☐	☐
4. I clearly stated my opinion about which option was best.	☐	☐
5. I supported my opinion with two key points, personal details, and examples.	☐	☐
6. I used signposts and transition words to effectively show the relationships between my ideas.	☐	☐

PROGRESSIVE PRACTICE: Go for the TOEFL Test

Listen to a statement about a familiar subject. After you hear the statement, you will have 15 seconds to prepare and 45 seconds to give your spoken response. 🎧 CD1, Track 50

TOEFL Speaking   VOLUME   HELP

Question 2 of 6

Some people believe that there are benefits to watching television, while others do not. Which position do you agree with and why?

Preparation Time: 15 Seconds

Response Time: 45 Seconds

NOTES:

Preparation time used: _____ seconds
Response time used: _____ seconds

To see and hear sample responses and possible scores, see page 196 and listen to CD2, Track 51.

Campus Matters Questions

For speaking task 3, you will answer a question by integrating information from a reading and a conversation. The reading is usually no more than 100 words long and appears on the screen for up to 45 seconds. Once the time is up, the text will disappear, so make sure to take notes! The reading may be an announcement, an article from the school newspaper, or another type of text that might be found on campus. It is <u>always</u> about a campus-related matter. Since the topics are related to university life in general, you won't need specific knowledge of any academic subject in order to respond effectively.

The reading passage is typically organized as follows:

- First, the author presents an issue related to campus matters, such as special assignments, proposed university plans, or changes to university policies.
- Next, the author provides two key points in support of that matter. These points may explain why a change is taking place or describe how a plan will benefit a part of or the entire university community.

You will hear the conversation <u>after</u> you read the text. Again, you should take notes during the given time because you will hear the conversation only once and will <u>not</u> be able to see the script on the screen. The listening passage is usually a conversation between two university students. The conversation is based on the information in the reading, and one of the students <u>always</u> has a strong opinion about the campus matter. The speaker will either support or oppose the change or plan and will give two reasons to support that position.

TEST TIP!

Practice recording your voice to prepare for the test. Make sure to time yourself. How does your voice sound? Is it easy to understand your pronunciation?

The question for campus matters tasks may be worded as follows:

» *The woman gives her opinion of the university's plan to repurpose the old English department. State her opinion and describe the reasons she gives for holding that opinion.*

» *The man expresses his opinion of the university's plan to change its parking policy. State his opinion and describe the reasons he gives for holding that opinion.*

» *The woman gives her opinion of the university's plan to raise tuition rates. State her opinion and describe the reasons she gives for holding that opinion.*

QUICK GUIDE: Campus Matters Questions

Definition	A campus matters task requires you to describe the opinion of a speaker based on the information provided in a reading passage and a conversation.
The Question	• After you read the passage and listen to the conversation, you will hear the narrator ask a question. • The question is based on both the reading and the conversation. The question will also appear on the screen until you have finished responding. • You will have 30 seconds after the beep to prepare your response. A clock will count down the time for you. • You will have 60 seconds to say your response into the microphone.
Targeted Skills	In order to achieve a high score for the campus matters question, you must: • identify the main points in the reading and the conversation. • identify a person's opinion and the support for that opinion. • analyze the prompt and understand what information you need to include in your response. • create an outline for your response. • connect information from both sources and correctly cite where the information came from. • organize your response so it is clear and easy to understand.
A Great Response	A top-scoring response will accurately and fluently address all of the information asked for in the question. It will provide a brief summary of the campus matter and the two key points used to support it. Additionally, a top-scoring response will give a complete description of the speaker's opinion (not your own opinion).
Things to Remember	1. First, analyze the prompt. What specific information will you include in your response? 2. Take careful notes for both the reading and the conversation. You will need these to create an outline before you speak. 3. Begin your answer by briefly describing the campus matter from the reading. Include two key points given in the reading as well. 4. State the speaker's opinion about the campus matter. Be sure to mention the supporting details from the conversation. Do not give your own opinion.

WALK THROUGH: Campus Matters Questions

A Below is a sample campus matters question. Read the announcement and then listen to the conversation between two students. While you read and listen, underline the information that you think is important in the announcement and the conversation.   🎧 CD2, Track 52

TOEFL Speaking   VOLUME   HELP

Question 3 of 6

Announcement

Starting next semester, the campus dining halls will close at 8 p.m. instead of 10 p.m. One reason for this change is that too few students visit the dining halls in the late evening. Over the last year, the cafeterias were busiest between 5 and 6 p.m. Next, the university hopes to save money by closing the dining halls earlier. The president of the university has said that he hopes to invest the money saved from paying late-shift workers on renovating the on-campus dining facilities.

Glossary:

⊜ POWERED BY COBUILD

renovate: to repair and improve something

SAMPLE SCRIPT ▶

for reference only, not available in test

Student 1: Did you hear about the decision to close the dining halls earlier next semester?

Student 2: Yes . . . and I really hope the university reconsiders.

Student 1: Really? I mean, it doesn't seem like that many people use the dining halls after eight o'clock anyway.

Student 2: That's the thing . . . there are a lot of people using the dining halls in the late evening, especially students who have seminars or discussion sections until late in the day. At least twice a week, my classes don't end until eight thirty. So being able to go to the dining hall later is really convenient. And I always see all of the people from my classes there at that time as well, so I'm sure that some people are going.

Student 1: I hadn't thought about that.

Student 2: Also, I'm really skeptical that cutting two hours is going to save very much money. My friend works during the late-night shift at the dining hall, and she said the student workers don't earn wages. Instead, they get a certain amount taken off of their tuition bill for the work they do. How does the university expect to save money if it's not really paying out money to run the shift?

Glossary:

⊜ POWERED BY COBUILD

skeptical: having doubts about something

tuition: the money paid for university classes

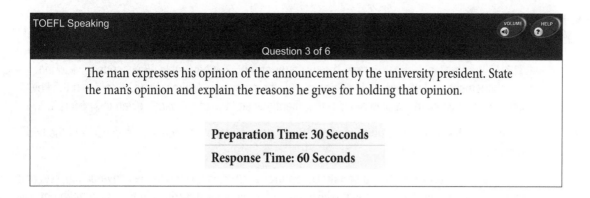

The man expresses his opinion of the announcement by the university president. State the man's opinion and explain the reasons he gives for holding that opinion.

Preparation Time: 30 Seconds

Response Time: 60 Seconds

B Now review the sample outline that the test taker made to prepare his response. Then, read the announcement and conversation again and circle the information that the test taker included in his outline. Compare the information you underlined with the circled information. Did you notice all of the important points?

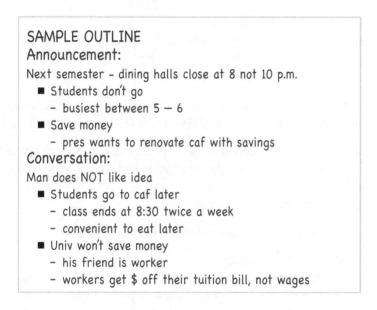

SAMPLE OUTLINE
Announcement:
Next semester - dining halls close at 8 not 10 p.m.
- Students don't go
  - busiest between 5 — 6
- Save money
  - pres wants to renovate caf with savings
Conversation:
Man does NOT like idea
- Students go to caf later
  - class ends at 8:30 twice a week
  - convenient to eat later
- Univ won't save money
  - his friend is worker
  - workers get $ off their tuition bill, not wages

C Below is a sample response for a campus matters task. While you listen, notice how the speaker turns his outline from Part B into a full response.   CD2, Track 53

SAMPLE RESPONSE ▶   The announcement is about the university's decision to close the dining halls at 8 p.m. instead of 10 p.m. According to the announcement, the university's decision is based on the low number of students who visit the dining halls after 6 p.m. Also, the university wants to save money. The man disagrees with the decision for two reasons. First, he says that many people rely on the dining halls being open later in the evening. He points out that he has classes until eight thirty two evenings out of the week, so it's convenient for him to eat in the dining hall later. Next, the student argues that the university probably won't save very much money. That's because the dining hall workers are students who don't earn wages. Instead, they get an amount taken off their tuition bill. The student says that the university can't save money if it isn't paying out to run the dining hall in the first place.

GET IT RIGHT: Tips and Tasks for Answering Correctly

» **TIP 1: Take notes while you read the announcement.** You have only 45 seconds to read the announcement, and you won't see it again after the time is up. Make sure to write down the key information, including the plan or change it mentions and the two reasons given to support it.

TASK 1: In **the announcement** on page 108, make a box around the topic sentence and the two reasons given to support it.

» **TIP 2: Listen carefully for the speakers' opinions.** When you listen to the conversation, one of the speakers will <u>always</u> have a strong opinion about the proposal described in the announcement. The speaker will usually state the opinion near the beginning of the conversation. Be sure to write the speaker's opinion in your notes. The speaker may use the expressions listed below to give opinions.

| Expressions for Giving Opinions ||
Support	*Oppose*
I think a lot of people will benefit from . . . *I can see why the university has decided to . . .* *It might help with . . .*	*I don't like the plan to . . .* *I think it's a bad idea.* *I hope the university reconsiders.* *I don't understand why . . .*

TASK 2: Circle one sentence in **the conversation** on page 108 that indicates the speaker's opinion. Remember to look for an expression listed in the table above! Does the man support or oppose the plan?

» **TIP 3: Write down the two key points and supporting details that the speaker uses to support the opinion.** Since you will hear the conversation only once, it's important to take good notes. By doing so, you will be able to create an effective response. Listen carefully for the key points and supporting details in the conversation and make sure to write them in your notes.

TASK 3: Underline two key points the man makes in **the conversation** on page 108.

» **TIP 4: Read the question carefully!** In order to give an effective response, you must address the question being asked. In addition to hearing the narrator say the question, you will see the question appear on your screen, where it will remain until you finish giving your response. Be sure to read it carefully and understand what information it is asking you for and make sure to answer the entire question in your response. This will help you include only the correct information in your response, not information that was never asked about. Remember, campus matters tasks will never ask about your opinion, so use only the information in the announcement and conversation in your response.

TASK 4: Underline two pieces of key information being asked for in **the question** on page 109.

» **TIP 5: Cite the sources correctly.** Since you have to connect information from the announcement and the conversation, you must correctly identify where the information came from. You should use expressions from the table below to cite the sources in your response.

TEST TIP!

. Make sure to give a
. complete summary of
. the campus matter in
. your response. Some-
. one who hasn't read the
. announcement or heard
. the conversation should
. know exactly what
. you're referring to.

Expressions for Citing Sources
The author / speaker thinks / feels that . . .   *The author / speaker agrees / disagrees / opposes / supports . . .*   *According to the passage / speaker . . .*   *In the conversation, the speaker says / argues / points out / makes the point that . . .*   *In the announcement / bulletin / article / passage, the author says . . .*   *The speaker / author supports X by saying / pointing out / arguing / giving an example of . . .*

TASK 5: Double underline five citation expressions in **the sample response** on page 109.

PROGRESSIVE PRACTICE: Get Ready

A Read the announcement. Then, listen to the conversation on the same topic. Look at the prompt and circle the two pieces of information that must be included in the response. 🎧 CD2, Track 54

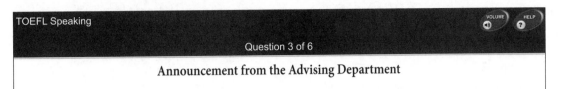

TOEFL Speaking   VOLUME   HELP

Question 3 of 6

Announcement from the Advising Department

Starting in the fall semester, City College will increase the mandatory number of advisory meetings to two per semester. Although students currently meet with advisors once a semester, the advising department feels that this is inadequate. By meeting with advisors more frequently, students will be better informed of required courses and changes in their majors. The additional meetings will also allow advisors to become more closely acquainted with each student. By getting to know every advisee well, advisors are better equipped to provide counsel and make recommendations.

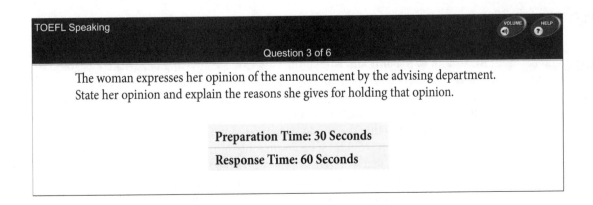

TOEFL Speaking   VOLUME   HELP

Question 3 of 6

The woman expresses her opinion of the announcement by the advising department. State her opinion and explain the reasons she gives for holding that opinion.

Preparation Time: 30 Seconds

Response Time: 60 Seconds

B Why did the test taker write down the information below? Answer the questions about the person's outline.

Announcement

↑ req.'d # of advisory meetings (now 2/semester) ❶
- Students have more info about req.'d courses / majors.
- Advisors will get to know students better. ❷
  - give better advice

Conversation

Woman - good idea ❸
- Advisor told her about missing writing class. ❹
  - She wouldn't be graduating on time w/o advisor's help.
- Advisor gave career advice and letter of rec.

---

1. What does item 1 in the notes tell us?

○ A change in university policy

○ The first reason to explain the change

2. What does item 2 in the notes tell us?

○ The first reason to explain the change

○ The second reason to explain the change

3. What does item 3 in the notes tell us?

○ The woman's opinion about the change

○ A change in university policy

4. What does item 4 in the notes tell us?

○ The first key point in support of the woman's opinion

○ The second key point in support of the woman's opinion

C Listen to a sample response to the prompt from Part A. Notice the words and expressions the speaker uses to introduce her topic sentences, introduce and talk about key points, and introduce and talk about supporting details. Then, listen again. Identify the purpose of each section in the sample response. Write the numbers of the phrases from the box below in front of the correct sentences.   🎧 CD2, Track 55

1. ~~Proposed Change~~	2. Reason 1 for Opinion	3. Reason 2 for Opinion
4. Reasons for Change	5. Student's Opinion	6. Supporting Detail 1
7. Supporting Detail 2		

SAMPLE RESPONSE ▶   [1] According to the announcement, the City College advising department is going to require students to meet with their advisors twice a semester instead of just once.

[   ] The college is doing this so that students will know which courses to take and also to help advisors get to know students better.

[   ] The woman thinks that the change is a great idea.

[   ] For one, the woman would not be graduating on time without her advisor's help.

[   ] She forgot to enroll in a required writing course her freshman year. But her advisor noticed that mistake, and the woman was able to take the course without delaying her graduation.

[   ] The woman also says that her advisor has helped with her career.

[   ] The advisor suggested places for the woman to apply and has written her a letter of recommendation. The woman believes that she wouldn't have gotten that help with just one meeting a semester.

D Now fill in the template below using your own words. Then, practice your response aloud. Record your response if you can.

> [*Proposed Change*] The announcement says that _____
> _____.
>
> [*Reason 1 for Change*] One reason for the change is that _____
> _____.
>
> [*Reason 2 for Change*] According to the announcement, the university also decided to
> _____ because _____
> _____.
>
> [*Student's Opinion*] In the conversation, the woman says that she thinks the change is a
> _____ idea and gives two personal details that _____ the reasons
> given in the announcement.
>
> [*Reason 1 for Opinion*] First, she explains that meeting with her advisor helped her _____
> _____.
>
> [*Supporting Detail 1*] That's because _____
> _____.
>
> [*Reason 2 for Opinion*] Next, the woman says that _____
> _____.
>
> [*Supporting Detail 2*] The student mentions that _____
> _____.

E Now think about your response or listen to it again if it was recorded. Then, read the statements below. Did your response meet the scoring requirements for campus matters questions? Check (✓) *Yes* or *No*. Keep practicing until you can check *Yes* for all of the statements.

Response Checklist: Campus Matters Questions	Yes	No
1. My response was thorough and complete. I answered the prompt directly and did not include unnecessary information.	☐	☐
2. My response was well-paced. It was neither too fast nor too slow, and I spoke for the full amount of time.	☐	☐
3. I used correct grammar, vocabulary, and pronunciation.	☐	☐
4. I gave a complete and clear description of the campus matter.	☐	☐
5. I clearly stated the student's opinion of the campus matter.	☐	☐
6. I used signposts and transition words to effectively show the relationships between my ideas.	☐	☐

PROGRESSIVE PRACTICE: Get Set

A Read the announcement. Then, listen to the conversation on the same topic. Look at the prompt and write the three pieces of information that must be included in the response.   🎧 CD2, Track 56

1. _____

2. _____

3. _____

TOEFL Speaking   VOLUME HELP

Question 3 of 6

Change in Policy at the Student Computer Lab

Effective immediately, students may no longer print documents at the student computer lab free of charge. Printing will now cost five cents per page. The reason for this policy change is that the price of ink and paper is simply too high to continue providing printing services without a charge. In addition, charging students for printing services will allow the computer lab to invest in more modern technology.

The money used to purchase ink will now be used to update software and computers.

TOEFL Speaking   VOLUME HELP

Question 3 of 6

The woman expresses her opinion of the university's plan to change its printing policy in the student computer lab. State her opinion and explain the reasons she gives for holding that opinion.

Preparation Time: 30 Seconds

Response Time: 60 Seconds

B Read the announcement and listen to the conversation again. Complete the notes below using information from both sources.   CD2, Track 56

Announcement

Students can't ❶ _____ docs at student comp lab for free. Cost 5¢/page (effective now)
■ The cost of ❷ _____ and paper is too high.
■ Money saved on ink costs will help lab ❸ _____ software and comps.

Conversation

Woman says printing fee is ❹ _____.
■ Students pay for printing.
■ They pay ❺ _____, which should cover all lab costs, including printing.
■ Comp lab doesn't need new tech.
   – 90% of students use lab for ❻ _____ and printing, so new ❼ _____ and comps aren't necessary.

C Use the notes above to complete the response template. Be sure to use transition words and citing expressions. Then, say your response aloud. Record your response if you can.

[*Summary of Announcement*] _____
_____ .

[*Reason 1 for Change*] _____
_____ .

[*Reason 2 for Change*] _____
_____ .

[*Student's Opinion*] _____
_____ .

[*Reason 1 for Opinion*] _____
_____ .

[*Supporting Detail 1*] _____
_____ .

[*Reason 2 for Opinion*] _____
_____ .

[*Supporting Detail 2*] _____
_____ .

D Now think about your response or listen to it again if it was recorded. Then, read the statements below. Did your response meet the scoring requirements for campus matters questions? Check (✓) *Yes* or *No*. Keep practicing until you can check *Yes* for all of the statements.

Response Checklist: Campus Matters Questions	Yes	No
1. My response was thorough and complete. I answered the prompt directly and did not include unnecessary information.	☐	☐
2. My response was well-paced. It was neither too fast nor too slow, and I spoke for the full amount of time.	☐	☐
3. I used correct grammar, vocabulary, and pronunciation.	☐	☐
4. I gave a complete and clear description of the campus matter.	☐	☐
5. I clearly stated the student's opinion of the campus matter.	☐	☐
6. I used signposts and transition words to effectively show the relationships between my ideas.	☐	☐

PROGRESSIVE PRACTICE: Go for the TOEFL Test

Read the announcement in 45 seconds. Begin reading now. 🎧 CD2, Track 57

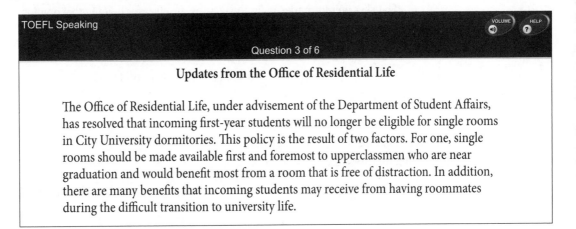

TOEFL Speaking   VOLUME 🔊   HELP ?

Question 3 of 6

Updates from the Office of Residential Life

The Office of Residential Life, under advisement of the Department of Student Affairs, has resolved that incoming first-year students will no longer be eligible for single rooms in City University dormitories. This policy is the result of two factors. For one, single rooms should be made available first and foremost to upperclassmen who are near graduation and would benefit most from a room that is free of distraction. In addition, there are many benefits that incoming students may receive from having roommates during the difficult transition to university life.

Note: The announcement will **not** appear on your screen after the 45 seconds are over.

Now listen to two students as they discuss the announcement. Take notes.

NOTES:

Now answer the question. You may use your notes.

The woman expresses her opinion of the announcement by the Office of Residential Life. State her opinion and explain the reasons she gives for holding that opinion.

Preparation Time: 30 Seconds

Response Time: 60 Seconds

Preparation time used: _____ seconds
Speaking time used: _____ seconds

To see and hear sample responses and possible scores, see page 197 and listen to CD2, Track 58.

Academic Reading and Lecture Questions

For speaking task 4, you will answer a question by integrating information from a reading and a lecture. The short reading appears on your computer screen for up to 45 seconds and is usually no more than 100 words long. Once the time is up, the text will disappear, so be sure to take notes! The reading is <u>always</u> about an academic subject. Sample topics for task 4 readings include the following:

- anthropology
- biology
- literature

- marketing
- psychology
- sociology

In your response, you will need to use only the provided information. You do <u>not</u> need to have specific knowledge of any academic subject in order to respond effectively. The reading typically provides an overview of an academic concept in abstract terms and gives a few specific examples.

The listening passage is an academic lecture given by a university professor. You will hear the professor's lecture <u>after</u> you read the text. You will hear the lecture only once, so take notes! The lecture is <u>always</u> related to the reading and includes two key points that are discussed in detail. These key points give more information about the topic presented in the reading by discussing applications of the concept or giving specific examples to illustrate the concept.

The question for academic reading and lecture tasks may be worded as follows:

» *The professor describes the characteristics of whale navigation. Explain how the characteristics are related to a whale's ability to migrate.*

» *The professor describes two novels. Describe these novels and explain why they are considered examples of gothic novels.*

TEST TIP!

You know that the lecture is related to the reading passage that comes before it. When you take notes for the passage, leave room under key points. Then, when you listen to the lecture, write down related ideas under the appropriate categories or headings. That way, your notes will be organized when it's time for you to prepare your response!

QUICK GUIDE: Academic Reading and Lecture Questions

Definition	An academic reading and lecture task requires you to describe and connect the information presented in a reading and lecture.
The Question	• After you read the passage and listen to the lecture, you will hear the narrator ask a question. • The question is based on both the reading and the lecture. The question will remain on your screen until you have completed your response. • You will have 30 seconds to prepare your response. A clock on the screen will show how much time you have left to prepare. • You will have 60 seconds to speak your response into the headset.
Targeted Skills	In order to achieve a high score for the academic reading and lecture question, you must: • identify the major points in the reading and the lecture. • understand the relationship between what you read and what the professor says. • analyze the prompt and understand what information you need to include in your response. • create an outline for your response. • connect information from both sources and correctly cite where the information came from. • organize your response so it is clear and easy to understand.
A Great Response	A top-scoring response will accurately and fluently address all of the information asked for in the question within the time provided. It will summarize the main idea of the reading and describe the purpose of the lecture. It will also connect information from both sources.
Things to Remember	1. First, analyze the prompt. Make sure you understand the specific information you should include in your response. 2. Use your notes to create an outline for your response during the preparation time. 3. Begin your response by briefly summarizing the main ideas of both the reading and the lecture. Be sure to describe how the sources are related. 4. Introduce both of the key points from the lecture. Include supporting details for each key point. Don't forget to describe how the key points relate to the reading!

WALK THROUGH: Academic Reading and Lecture Questions

A Below is a sample academic reading and lecture question. Read the passage and then listen to the lecture from a marketing class. While you read and listen, underline the information that you think is important in the reading and the script. 🎧 CD3, Track 2

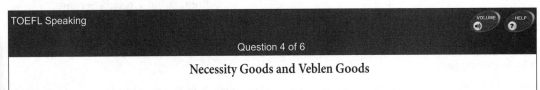

TOEFL Speaking   VOLUME HELP

Question 4 of 6

Necessity Goods and Veblen Goods

When the price of a good increases, consumers typically buy less of it. Yet two types of goods do not follow this pattern. Necessity goods are products that people always buy, even when prices rise. Consumers purchase necessity goods because they need them. Even if a necessity good doubles in price, people will always attempt to buy it.

Veblen goods, conversely, are products that people buy more of because of the goods' high prices. However, people buy these goods, even when they are expensive, for different reasons. People purchase Veblen goods despite their high prices because many consumers equate high prices with quality and status. By buying Veblen goods, consumers feel that they are getting a better product than they would with lower-priced goods that perform the same function.

SAMPLE SCRIPT ▶
for reference only, not available in test

Professor: So last time, we talked about necessity and Veblen goods. But I think the best way to understand them is to imagine buying them. Let's see why people will keep buying products even though the price is higher.

So first, necessity goods. Imagine that you live in a very cold area, and you use oil to heat your home. If the price of oil goes up, are you going to stop buying oil? No. You can't stop buying oil or you'll freeze. That's why people keep buying it—they need to. In fact, they'll stop buying other products just to have money for oil.

Now, Veblen goods are something different. This time, think of yourself as a wealthy person who is looking to buy a car. You find two models that are almost identical. They use the same amount of gas per mile, they have the same number of seats, and they passed the same safety tests. But one of them is several thousand dollars more expensive, and it's made by a manufacturer known for producing luxury cars. And you choose the more expensive car. Why? Because people generally feel that if a car is more expensive, it's of higher quality.

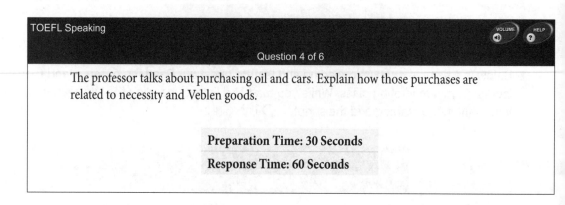

TOEFL Speaking

VOLUME   HELP

Question 4 of 6

The professor talks about purchasing oil and cars. Explain how those purchases are related to necessity and Veblen goods.

Preparation Time: 30 Seconds

Response Time: 60 Seconds

TEST TIP!

The lecture is related to the reading passage that comes before it. When you take notes on the passage, leave room under key points. Then, when you listen to the lecture, write down related ideas under the appropriate categories or headings. That way, your notes will be organized when it's time for you to prepare your response!

B Now review the sample outline that the test taker made to prepare her response. Then, read the passage and lecture again and circle the information that the test taker included in her outline. Compare the information you underlined and the circled information.

SAMPLE OUTLINE
Reading
2 goods ppl buy even if price ↑
- necessity goods
  - ppl need them
- Veblen goods
  - ppl buy b/c of high price
  - they think high cost = high quality / status

Lecture
Examples of 2 goods
- necessity g'd: oil
  - ppl will buy even if exp's've b/c they need it to heat homes
- Veblen g'd: luxury car
  - 2 models nearly identical
  - ppl buy expensive 1 b/c they think it is higher quality / status

C Below is a sample response for an academic reading and lecture question. While you listen, notice how the speaker turns her outline from Part B into a full response.
CD3, Track 3

SAMPLE RESPONSE ▶

Both the reading and the lecture are about necessity and Veblen goods. The reading defines necessity and Veblen goods, and the professor expands upon this topic by describing two examples of each type of good.

First, the reading passage says that necessity goods are products that people buy regardless of their price because people need them. Then, the professor gives an example of a specific necessity good: oil. According to the professor, people in cold areas will always buy oil because they will freeze if they don't buy it to heat their homes with.

Second, the reading passage says that Veblen goods are products that people relate with high quality and status as a result of their high price. The professor explains that a consumer might choose an expensive car over an affordable one, even though the cars are almost identical. That's because some people are willing to pay more if they relate the product with high quality or status.

GET IT RIGHT: Tips and Tasks for Answering Correctly

» **TIP 1: Read the title of the reading passage.** Each reading passage has a title. By reading the title, you will get a general sense of the main idea of the passage and lecture.

TASK 1: What's the title of **the reading** on page 121?

» **TIP 2: Take notes on the major points of the reading and listening.** You will have only about 45 seconds to read the passage, and you will hear the lecture only once. So don't forget to take notes during the reading and the listening! Taking notes will help you create a complete response that includes information from both sources.

TASK 2: Draw a box around the main idea and two key points presented in **the reading passage** on page 121. Then, draw a box around the main idea and two key points presented in **the lecture** on page 121.

» **TIP 3: Read the prompt carefully!** By reading the prompt carefully, you will know exactly what information you are expected to include in your response. If you don't address <u>all</u> of the points asked about in the prompt, your score may be lower.

TASK 3: Underline two important pieces of information in **the prompt** on page 122.

» **TIP 4: Start your response by stating the relationship between the reading and the lecture.** By realizing how the two sources are related, you will be able to give a stronger response. Below are ways to state possible relationships between Task 4 sources.

Stating the Relationship Between Two Sources
In the lecture, the professor gives two examples of the idea mentioned in the reading.
The reading discusses X, and the professor gives more information on this by giving examples / describing personal experiences / discussing two types of X.
The professor talks about two types / examples of the X described in the reading.
The professor mentions a study that used the idea of X, which was described in the reading.

TASK 4: Underline one sentence in **the sample response** on page 122 that states the relationship between the two sources.

» **TIP 5: Be sure to cite your sources!** For this task, you must connect information from the reading and the listening. When you discuss the information, be sure to say what source it came from. This will help make your response clearer. See the table titled *Expressions for Citing Sources* on page 110 for expressions you can use to cite your sources.

TASK 5: Double underline five citation expressions in **the sample response** on page 122.

PROGRESSIVE PRACTICE: Get Ready

A Read the passage. Then, listen to the lecture on the same topic. Look at the prompt and circle the two pieces of information that must be included in the response. 🎧 CD3, Track 4

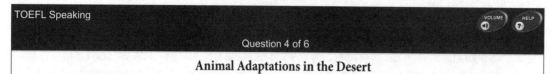

TOEFL Speaking   VOLUME   HELP

Question 4 of 6

Animal Adaptations in the Desert

In the desert, the heat and lack of water have led animals to take on two specific adaptations that encourage survival. Some animals adapt to the limited food supply by expanding the types of food they ingest. Unlike animals that only either eat plants or hunt to survive, some desert animals eat any plant or animal they can. By doing so, these animals increase the likelihood of ingesting enough water and nutrients to survive.

Others maximize their opportunities to locate food by hunting at peak hours of prey activity throughout the day, like the early evening and early morning. This provides opportunities to hunt creatures that are active at night as well as those that are active during the day.

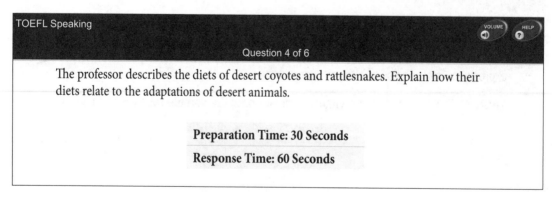

TOEFL Speaking   VOLUME   HELP

Question 4 of 6

The professor describes the diets of desert coyotes and rattlesnakes. Explain how their diets relate to the adaptations of desert animals.

Preparation Time: 30 Seconds

Response Time: 60 Seconds

B Why did the test taker write down the information below? Answer the questions about the person's outline.

Reading
- ■ Animal adaptations in the desert ❶
  - – 2 adpt'tns
    - – eat a lot of diff foods
      - – any food they find
      - – get enough water and nutrients
    - – hunt during busy times ❷
      - – early evening, morning
      - – catch animals that are active day and night

Lecture
- ■ Coyotes (wild dog) ❸
  - – diverse diet
  - – eat animals, plants, dead animals; hunt for large and small animals
- ■ Rattlesnakes
  - – eat mice (morning) and squirrels (night) ❹
  - – hunt when prey is active, double chances of finding food

1. What does item 1 in the notes tell us?

○ The main topic of the reading and lecture

○ The relationship between the reading and lecture

2. What does item 2 in the notes tell us?

○ The first type of desert adaptation

○ The second type of desert adaptation

3. What is item 3?

○ An example of an animal that uses the first type of adaptation

○ An example of an animal that uses the second type of adaptation

4. What is item 4?

○ A supporting detail for why rattlesnakes hunt at different times of the day

○ A supporting detail for why rattlesnakes have a diverse diet

C Listen to a sample response to the prompt from Part A. Notice the words and expressions the speaker uses to introduce his topic sentences, introduce and talk about key points, and introduce and talk about supporting details. Then, listen again. Identify the purpose of each section in the sample response. Write the numbers of the phrases from the box below in front of the correct sentences. 🎧 CD3, Track 5

1. Key Point 1 from Reading	2. Key Point 2 from Reading
3. ~~Reading and Lecture Topic~~	4. Relationship Between Sources
5. Support 1 from Lecture	6. Support 2 from Lecture

SAMPLE RESPONSE ▶

[3] The reading passage and the lecture are both about adaptations of desert animals.

[ ] The reading describes two types of adaptations, and the professor gives examples of two animals that each use one of the adaptations mentioned in the reading.

[ ] First, the reading passage states that some desert animals will eat any plant or animal they can.

[ ] The professor uses coyotes, a type of wild dog, as an example of an animal that uses this adaptation. She explains that coyotes will eat fruit, vegetables, small or large prey, and even dead animals. Having a diverse diet allows coyotes to survive in deserts.

[ ] The second adaptation mentioned in the reading is that some animals hunt in the early morning and early evening to catch prey that is active during the day or night.

[ ] According to the professor, rattlesnakes are an example of animals that use the second adaptation. The professor says that rattlesnakes depend on squirrels and mice for food but that these prey are active at different times. By hunting in the early morning and night, rattlesnakes have twice as many chances to catch these animals.

D Now fill in the template with your own words. Then, practice your response aloud. Record your response if you can.

[*Reading and Lecture Topic*] Both the reading and the lecture are about _____
_____ .

[*Relationship Between Sources*] The professor gives _____
_____ that are mentioned in the reading.

[*Key Point 1 from Reading*] The first desert adaptation from the reading is that animals
_____ .

[*Support 1 from Lecture*] In the lecture, the professor talks about _____ to show
an animal that uses this first adaptation. According to the professor, _____
_____ .
_____
_____ .

[*Key Point 2 from Reading*] The next desert adaptation discussed in the reading is that
_____ .

[*Support 2 from Lecture*] To illustrate this point, the professor uses the example of
_____ . She says that _____ ,
when their two main prey, _____ , are active. By hunting during
these periods, _____
_____ .

E Now think about your response or listen to it again if it was recorded. Then, read the statements below. Did your response meet the scoring requirements for academic reading and lecture questions? Check (✓) *Yes* or *No*. Keep practicing until you can check *Yes* for all of the statements.

Response Checklist: Academic Reading and Lecture Questions	Yes	No
1. My response was thorough and complete. I answered the prompt directly and did not include unnecessary information.	☐	☐
2. My response was well-paced. It was neither too fast nor too slow, and I spoke for the full amount of time.	☐	☐
3. I used correct grammar, vocabulary, and pronunciation.	☐	☐
4. I used signposts and transition words to effectively show the relationships between my ideas.	☐	☐
5. I clearly explained how the reading and the lecture are related.	☐	☐
6. I mentioned both of the key points from the reading and provided supporting details from the lecture for both points.	☐	☐

PROGRESSIVE PRACTICE: Get Set

A Read the passage. Then, listen to the lecture on the same topic. Look at the prompt and write the two pieces of information that must be included in the response. 🎧 CD3, Track 6

1. _____

2. _____

TOEFL Speaking   VOLUME   HELP

Question 4 of 6

Method Acting

Method acting provides actors with tools they can use to realistically depict the characters they are playing. One tool of method acting, affective memory, helps actors display believable emotions. Affective memory requires actors to consider how their characters would feel and to then recall a memory from their own lives that brings up a similar feeling.

   Another tool, the object of attention, assists actors in focusing on the world in which their characters reside. Actors create an object of attention by focusing on some aspect of the world in a play. They choose some detail of a play's setting to remember at all times, which makes their characters' actions more realistic.

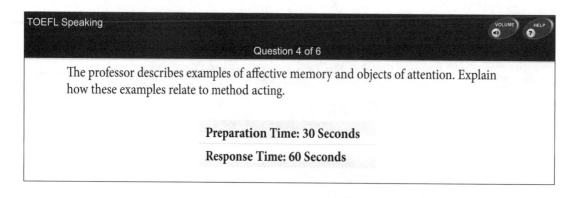

TOEFL Speaking   VOLUME   HELP

Question 4 of 6

The professor describes examples of affective memory and objects of attention. Explain how these examples relate to method acting.

Preparation Time: 30 Seconds

Response Time: 60 Seconds

B Read the passage and listen to the lecture again. Complete the notes below using the information from both sources. 🎧 CD3, Track 6

Reading
- ■ Method acting: tools for actors
  - ❶ _____ : helps create believable ❷ _____
    - use memories and personal experiences
  - obj of ❸ _____ : helps focus on character's world
    - think of a detail in the ❹ _____

Lecture
- ■ How to use these tools
  - affective memory:
    - role of disappointed queen
    - think of feeling ❺ _____ in life
  - obj of attn: makes character's world more real to actor
    - setting is ❻ _____ outdoors — focus on this detail
    - rub and blow on hands, ❼ _____

C Use the notes above to complete the response template. Be sure to use transition words and citing expressions. Then, say your response aloud. Record your response if you can.

[*Reading and Lecture Topic*] _____

_____

[*Relationship Between Sources*] _____

_____

_____

[*Key Point 1 from Reading*] _____

_____

[*Support 1 from Lecture*] _____

_____

_____

_____

[*Key Point 2 from Reading*] _____

_____

[*Support 2 from Lecture*] _____

_____

_____

_____

D Now think about your response or listen to it again if it was recorded. Then, read the statements below. Did your response meet the scoring requirements for academic reading and lecture questions? Check (✓) *Yes* or *No*. Keep practicing until you can check *Yes* for all of the statements.

Response Checklist: Academic Reading and Lecture Questions	Yes	No
1. My response was thorough and complete. I answered the prompt directly and did not include unnecessary information.	☐	☐
2. My response was well-paced. It was neither too fast nor too slow, and I spoke for the full amount of time.	☐	☐
3. I used correct grammar, vocabulary, and pronunciation.	☐	☐
4. I used signposts and transition words to effectively show the relationships between my ideas.	☐	☐
5. I clearly explained how the reading and the lecture are related.	☐	☐
6. I mentioned both of the key points from the reading and provided supporting details from the lecture for both points.	☐	☐

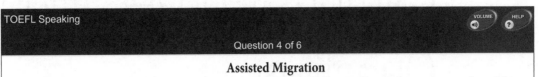

PROGRESSIVE PRACTICE: Go for the TOEFL Test

Read the passage in 45 seconds. Begin reading now. 🎧 CD3, Track 7

TOEFL Speaking　　　　　　　　　　　　　　　　　　VOLUME　HELP

Question 4 of 6

Assisted Migration

Assisted migration refers to the practice of relocating a population of organisms to a new place. The goal of assisted migration is for the relocated species to establish permanent residence in the new area.

　　The most common reason that scientists undertake assisted migration projects is to protect endangered species. Often, the survival of a species becomes threatened due to the unsuitability of the environment, especially in terms of providing food or shelter. An environment may become inadequate for certain populations due to factors like climate change or human development. By moving a threatened species to a new area, scientists help the species access an environment that can meet the organisms' survival needs and thus ensure their continued existence.

Note: The passage will <u>not</u> appear on your screen after the 45 seconds are over.

Now listen to part of a lecture in an environmental science class and take notes.

NOTES:

Now answer the question. You may use your notes.

TOEFL Speaking　　　　　　　　　　　　　　　　　　VOLUME　HELP

Question 4 of 6

The professor talks about checkerspot butterflies and the North American pika. Explain the aspects of these animals' original habitats that make them good candidates for assisted migration.

Preparation Time: 30 Seconds

Response Time: 60 Seconds

Preparation time used: _____ seconds
Speaking time used: _____ seconds

To see and hear sample responses and possible scores, see page 199 and listen to CD3, Track 8.

Campus Conversation Questions

For speaking task 5, you will answer a question that is based on a conversation between two university students. The conversation is between 60 and 90 seconds long, and you will hear it only once, so take notes! The conversation usually focuses on a problem that a university student might face. Sample problems might relate to the following:

- failing a class
- scheduling issues
- problems with housing
- absences from class
- financial problems
- transportation issues

No knowledge of daily life at North American universities will be needed in order to understand the conversation or respond to the question. In the conversation, the speakers will discuss two possible solutions to the problem and mention the advantages and disadvantages of the possible solutions.

The question for campus conversation tasks may be worded as follows:

» *The students discuss two solutions to the man's problem. Describe the problem. Then, state which of the two solutions you prefer and explain why.*

QUICK GUIDE: Campus Conversation Questions

Definition	The campus conversation task requires you to listen to a conversation between two students. The conversation is mainly about a problem that one of the speakers is having. Then, you will be asked a question based on the conversation.
The Question	After you listen to the conversation, you will hear the narrator asking a question. The question will appear on the screen until you have finished responding. It asks for the following three key pieces of information: **1.** the problem that the speakers are discussing. **2.** the problem's possible solutions that are mentioned by the speakers. **3.** your recommendation. • You will have 20 seconds to prepare your response after the beep. A clock will count down the time for you. • You will have 60 seconds to say your response into the microphone.
Targeted Skills	In order to achieve a high score for the campus conversation question, you must: • identify the main problem and two possible solutions in the conversation. • analyze the prompt and understand what information you need to include in your response. • create an outline for your response. • make a recommendation and explain the reasons for that recommendation. • organize your response so it is clear and easy to understand.
A Great Response	A top-scoring response will accurately and fluently address all of the information asked for in the question within the time provided. It will provide a brief summary of the problem and of the two options available to the student. Furthermore, a great response will give a well-reasoned recommendation about which option is best.
Things to Remember	**1.** First, analyze the prompt. What specific information will you include in your response? **2.** Take careful notes while you listen to the conversation. Listen for information about the main problem, the two possible solutions, and the advantages and disadvantages of both solutions. **3.** Begin your response by summarizing the problem. You should also briefly describe the two options that were mentioned in the conversation. Do <u>not</u> provide any options that weren't mentioned in the conversation. **4.** Make a recommendation about which of the two possible solutions is best. Provide at least two reasons to justify your recommendation. Be sure to support both of your reasons with details from the conversation.

WALK THROUGH: Campus Conversation Questions

A Below is a sample campus conversation question. Listen to the conversation between two students. While you listen, underline the information that you think is important in the conversation.   🎧 CD3, Track 9

SAMPLE SCRIPT ▶
for reference only, not available in test

Speaker 1: Good morning, Carol. What are you doing here? I thought you were usually working at this hour.

Speaker 2: Hi, Mark. Yeah, I used to work the morning shift at the bookstore. But now that the busy season is over, the manager cut back on everyone's hours.

Speaker 1: That's not good. Are you going to make enough money to get by?

Speaker 2: Well, that's the problem. I think that I'll be able to pay my bills, but just barely. I certainly won't be able to save up any money. And I like having some cash set aside, just in case there's an emergency.

Speaker 1: I see. Can't you just ask your manager at the bookstore for some more hours?

Speaker 2: I already did. But she said there's nothing available right now. Basically, I have to hope that someone leaves and I get to pick up those shifts or that the bookstore gets busy again and they need people to work more.

Speaker 1: Is that what you're going to do?

Speaker 2: I don't know. If I do that, I'll really have to be careful about how much money I spend until I get more shifts. And really, there's no guarantee that the extra hours will become available.

Speaker 1: That's true. It might be a good idea just to find another job, don't you think?

Speaker 2: I thought of that, too. But the only jobs available these days are off campus. There's actually a bookstore in the mall that's hiring, so I'm pretty sure I could get the job. The pay is better, and I'd be able to get as many hours as I want.

Glossary:

ⓒ POWERED BY COBUILD

shift: a set period of work time

guarantee: a promise or something that is certain

TOEFL Speaking   VOLUME   HELP

Question 5 of 6

The students discuss two solutions to the woman's problem. Describe the problem. Then, state which of the two solutions you prefer and explain why.

Preparation Time: 20 Seconds

Response Time: 60 Seconds

B Now review the sample notes that the student made to prepare her response. Then, read the conversation again and circle the information that the student included in her notes. Compare the information you underlined and the circled information. Did you notice all of the important points?

Sample Notes

W not getting enough hrs @ bookstore; barely enough $ / can't save $

- Ask for more hrs
  - no extra hrs available
  - pick up hrs only if someone leaves
  - wait until store gets busy again
  - no guarantee more hrs will become avail.
- Find another job
  - off campus
  - could get job at mall bookstore

C Below is a sample response for a campus conversation question. While you listen, notice how the speaker turns her outline from Part B into a full response. 🎧 CD3, Track 10

SAMPLE RESPONSE ▶

The woman's problem is that her employer reduced her hours, which means she'll barely make enough money to get by. She can keep her job and hope that more shifts become available, although she would have to spend very carefully and wouldn't be able to save money for emergencies. She can also get another job off campus. I think that getting a different job off campus is the best solution to her problem. For one, it's important to save money in case she has an emergency. For example, she might not be able to pay medical bills if she got sick. Another reason why I think getting a new job is the best solution is that it is guaranteed to get her more money. She says that the job at the mall pays better than the bookstore job. Also, she can pick a job that gives her enough hours. But the on-campus bookstore may never give her the shifts she wants.

TEST TIP!

When giving your response, remember that there is no right or wrong answer to the question. As long as you provide good support for the option you've chosen, you will increase your chances of getting a high score.

GET IT RIGHT: Tips and Tasks for Answering Correctly

» **TIP 1: Know what to listen for.** The conversations for campus conversation tasks <u>always</u> include the description of a problem and two possible solutions. Because you know that the conversation will definitely include this information, make sure to write these facts in your notes.

TASK 1: What is the main problem in **the conversation** on page 134 and what are the two possible solutions?

» **TIP 2: Listen carefully for the two possible solutions.** Speakers often use specific phrases in order to make recommendations. Listen for the phrases listed below in order to easily identify the two possible solutions.

Making Recommendations
Can't you . . . ?
It might be a good idea to X, don't you think?
You should . . .
Maybe you should . . .
Could you . . . ?
It wouldn't hurt to . . .
Why don't you . . . ?

TASK 2: Draw a box around two expressions in **the conversation** on page 134 that are used to make a recommendation. Remember to look for expressions from the table above.

» **TIP 3: Organize your notes while you listen.** Because you know what type of information to expect in the conversation, you can easily organize your notes while you listen. When you write your notes, you should put the main problem at the top of the page. Then, write each possible solution as it's mentioned. Under each solution, write down the details mentioned by the speakers. To help you quickly decide which option you want to recommend in your response, you should write a plus sign (+) or a minus sign (-) next to each detail to indicate whether it is mentioned as an advantage or a disadvantage of choosing the possible solution. That way, when the conversation is over, you can quickly assess which solution you could support the best.

TASK 3: Write a plus sign (+) next to the positive details and a minus sign (-) next to the negative details in **the sample notes** on page 135. Which solution has the most advantages?

» **TIP 4: Read the prompt carefully to find out the what information you need to include.** Campus conversation questions always ask for the following key information:
1) the problem being discussed
2) the solution you recommend
3) a justification for your recommendation

Be sure to address all three points in your response. By knowing what information you need, you can focus on organizing your response in the best way.

TASK 4: Read **the prompt** on page 134 and underline three pieces of key information that the question asks for.

» **TIP 5: Start your response by giving a brief summary of the problem.** Because the entire response is based on the problem, stating the problem is a good way to begin. Your summary should be brief but give enough information that someone who has <u>not</u> heard the conversation will understand the main issue. Use the expressions on the next page to summarize the problem.

Summarizing the Problem

The speakers in the conversation are discussing . . .
The problem that the man is having is that . . .
The woman's problem is that . . .
The problem is that . . .

TASK 5: In **the sample response** on page 135, underline the summary of the problem.

» **TIP 6: State both of the possible solutions to the problem.** By stating both solutions, you show that you understand the two options that the speakers were talking about. Use the expressions below to briefly state possible solutions.

Stating the Possible Solutions

One solution is . . . / The second solution is . . .
The possible solutions are X and Y.
The first solution is to . . . / The other solution is to . . .
The two solutions that the speakers mention are . . .

TASK 6: Circle the two possible solutions described in **the sample response** on page 135.

» **TIP 7: Clearly state your recommendation.** In order to give an effective response, you must make a recommendation about what the speaker should do based on the solutions given in the conversation. Use the expressions below to state recommendations.

Making a Recommendation

My recommendation is . . .
If I were her, I would . . .
I think that the best thing to do in this situation is to . . .
I think that X is the best solution to his problem.
I suggest that the man . . .

TASK 7: Draw a box around the speaker's recommendation in **the sample response** on page 135.

» **TIP 8: Use details from the conversation to justify your recommendation.** You can justify, or support, your recommendation by stating an advantage of the recommended solution. You can also justify your position by describing why the other option is not as good.

TASK 8: Double underline the two justifications in **the sample response** on page 135 that the speaker uses to explain her position. Do the justifications relate to the advantages of the speaker's recommendation or to the disadvantages of the other solution?

PROGRESSIVE PRACTICE: Get Ready

A Listen to a conversation between two students. Then, look at the prompt and circle the three pieces of information that must be included in the response.   CD3, Track 11

TOEFL Speaking

VOLUME   HELP

Question 5 of 6

The students discuss two solutions to the woman's problem. Describe the problem. Then, state which of the two solutions you prefer and explain why.

Preparation Time: 20 Seconds

Response Time: 60 Seconds

B Why did the test taker write down the information below? Answer the questions about the person's outline.

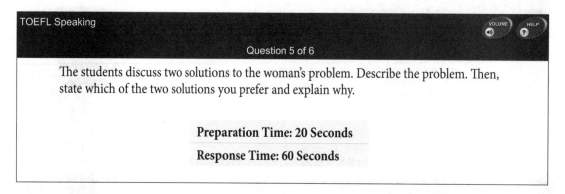

Woman can't study — noisy neighbors in apt building ❶
- Study at the library ❷
  - time and $ (−)
    - has to drive to campus
    - pay for parking
    - lives far from campus
- Move back into dorms ❸
  - help her grades (+) ❹
  - lose deposit (−)

1. What does item 1 in the notes tell us?
   ○ The problem that the speakers are discussing
   ○ The man's recommendation

2. What does item 2 in the notes tell us?
   ○ The first possible solution
   ○ The second possible solution

3. What does item 3 in the notes tell us?
   ○ The man's recommendation
   ○ The first possible solution

4. What does item 4 in the notes tell us?
   ○ The first supporting detail for the man's recommendation
   ○ The second supporting detail for the man's recommendation

C Listen to a sample response to the prompt from Part A. Notice the words and expressions the speaker uses to introduce his topic sentences, introduce and talk about his recommendation, and introduce and talk about supporting details. Then, listen again. Identify the purpose of each section in the sample response below. Write the numbers of the phrases from the box below in front of the correct sentences.

🎧 CD3, Track 12

1. ~~Summary of Problem~~	2. Reason 1 for Recommendation
3. Reason 2 for Recommendation	4. Speaker's Recommendation
5. Two Possible Solutions	6. Supporting Detail 1
7. Supporting Detail 2	

SAMPLE RESPONSE ▶   [1] The woman's problem is that her neighbors at her new apartment are so noisy that she has difficulty studying.

[   ] She could study at the library when her neighbors are noisy, but the drive would take a long time and she would have to pay for parking. She could also move out of her apartment and back into the dorms, but she would lose her deposit on the apartment.

[   ] In my opinion, moving out of her apartment is the best solution. I believe this for two reasons.

[   ] First, she won't be able to study as much if she drives to the library.

[   ] That's because every time she drives back and forth from the library, she loses time that she could have spent studying.

[   ] Second, her top priority should be her grades, not her finances.

[   ] In the end, getting poor grades would have a larger effect on her life than losing the deposit on her apartment.

D Now fill in the template in your own words. Then, practice your response aloud. Record your response if you can.

[*Summary of Problem*] The problem that the woman is having is that _____

_____.

[*Description of Possible Solutions*] One possible solution to her problem is _____

_____.

The second possible solution is to _____

_____.

[*Recommendation*] My recommendation for the woman is to _____

_____. This is the best solution for two reasons.

[*Reason 1*] First, _____

_____.

[*Supporting Detail 1*] By doing this, she will be able to _____

_____

_____

[*Reason 2*] Next, _____ is a good idea because

_____

_____.

[*Supporting Detail 2*] This will help her _____

_____

_____

_____.

E Now think about your response or listen to it again if it was recorded. Then, read the statements below. Did your response meet the scoring requirements for campus conversation questions? Check (✓) *Yes* or *No*. Keep practicing until you can check *Yes* for all of the statements.

Response Checklist: Campus Conversation Questions	Yes	No
1. My response was thorough and complete. I answered the prompt directly and did not include unnecessary information.	☐	☐
2. My response was well-paced. It was neither too fast nor too slow, and I spoke for the full amount of time.	☐	☐
3. I used correct grammar, vocabulary, and pronunciation.	☐	☐
4. I summarized the problem and the two possible solutions in a clear manner.	☐	☐
5. I provided a clear recommendation with support from the conversation.	☐	☐
6. I used signposts and transition words to effectively show the relationships between my ideas.	☐	☐

PROGRESSIVE PRACTICE: Get Set

A Listen to a conversation between two students. Then, look at the prompt and write the three pieces of information that must be included in the response.

1. _____

2. _____

3. _____

🎧 CD3, Track 13

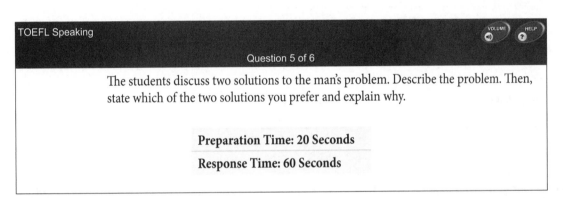

TOEFL Speaking

VOLUME   HELP

Question 5 of 6

The students discuss two solutions to the man's problem. Describe the problem. Then, state which of the two solutions you prefer and explain why.

Preparation Time: 20 Seconds

Response Time: 60 Seconds

B Listen to the conversation again. Complete the notes below using the information from the conversation.

🎧 CD3, Track 13

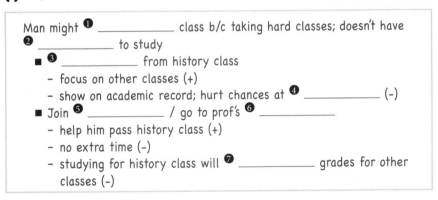

Man might ❶ _____ class b/c taking hard classes; doesn't have
❷ _____ to study
  ■ ❸ _____ from history class
    – focus on other classes (+)
    – show on academic record; hurt chances at ❹ _____ (-)
  ■ Join ❺ _____ / go to prof's ❻ _____
    – help him pass history class (+)
    – no extra time (-)
    – studying for history class will ❼ _____ grades for other
      classes (-)

C Use the notes to complete the response template below. Be sure to use transition words. Then, say your response aloud. Record your response if you can.

[*Summary of Problem*] _____

_____

[*Description of Possible Solutions*] _____

_____

_____

_____

[*Recommendation*] _____

_____

[*Reason 1*] _____

_____

[*Supporting Detail 1*] _____

_____

_____

[*Reason 2*] _____

_____

[*Supporting Detail 2*] _____

_____

_____

D Now think about your response or listen to it again if it was recorded. Then, read the statements below. Did your response meet the scoring requirements for campus conversation questions? Check (✓) *Yes* or *No*. Keep practicing until you can check *Yes* for all of the statements.

Response Checklist: Campus Conversation Questions	Yes	No
1. My response was thorough and complete. I answered the prompt directly and did not include unnecessary information.	☐	☐
2. My response was well-paced. It was neither too fast nor too slow, and I spoke for the full amount of time.	☐	☐
3. I used correct grammar, vocabulary, and pronunciation.	☐	☐
4. I summarized the problem and the two possible solutions in a clear manner.	☐	☐
5. I provided a clear recommendation with support from the conversation.	☐	☐
6. I used signposts and transition words to effectively show the relationships between my ideas.	☐	☐

PROGRESSIVE PRACTICE: Go for the TOEFL Test

Listen to a conversation between two students and take notes.

🎧 CD3, Track 14

NOTES:

Now answer the question. You may use your notes.

TOEFL Speaking

VOLUME   HELP

Question 5 of 6

The students discuss two solutions to the man's problem. Describe the problem. Then, state which of the two solutions you prefer and explain why.

Preparation Time: 20 Seconds

Response Time: 60 Seconds

Preparation time used: _____ seconds

Speaking time used: _____ seconds

To see and hear sample responses and possible scores, see page 200 and listen to CD3, Track 15.

Academic Summary Questions

For speaking task 6, you will be asked a question that is based on an academic lecture. The lecture is between 60 and 90 seconds long! You will hear the lecture only once, so be sure to take notes while you listen. The topics of the academic lectures are drawn from a number of academic subjects, including the following:

- sociology
- biology
- literature
- psychology
- anthropology
- astronomy

In your response, you will need to use only the information provided in the lecture. You do <u>not</u> need to have specific knowledge of any academic subject in order to respond effectively.

The lecture usually consists of a brief introduction, during which the professor describes the main focus of the lecture. It is common for the professor to define key terms at the beginning of the lecture. Next, the professor presents two key points to support the main idea. The professor often relates the key points to the main idea by:
- providing examples or applications of a concept.
- describing a cause and effect relationship.
- explaining the steps in a process.

After you listen to the lecture, you will hear a question that is based on the lecture.

The question for academic summary tasks may be worded as follows:

» *Using the points and examples from the lecture, explain how Emerson's work demonstrated the ideals of transcendentalism.*

» *Using the points and examples from the talk, explain two benefits of protective coloring in animals.*

» *Using the points and examples from the lecture, explain two ways that plants defend themselves from animals.*

QUICK GUIDE: Academic Summary Questions

Definition	The academic summary task requires you to listen to part of an academic lecture. Then, you will answer a question that is based on the lecture.
The Question	• After you listen to the lecture, the narrator will ask you a question based on it. The question will remain on your screen until you have completed your response. • You will have 20 seconds to prepare your response. A clock on the screen will show how much time you have left to prepare. • You will have 60 seconds to say your response into the microphone.
Targeted Skills	In order to achieve a high score for the academic summary question, you must: • identify the main idea and two key points from the lecture. • understand how the two key points relate to and support the main idea. • analyze the prompt and understand what information you need to provide in your response. • create an outline for your response. • organize your response so it is clear and easy to understand.
A Great Response	A top-scoring response will accurately and fluently address all of the information asked for in the question within the time provided. It will clearly state the main theme of the lecture. It will also describe both key points provided by the professor.
Things to Remember	**1.** First, take notes while you listen to the lecture. Be sure to write down the main idea of the lecture and the two key points that the professor uses to support the main idea. Also, don't forget to write down any key definitions. **2.** Analyze the prompt. Make sure you understand the specific information you should include in your response. **3.** Next, use your notes to quickly write an outline. **4.** Begin your response by explaining the main idea of the lecture. Then, answer the question by using details from the lecture.

WALK THROUGH: Academic Summary Questions

A Below is a sample academic summary question. Listen to part of a lecture about important inventions of the nineteenth century. While you listen, underline the information in the lecture that you think is important.   🎧 CD3, Track 16

SAMPLE SCRIPT ▶
for reference only, not available in test

Professor: The sewing machine was one of the most significant inventions of the nineteenth century, especially when we consider how it impacted Western society. This influence was particularly obvious in two areas: production rates for clothing and access to quality goods.

First, let's look at production rates, which are basically just the rates at which things are made. In other words, it refers to how fast an item is created. OK, so before the sewing machine was invented, it took a skilled seamstress or tailor about two hours to produce a pair of pants. With a sewing machine, making the same pair of pants took just 38 minutes! That means that a tailor who made 10 pairs of pants a week before was able to make more than twice as many with the help of a sewing machine. Of course, the increased production rates affected the cost of the pants. Because it took much less time to make them, tailors could sell their products for a lower price.

Second, because of its effect on consumer prices, the sewing machine also increased access to quality goods. Prior to the invention of the sewing machine, the average worker wore clothing that was made at home. While these clothes were functional, they were not of the same quality and craftsmanship as the clothing that wealthy people purchased in stores. But with the sewing machine, the same high-quality clothes became available for everyone. A factory worker could now afford to wear the same pants as the factory owner.

Glossary:

⊜ POWERED BY COBUILD

significant: important

craftsmanship: the quality that something made by hand has

TOEFL Speaking   VOLUME   HELP

Question 6 of 6

Using the points and examples from the lecture, explain two ways in which the sewing machine influenced Western society.

Preparation Time: 20 Seconds

Response Time: 60 Seconds

B Now review the sample notes that the test taker made to prepare her response. Then, read the lecture again and circle the information that the test taker included in her outline. Compare the information you underlined and the circled information. Did you notice all of the important points?

> SAMPLE NOTES
> Effect of sew'g mach. on W. soc.
> ■ Prod. rates (how fast sometg is created)
>   – before: 2 hrs/pants
>   – after: 38 mins/pants
>   – ↑ prod = less $ for clothes
> ■ Access to qual. goods
>   – before ppl wore homemade clths; rich bought in stores
>   – sew'g mach. = high quality avail. to everyone

C Listen to a sample response for an academic summary question. While you listen, notice how the speaker turns her outline from Part B into a full response. 🎧 CD3, Track 17

SAMPLE RESPONSE ▶

In the lecture, the professor talks about the impact that the sewing machine had on Western society. The professor mentions two ways that the sewing machine influenced society: the rate of production and access to quality clothing.

According to the professor, the sewing machine increased the rate of production and drove down the cost of clothes. To show this, he gives the example of a pair of pants. Before the sewing machine was invented, a pair of pants took two hours to sew. With a sewing machine, it took less than one hour. This made it quicker to produce pants, and they could be sold for much less.

The second major impact the professor mentions is that more people had access to high-quality clothes. Before the sewing machine, clothes were mostly made at home. This made it hard for people with a lower income to have really nice clothes. The professor suggests that the sewing machine allowed high-quality clothes to be made cheaply, so the same clothes were available for everyone.

GET IT RIGHT: Tips and Tasks for Answering Correctly

» **TIP 1: Listen for key information.** Remember, the lecture will always include a description of the main idea and two key points to support the main idea. The main idea typically appears at the beginning of the lecture. The key points are often introduced by using sequence language, so listening for these words will help you identify the key points. Sequence language includes words or expressions that indicate the order in which the information is presented (e.g., *First, Second, In addition*).

TASK 1: Draw a box around the main idea and the two key points in **the lecture** on page 146. Underline two sequence words that help you find the key points.

» **TIP 2: Read the prompt carefully and think about the key points from the lecture before responding.** The prompt is based on the lecture, but you will have to understand exactly what the question is asking in order to give a good response. One way you can better understand the prompt is to think about how the two key points from the lecture relate to the main idea of the prompt. Are the key points examples of the main idea? Do the key points describe a process?

TASK 2: Read the question and circle the main information you need to include. Then, compare that to the key points from the lecture. Are the key points reasons? examples? something else?

» **TIP 3: Start your response by rewording the main idea of the passage**. To give your response a clear focus, be sure to describe in your own words the main idea of the passage. The rewording of the main idea should go at the beginning of your response.

TASK 3: In **the sample response** on page 147, underline the rewording of the main idea.

» **TIP 4: Use reported speech phrases to provide details from the lecture.** Reported speech phrases are expressions used to describe what somebody said. By using reported speech phrases, you will be able to provide clear support from the lecture and give a stronger response. Use the expressions below to describe what somebody said.

Reported Speech Phrases
In the lecture, the professor talks about . . .
The professor mentions . . .
To show this, the professor gives the example of . . .
According to the professor . . .
The professor suggests . . .
The second X that was mentioned by the professor was . . .

TASK 4: Circle six reported speech phrases you see in **the sample response** on page 147.

PROGRESSIVE PRACTICE: Get Ready

A Listen to part of a lecture in a psychology class. Then, look at the prompt and circle two pieces of information that will help you respond to the prompt.

🎧 CD3, Track 18

TOEFL Speaking

Question 6 of 6

Using the points and examples from the lecture, explain two processes that humans use for short-term memory.

Preparation Time: 20 Seconds

Response Time: 60 Seconds

B Why did the test taker write down the information below? Answer the questions about the person's outline.

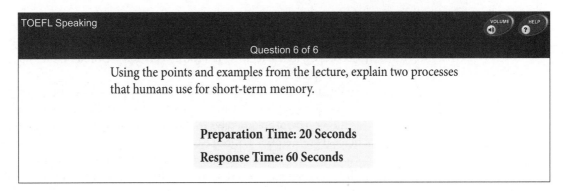

Short-term memory: to rem. phone #s, names, directions ❶
- Processes for ST mem
  - chunking ❷
    - break up long info into small pieces
    - ex: phone #, 3–4 #s at a time, remember the whole ❸
  - phonological loop ❹
    - replay info in head
    - ex: directions, r-l-2m-3ʳᵈl (repeat in head to rm'mbr)

1. What does item 1 in the notes tell us?
   ○ The main topic of the lecture
   ○ The relationship between the main topic and the key points

2. What does item 2 in the notes tell us?
   ○ The first process used in short-term memory
   ○ The second process used in short-term memory

3. What does item 3 in the notes tell us?

○ An example of the first process used in short-term memory

○ An example of the second process used in short-term memory

4. What does item 4 in the notes tell us?

○ The first process used in short-term memory

○ The second process used in short-term memory

C Listen to a sample response to the prompt from Part A. Notice the words and expressions the speaker uses to introduce his topic sentences, introduce and talk about his recommendation, and introduce and talk about supporting details. Then, listen again. Identify the purpose of each section in the sample response. Write the numbers of the phrases from the box below in front of the correct sentences.   CD3, Track 19

1. Key Point 1	2. Key Point 2	3. Main Topic of Lecture
4. Support for Key Point 1	5. Support for Key Point 2	

SAMPLE RESPONSE ▶   [**3**] The lecture is about short-term memory. The professor discusses two different ways our brains create short-term memories: chunking and the phonological loop.

[   ] According to the lecture, chunking is when we break up a long piece of information into smaller pieces.

[   ] To illustrate how this works, the professor gives an example of how we use chunking to remember telephone numbers. Usually, we divide the long number into three smaller sections. The professor says that by breaking up the information into these "chunks," it helps us remember it more easily.

[   ] The second method mentioned in the lecture is the phonological loop.

[   ] The professor explains that this is when a person repeats information over and over again in the mind. The example given in the lecture is of directions to a place. Our brains use the phonological loop to repeat the steps over and over again, which helps us remember them.

D Now fill in the template below in your own words. Then, practice your response aloud. Record your response if you can.

> [*Main Topic of Lecture*] In the lecture, the professor discusses _____, which is a memory that we remember for a short time only. The professor talks about two processes that we use to create _____.
>
> [*Key Point 1*] The first process mentioned by the professor is called _____. This is when _____ _____.
>
> [*Support for Key Point 1*] To demonstrate this, the professor talks about remembering _____. She says that _____ _____ _____.
>
> [*Key Point 2*] The second process that the professor talks about is the _____ _____. This is when _____ _____.
>
> [*Support for Key Point 2*] To show how the phonological loop works, the professor talks about remembering _____. She says _____ _____ _____.

E Now think about your response or listen to it again if it was recorded. Then, read the statements below. Did your response meet the scoring requirements for academic summary questions? Check (✓) *Yes* or *No*. Keep practicing until you can check *Yes* for all of the statements.

Response Checklist: Academic Summary Questions	Yes	No
1. My response was thorough and complete. I answered the prompt directly and did not include unnecessary information.	☐	☐
2. My response was well-paced. It was neither too fast nor too slow, and I spoke for the full amount of time.	☐	☐
3. I used correct grammar, vocabulary, and pronunciation.	☐	☐
4. I described the main topic and two key points from the lecture.	☐	☐
5. I provided details from the lecture to support the key points.	☐	☐
6. I used signposts and transition words to effectively show the relationships between my ideas.	☐	☐

PROGRESSIVE PRACTICE: Get Set

A Listen to part of a lecture in a marketing class.
Then, look at the prompt and write the main piece of
information that must be included in the response.

1. _____

🎧 CD3, Track 20

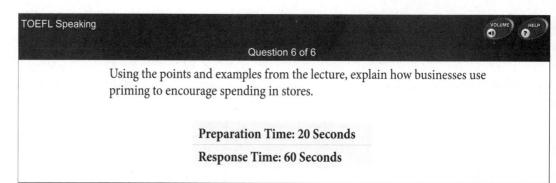

TOEFL Speaking

VOLUME   HELP

Question 6 of 6

Using the points and examples from the lecture, explain how businesses use
priming to encourage spending in stores.

Preparation Time: 20 Seconds

Response Time: 60 Seconds

B Listen to the lecture again. Complete the notes below using the information from the lecture.

> Priming — stores use it to encourage ❶ _____
> ■ Placement
>   – products put in a specific ❷ _____ in store
>   – example: ❸ _____ by door in grocery store — leads customers
>   to believe products are ❹ _____, fragrant, and beautiful
> ■ ❺ _____
>   – how products are presented in store
>   – example: ❻ _____ and vegs arranged to look like farmers'
>   ❼ _____ (freshness)

C Use the notes on the previous page to complete the response template. Be sure to use transition words. Then, say your response aloud. Record your response if you can.

[*Main Topic of Lecture*] _____

_____

_____

[*Key Point 1*] _____

_____

[*Support for Key Point 1*] _____

_____

_____

[*Key Point 2*] _____

_____

[*Support for Key Point 2*] _____

_____

_____

D Now think about your response or listen to it again if it was recorded. Then, read the statements below. Did your response meet the scoring requirements for academic summary questions? Check (✓) *Yes* or *No*. Keep practicing until you can check *Yes* for all of the statements.

Response Checklist: Academic Summary Questions	Yes	No
1. My response was thorough and complete. I answered the prompt directly and did not include unnecessary information.	☐	☐
2. My response was well-paced. It was neither too fast nor too slow, and I spoke for the full amount of time.	☐	☐
3. I used correct grammar, vocabulary, and pronunciation.	☐	☐
4. I described the main topic and two key points from the lecture.	☐	☐
5. I provided details from the lecture to support the key points.	☐	☐
6. I used signposts and transition words to effectively show the relationships between my ideas.	☐	☐

PROGRESSIVE PRACTICE: Go for the TOEFL Test

Listen to part of a lecture in a biology class and take notes. 🎧 CD3, Track 21

NOTES:

Now answer the question. You may use your notes.

TOEFL Speaking

VOLUME   HELP

Question 6 of 6

Using the points and examples from the lecture, explain the impact of colony collapse disorder on agricultural productivity and food prices.

Preparation Time: 20 Seconds

Response Time: 60 Seconds

Preparation time used: _____ seconds

Speaking time used: _____ seconds

To see and hear sample responses and possible scores, see page 201 and listen to CD3, Track 22.

Speaking Review Test

The following section is designed to put the skills you learned to the test. In the Speaking Review Test, you will encounter all six questions types as they appear on the speaking section. Furthermore, the questions are the same difficulty as those on the TOEFL test.

In order to follow the test as closely as possible, please be sure to follow the directions on the page. When you play the CD tracks that are listed on the page, you will hear beeps that let you know when to start preparing your response, when to begin speaking your response, and when your response time is over. The following timing guide shows how much time you will have to prepare and speak your response for each question type on the speaking section:

Speaking Section Timing Guide			
Question	Reading Time	Preparation Time	Response Time
Question 1: Personal Experiences	n/a	15 seconds	45 seconds
Question 2: Paired Choices	n/a	15 seconds	45 seconds
Question 3: Campus Matters	45 seconds	30 seconds	60 seconds
Question 4: Academic Reading and Lecture	45 seconds	30 seconds	60 seconds
Question 5: Campus Conversations	n/a	20 seconds	60 seconds
Question 6: Academic Summary	n/a	20 seconds	60 seconds

For the best results, you should record your responses for each question. After the review test, you will find two model responses for each question. The model responses have been rated and are accompanied by a rater's analysis that explains the good and bad points of each response. Use these evaluations along with the scoring guides in the Guide to Speaking to determine what score you would have received.

When evaluating your responses, try to identify your weaknesses. Are your responses under-developed or is your pronunciation unclear? By understanding your weaknesses, you will know exactly what sections to review in order to improve.

QUESTION 1

You will hear a statement about a familiar subject. After you hear the statement, you will have 15 seconds to prepare and 45 seconds to give your spoken response

CD3, Track 23

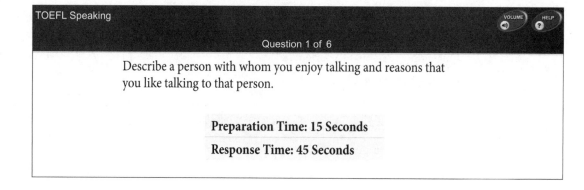

NOTES:

Preparation time used: _____ seconds

Speaking time used: _____ seconds

To hear sample responses, listen to CD 3, Track 24.

QUESTION 2

Now, you will hear a statement about a familiar subject. After you hear the statement, you will have 15 seconds to prepare and 45 seconds to give your spoken response. CD3, Track 25

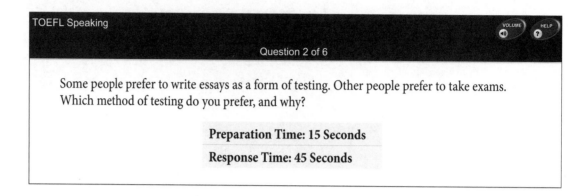

TOEFL Speaking

Question 2 of 6

Some people prefer to write essays as a form of testing. Other people prefer to take exams. Which method of testing do you prefer, and why?

Preparation Time: 15 Seconds

Response Time: 45 Seconds

NOTES:

Preparation time used: _____ seconds

Speaking time used: _____ seconds

To hear sample responses, listen to CD 3, Track 26.

QUESTION 3

Read the announcement in 45 seconds. Begin reading now. 🎧 CD3, Track 27

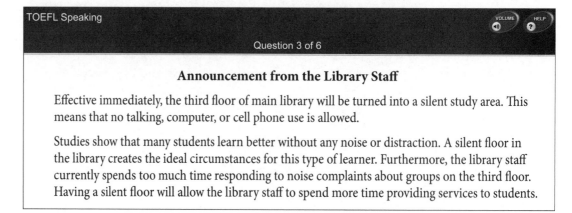

Note: The announcement will <u>not</u> appear on your screen after the 45 seconds are over.

Now listen to two students as they discuss the announcement and take notes.

Now get ready to answer the question. You may use your notes.

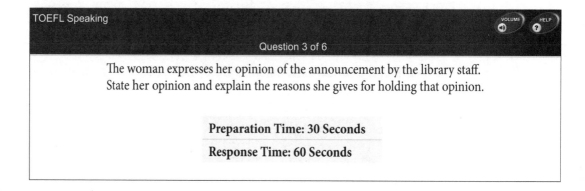

NOTES:

Preparation time used: _____ seconds

Speaking time used: _____ seconds

To hear sample responses, listen to CD 3, Track 28.

QUESTION 4

Read the passage in 45 seconds. Begin reading now. 🎧 CD3, Track 29

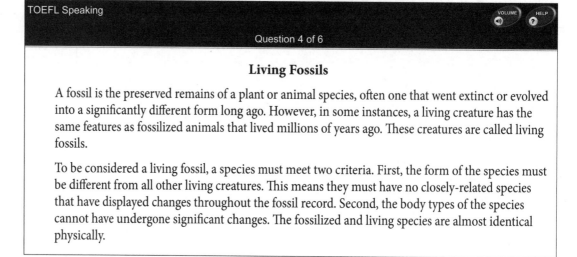

Note: The passage will <u>not</u> appear on your screen after the 45 seconds are over.

Now listen to part of a lecture in a biology class and take notes.

Now get ready to answer the question. You may use your notes.

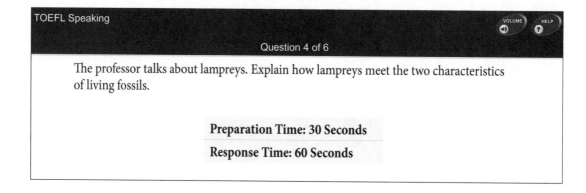

NOTES:

Preparation time used: _____ seconds

Speaking time used: _____ seconds

To hear sample responses, listen to CD 3, Track 30.

QUESTION 5

Listen to a conversation between two students and take notes. 🎧 CD3, Track 31

Now get ready to answer the question. You may use your notes.

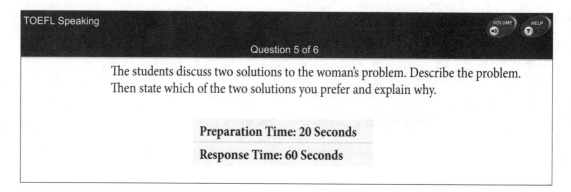

TOEFL Speaking

Question 5 of 6

The students discuss two solutions to the woman's problem. Describe the problem. Then state which of the two solutions you prefer and explain why.

Preparation Time: 20 Seconds

Response Time: 60 Seconds

NOTES:

Preparation time used: _____ seconds

Speaking time used: _____ seconds

To hear sample responses, listen to CD 3, Track 32.

QUESTION 6

Listen to part of a lecture in a biology class and take notes. 🎧 CD3, Track 33

Now get ready to answer the question. You may use your notes.

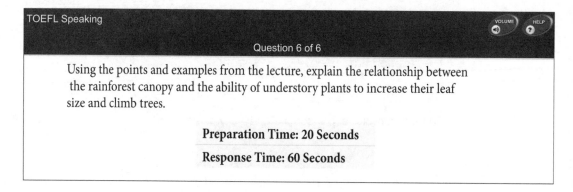

Using the points and examples from the lecture, explain the relationship between the rainforest canopy and the ability of understory plants to increase their leaf size and climb trees.

Preparation Time: 20 Seconds

Response Time: 60 Seconds

NOTES:

Preparation time used: _____ seconds

Speaking time used: _____ seconds

To hear sample responses, listen to CD 3, Track 34.

Answer Key

Listening

Lesson 1: Main Idea Questions and Detail Questions

Walk Through: Main Idea Questions
1. The positive impact of exchanges between cultures

Get It Right: Main Idea Questions
Task 1: *See, there was something we didn't get to talk about in class last time: the advantages of the Columbian Exchange. That's what we'll be addressing today.* **Task 2:** *negative effects, advantages, one advantage;* Pros / Cons **Task 3:** *That's what we'll be addressing today.* **Task 4:** Christopher Columbus or the negative effects of the Columbian Exchange **Task 5:** The exchange of animals that resulted from the Columbian Exchange **Task 6:** The positive impact of exchanges between cultures

Walk Through: Detail Questions
1. They contain components that move.

Get It Right: Detail Questions
Task 1: *move* **Task 2:** *So this is important, now; In fact; You don't really have to know that much about that* **Task 3:** "Kinetic" means "moving." **Task 4:** They contain components that move.

Get Set
A 1. 3600   **2.** 1200   **3.** ironworkers   **4.** iron
   5. bronze   **6.** smelt   **7.** soft

B 1. D, C, B, A   **2.** C, B, A, D   **3.** D, C, B, A   **4.** B, C, A, D   **5.** B, A, C, D

Go for the TOEFL Test
1. The history of early photography   **2.** It is a relatively recent art form.   **3.** It led to the invention of the camera obscura.   **4.** It was modified to produce clearer images.; It became more portable.   **5.** It enabled photographers to capture images with light-sensitive material.   **6.** They were destroyed when exposed to light.

Lesson 2: Purpose Questions and Inference Questions

Walk Through: Purpose Questions
1. To ask the professor for extra time to write her paper

Get It Right: Purpose Questions
Task 1: student and astronomy professor; office hours **Task 2:** *I wanted to talk about; what I'm hoping is* **Task 3:** *Problem: The thing is, I've had to write a lot of papers this semester. I had to write two research papers for other classes. So . . . I've been overloaded.; Request: Anyway, what I'm hoping is . . . maybe I can get an extension.* **Task 4:** *Let me guess . . .; The student rejects the guess.* **Task 5:** To find out more about a topic discussed in class

Walk Through: Inference Questions
1. Scientists may be able to forecast them in the future.

Get It Right: Inference Questions

Task 1: The professor is speaking seriously.   **Task 2:** Current methods can accurately predict their severity.   **Task 3:** Animals have better sensory systems than humans.   **Task 4:** A small percentage of animals can predict them.

Get Set

A 1. professor   **2.** office hours   **3.** midterm   **4.** unexcused
   5. flu   **6.** biology   **7.** justification

B 1. B, D, C, A   **2.** C, A, B, D   **3.** C, B, A, D   **4.** D, C, A, B   **5.** C, A, D, B

Go for the TOEFL Test

1. To ask about the availability of a video   **2.** The student is mistaken.   **3.** She teaches an astronomy class.   **4.** The professor will not watch it with her students.   **5.** The student must tell the professor to reserve the movie.

Lesson 3: Function Questions and Attitude Questions

Walk Through: Function Questions

1. To emphasize the potential value of underwater archaeology

Get It Right: Function Questions

Task 1: *And who knows how much we can learn from those wrecks.*; To suggest that underwater archaeology is not scientifically valid   **Task 2:** *But, of course, underwater archaeologists have to deal with problems that archaeologists on land rarely face.*   **Task 3:** *And who knows how much we can learn from those wrecks.*   **Task 4:** *artifacts they collect are just saturated with water—they're soaked*

Walk Through: Attitude Questions

1. It explains the variety of personalities.

Get It Right: Attitude Questions

Task 1: *one of my favorite theorists is*; *if you ask me*   **Task 2:** sympathetic   **Task 3:** *But the beauty of the theory, if you ask me*   **Task 4:** It is one of his favorite theories in psychology.   **Task 5:** It ignores individual differences in personality.

Get Set

A 1. professor   **2.** paper topic   **3.** brainstorm   **4.** cultural diffusion
   5. definition   **6.** cultural capitals   **7.** the Internet

B 1. C, B, A, D   **2.** C, D, A, B   **3.** C, A, D, B   **4.** D, B, C, A   **5.** A, D, C, B

Go for the TOEFL Test

1. To compliment the student for his knowledge   **2.** They can't be used for learning in most cases.
3. To clarify the location of a part of the Chola empire   **4.** To offer a reason for the Cholas' literary success   **5.** She is certain of its continued significance.   **6.** She admires their high level of skillfulness.

Lesson 4: Organization Questions and Connecting Content Questions

Walk Through: Organization Questions

1. By mentioning steps in a process

Get It Right: Organization Questions

Task 1: *Organizational Structure for a Definition: means to*; *Direct Definition: means to incorporate a substance into another one or means to attract and capture molecules or particles*   **Task 2:** The entire last paragraph of the lecture describes a way to treat water.   **Task 3:** *let me give you an example; imagine the dust*

Walk Through: Connecting Content Questions

1.

	Wind	Water	Animals
Dandelion Seeds	✓		
Burrs			✓
Coconuts		✓	

Get It Right: Connecting Content Questions

Task 1: definition   **Task 2:** *And this process, um, the process of spreading seeds, it's called seed dispersal. Let's talk about this.*   **Task 3:** burrs / dog's fur; dandelion seeds / wind; coconuts / water
Task 4: dandelion seeds, burrs, coconuts

Get Set

A 1. e-mailed   **2.** nanotechnology   **3.** millimeters   **4.** molecules
   5. meter   **6.** nanoparticles   **7.** sun
B 1. B, D, C, A   **2.** A, B, D, C   **3.** A, B, C, D   **4.** D, C, B, A

Go for the TOEFL Test

1. To describe one of the features that all birds possess   **2.** He wants to relate a previously mentioned detail to the main topic.   **3.** By describing the way in which a kite flies

4.

	Feathers	Skeleton	Neither
Lets the bird fly without using a lot of energy		✓	
Allows the bird to move upward and off the ground	✓		
Permits the bird to travel over long distances without getting lost			✓
Helps the bird control the direction it is flying in	✓		

Listening Review Test

Part 1

1. To discuss the best project format for her

2. She has enjoyed working with them.

3. Share her research with them

4. Whether she has found a specific topic for her paper

5. Visit the library

6. The advantages and disadvantages of a flextime scheduling system

7. Flextime is fairly common amongst people with full-time jobs.

8. To describe how flextime can be useful for working parents

9. It builds loyalty among workers.

10. It is probably not offered at jobs where managers must closely observe employees.

11.

	Condensed Schedule	Altered Schedule	Neither
Permits employees to work full-time in fewer than five days; Good for people who are able to work more than eight hours a day	✓		
Helps working parents		✓	
Allows employees to work fewer than 40 hours a week			✓

12. Why some organisms use diel vertical migration

13. To suggest that the professor's definition was incomplete

14. To give an example of an organism that uses diel vertical migration

15. It doesn't occur as often as diel vertical migration.

16. They hunt primarily by using their sense of sight.

17.

	Correct	Incorrect
Provides security for animals; Protects animals from damaging sunlight; Occurs in oceans and lakes	✓	
Helps animals find new sources of food		✓

Part 2

18. To request to live off campus

19. She can't study in her room.

20. It provides students with social support.; It gives students access to important services.

21. She thinks it's a good option for her.

22. Apply to live in the Quiet Dorm

23. The medicinal uses of biotoxins

24. To help the students understand the definition of a key term

25. To emphasize how common biotoxins are

26. Most people don't consider them living organisms.

27. There are many types currently available.

28.

	Botulinum Type A	Conotoxin	Both
Must be purified before it can be used as medication; Can be used to cure migraines	✓		
Can be used as a painkiller		✓	
Produced by a living organism			✓

29. The basic characteristics of its climate

30. To illustrate why scientists are interested in studying the Martian climate

31. To explain the length of Martian seasons

32. They change according to location and time.

33. It will be less windy there in the future.

34. They're occurring less frequently because of colder weather.

Speaking

Lesson 1: Personal Experience Questions

Get It Right

Task 1: older sister, Helen; very hard worker; often stays late at work; she is reliable; No matter how busy or tired she is; she always fulfills her commitments   **Task 2:** My older sister, Helen, is someone who inspires me in a number of ways.   **Task 3:** For one, my sister is a very hard worker.; Another reason I am inspired by my sister is that she is reliable.   **Task 4:** For example, she often stays late at work, even though she has to go to school early in the morning. In fact, last week she worked until 11 o'clock one night to finish a project! Seeing her dedication makes me want to work hard, too.; One time, she promised me she would help me with a school project. That week, she was very busy, but she made time to help me anyway. No matter how busy or tired she is, she always fulfills her commitments.

Get Ready

A a type of music that you enjoy; explain why you like listening to it

B **1.** The topic of the speaker's response   **2.** The personal details for the speaker's first reason
   3. The second key point to support the topic   **4.** The personal details for the speaker's second reason

C **1.** Topic Sentence; Key Point 1;   **3.** Personal Details 1;   **2.** Key Point 2;   **4.** Personal Details 2

D *Sample Response:* A genre of music that I like listening to is rock and roll. I like rock and roll for two reasons. First of all, rock and roll is fun to dance to. For example, when my friends and I get together, I always play rock music. No matter how tired we are, we always end up dancing because rock is great dance music. The next reason that I like listening to rock and roll is that it's cool. For me, every time I listen to rock music, I feel like the coolest kid ever. In fact, sometimes when I'm nervous, I think of my favorite rock song. Immediately, I feel cooler and I feel like I can do anything.

Get Set

A **1.** Describe an activity that you like to do.   **2.** Explain why you like doing it.   **3.** Include specific details in your explanation.

B **5.** Topic Sentence;   **1.** Key Point 1;   **3.** Personal Details 1;   **2.** Key Point 2;   **4.** Personal Details 2

C 2, 5, 3, 1, 4

D *Sample Response:* An activity that I enjoy doing is walking. I enjoy walking for a number of reasons. First, it's fun to walk with friends. With some activities, it's too difficult to do it with all of my friends because you have to be really in shape. For example, my friend Brooke likes to play tennis. But I'm just not athletic enough to play tennis. With walking, all of my friends can participate, and you don't need any special equipment or skills. Next, walking doesn't cost much at all. In fact, good sneakers are all you really need to spend money on. Besides that, you don't need to spend any money at all. Also, you don't need to spend money to be part of a gym or anything. You can just walk around your neighborhood or a local park.

Go for the TOEFL Test

Sample Response #1:	Sample Response #2:
Two places that I have traveled to are Hong Kong and Miami. These two trips were different in at least two ways. First of all, the food in each country was completely distinct. In Hong Kong, I ate a lot of noodle dishes that had soy sauce. On the other hand, I ate a lot of spicy foods in Miami, like tacos. Another way that my trips to each country were different was the general pace of life. I found that in Hong Kong, people walked faster and always seemed to be in a rush to get somewhere. In Miami, people walked pretty slowly and were not as rushed. Life there seemed to be more relaxed in general.	I've been to New York City and to Paris. New York City is very big, like Paris. There are so many people in both places. And they're both really expensive. I spent a lot more money in both places than I thought I would. Also, New York City has the Statue of Liberty. It is very tall, and many people visit it. When I went, I waited in line for three hours. That's a long time. Paris doesn't have the Statue of Liberty. Paris has the Eiffel Tower.

<table>
<tr><td>

Sample Score #1:

This response scored a 4 because it was complete, well organized, and displayed a high level of language usage. In the first two sentences, the speaker addressed the two points asked about in the prompt. The speaker used transition and sequence language appropriately to introduce two key points and personal details, which gave the response an organization that was clear and easy to follow. The speaker's speech was easy to understand and included a variety of sentence structures. Finally, the speaker used a wide range of vocabulary in the response.

</td><td>

Sample Score #2:

This response scored a 2 because it didn't fully address the prompt, it lacked focus, and the language usage was relatively low. While the prompt asks for the speaker to describe two places and how they are different, the speaker spends two sentences talking about how the cities are similar. Furthermore, the speaker provides personal details, but they are not always relevant to the point. For example, the speaker describes waiting in line for three hours at the Statue of Liberty. However, this detail does not support the point that New York City is different from Paris. Notice that the vocabulary in the response is not high and that, overall, the topic is underdeveloped.

</td></tr>
</table>

Lesson 2: Paired Choice Questions

Get It Right

Task 1: others say that their success comes only through hard work   **Task 2:** athletes gain their skills through hard work; Take me, for example; My next reason is because improvement comes through practice; For instance, when I lost against those shorter kids at basketball, it made me want to win.   **Task 3:** In my opinion, successful athletes gain their skills through hard work rather than through natural ability. I hold this opinion for several reasons.   **Task 4:** First of all, in some cases, natural advantages can work against you.; My next reason is because improvement comes through practice.   **Task 5:** However, because of my height, I thought that I didn't have to work as hard as shorter people. Imagine my surprise when I played basketball against shorter kids and I lost! It was because I thought my height was all I needed to win, while my shorter opponents worked harder to gain skills.; For instance, when I lost against those shorter kids at basketball, it made me want to win. So I started practicing every day, and sure enough, I got better. The next time I played them, I won!

Get Ready

A Some people think it is a good idea for university students to have jobs during college.; Which do you think is better and why?
C 1. The position of the response   **2.** The first key point of the response   **3.** The personal details for the first key point
4. The personal details for the second key point
D 5. Topic Sentence;   **1.** Key Point 1;   **3.** Personal Detail 1;   **2.** Key Point 2;   **4.** Personal Detail 2
E *Sample Response:* I know that some people may think differently, but in my opinion, it is a bad idea to work during college. I have this opinion for several reasons. First of all, working during college is stressful. For example, last semester I had a part-time job. Even though I worked only 10 hours a week, I felt a lot more stressed than I did before I started working. I hardly ever had any free time, and I was too tired and stressed to do anything fun if I did have a night off. The next reason that I think that it's bad to work during college is that it distracts from school. In my case, I often stayed late at work to help, but I ended up missing homework assignments as a result. I had straight As before I started working, but afterward, I struggled just to get passing grades because I was so distracted.

Get Set

A 1. Some people think it's necessary to make your own mistakes in order to learn important lessons.
2. Others think that it's best to learn from the mistakes of others.   **3.** Which do you think is best and why?
B 5. Topic Sentence;   **1.** Key Point 1;   **3.** Personal Detail 1;   **2.** Key Point 2;   **4.** Personal Detail 2
C 3, 5, 1, 4, 2
D *Sample Response:* I realize that some people think it's good to learn from the mistakes of others, but I am of the opinion that it's better to learn important lessons on my own. I think this for several reasons. To start with, I learn best by doing. For instance, I can read about an experiment, but I don't really learn until I do the experiment myself. Basically, if I don't experience it myself, I just won't learn. Furthermore, I think that it helps build my character to learn important lessons on my own. Once, I was working on an important assignment for class. I was having trouble with it, but my pride kept me from asking my professor for help. Eventually, I did ask my professor, and it made things a lot easier. Now I know that it's OK to ask for help and that it's part of my character.

Go for the TOEFL Test

Sample Response #1:	Sample Response #2:
While some people think that there are no benefits to watching television, I disagree because I've found that watching television can be both educational and relaxing. To start with, a lot of television shows are actually educational. For example, my favorite shows are about astronomy and biology. By watching these shows, I have a better understanding of these fields. Plus, the shows feature the latest discoveries, so I have access to recent research. Next, watching television is relaxing, which is very beneficial. No matter how stressful my day is, I always feel better after watching a half hour of television. Because I've had the chance to unwind, my mind is clear when it's time to do homework, so I can do a better job.	Everybody knows that watching television is really bad for you. I don't even know how watching a lot of TV is good. For one thing, it makes you lazy because you will not want to go outside to do anything. You will just stay inside all day long and watch all your favorite shows. And you'll probably eat a lot, too. So it makes life bad. TV has too many commercials, so it's boring, too. I can't even tell what the commercials are for. Sometimes I see a commercial and I don't know what product they are talking about.
Sample Score #1:	**Sample Score #2:**
This response received a 4 because the speaker uses the full time given to produce a well-organized response with few pauses. He clearly states his opinion in the opening sentence of the response. Then, he supports his opinion by describing two benefits of watching television. Rather than just saying that TV is educational, he describes his favorite shows and how they help him learn about subjects that interest him. The speaker also uses a variety of sentence structures in his response, which makes it sound more natural and fluent.	This response received a 2 because it is difficult to understand and demonstrates a limited vocabulary. The woman's speech is slow and contains a lot of pauses. Furthermore, the speaker does not develop her ideas past the sentence level. For example, she jumps from the idea of television making people lazy to the notion that television makes life bad. If she had used more transition language, her progression of ideas might have been easier to follow.

Lesson 3: Campus Matters Questions

Get It Right

Task 1: Starting next semester, the campus dining halls will close at 8 p.m. instead of 10 p.m.; too few students visit the dining halls in the late evening; the university hopes to save money by closing the dining halls earlier   **Task 2:** Yes . . . and I really hope the university reconsiders.; The man opposes the plan.   **Task 3:** That's the thing . . . there *are* a lot of people using the dining halls in the late evening, especially students who have seminars or discussion sections until late in the day.; Also, I'm really skeptical that cutting two hours is going to save very much money.   **Task 4:** State the man's opinion; explain the reasons he gives for holding that opinion   **Task 5:** According to the announcement; he says; He points out; the student argues; The student says

Get Ready

A State her opinion; explain the reasons she gives for holding that opinion

B 1. A change in university policy   **2.** The second reason to explain the change   **3.** The woman's opinion about the change   **4.** The second key point in support of the woman's opinion

C 1. Proposed Change;   **4.** Reasons for Change;   **5.** Student's Opinion;   **2.** Reason 1 for Opinion;   **6.** Supporting Detail 1;   **3.** Reason 2 for Opinion;   **7.** Supporting Detail 2

D *Sample Response:* The announcement says that in the fall semester, City College is going to start requiring students to meet with advisors twice a semester. One reason for the change is that the advising department thinks that it gives students an opportunity to get more information about required courses and major requirements. According to the announcement, the university also decided to increase the number of mandatory advisory meetings per semester because it will help advisors get to know students better. In the conversation, the woman says that she thinks the change is a good idea and gives two personal details that support the reasons given in the announcement. First, she explains that meeting with her advisor helped her graduate on time. That's because her advisor told her she was missing some required classes. Next, the woman says that her advisor wrote her a letter of recommendation and gave her good career advice. The student mentions that she couldn't have gotten all of that if she had met with her advisor only once a semester.

Get Set

A 1. university's plan to change its printing policy in the student computer lab **2.** State her opinion

3. explain the reasons she gives for holding that opinion

B 1. print **2.** ink **3.** update **4.** unfair **5.** a technology fee **6.** research **7.** software

C Sample Response: [*Summary of Announcement*] The announcement states that the computer lab will no longer allow students to print for free. [*Reason 1 for Change*] It is making this change because ink and paper are becoming too expensive. [*Reason 2 for Change*] The other reason for the change is to free up more money to update software and computers. [*Student's Opinion*] The woman feels that the change is unfair, and she offers two reasons why she feels this way. [*Reason 1 for Opinion*] First, she states that students are already charged for printing. Every student pays a technology fee that should cover any costs of printing in the computer lab. [*Supporting Details*] The woman's second reason why the change is unfair is that the computer lab does not need new software or computers. [*Reason 2 for Opinion*] She says that most of the students use the computers only for research and typing. [*Supporting Details*] She doesn't believe that new or expensive software is necessary to do that.

Go for the TOEFL Test

Sample Response #1:	Sample Response #2:
The notice from the Office of Residential Life states that freshmen cannot get into single rooms at City University. The reasons for the decision are that upperclassmen need their own rooms because they take more difficult classes and that freshmen benefit from having roommates. The woman says that the decision is a smart one. She mentions two reasons why she supports the decision. First, she states that her upper-level chemistry classes are much harder than her freshman courses. If she didn't have her own room, she would have trouble studying as much as she needs to. Second, she explains that if she had not lived with a roommate her freshman year, she might have left the university. The woman had been nervous and afraid until she became friends with her roommate. That friendship helped her finish her first year at the university.	I think the university made a good decision. Upper-level students deserve the privacy more than incoming students. When my friend Max was in his third year of university, he always said he was happy to have a single room. His classes were really hard. In my opinion, first-year students don't really have to worry about really hard classes. Another reason is that first-year students need to be social. If they are shy, they will have trouble if they live in a single room. Maybe they will leave the university and study somewhere closer to their families, like the lady said.
Sample Score #1:	Sample Score #2:
This response scored a 4 because the response is clear and well organized. The speaker uses all of the response time and speaks at a pace that makes her easy to understand. In the first sentence, she describes the change that the university plans to make. Then, she clearly describes the woman's opinion of the change. She uses sequence language to connect her points and details from the conversation to support her response.	This response scored a 2 for a number of reasons. While he states an opinion, the speaker describes his own opinion rather than the opinion of the woman in the conversation. The speaker provides some relevant information to support the opinion, but he also provides personal examples that don't support why the woman holds her opinion. The response is also short and does not use all of the response time.

Lesson 4: Academic Reading and Lecture Questions

Get It Right

Task 1: Necessity Goods and Veblen Goods **Task 2:** *Reading Passage:* Yet two types of goods do not follow this pattern.; Necessity goods are products that people always buy, even when prices rise.; Veblen goods, conversely, are products that people buy more of because of the goods' high prices. *Lecture:* But I think the best way to understand them is to imagine buying them.; Imagine that you live in a very cold area, and you use oil to heat your home.; This time, think of yourself as a wealthy person who is looking to buy a car. **Task 3:** The professor talks about purchasing oil and cars.; Explain how those purchases are related to necessity and Veblen goods. **Task 4:** The reading defines necessity and Veblen goods, and the professor expands upon this topic by describing two examples of each type of good. **Task 5:** the reading passage says; the professor gives an example of; According to the professor; the reading passage says; The professor explains

Get Ready

A describes the diets of desert coyotes and rattlesnakes; how their diets relate to the adaptations of desert animals.

B **1.** The main topic of the reading and lecture **2.** The second type of desert adaptation **3.** An example of an animal that uses the first type of adaptation **4.** A supporting detail for why rattlesnakes have a diverse diet

C **3.** Reading and Lecture Topic; **4.** Relationship Between Sources; **1.** Key Point 1 from Reading; **5.** Support 1 from Lecture; **2.** Key Point 2 from Reading; **6.** Support 2 from Lecture

D *Sample Response:* Both the reading and the lecture are about adaptations that help desert animals survive. The professor gives examples of two animals that use each of the adaptations that are mentioned in the reading. The first desert adaptation from the reading is that animals often have very diverse diets. In the lecture, the professor talks about coyotes to show an animal that uses this first adaptation. According to the professor, coyotes eat plants, animals, and even dead animals. By having such a diverse diet, they are always sure to get enough food and water to survive. The next desert adaptation discussed in the reading is that some animals will hunt during their prey's peak active hours. To illustrate this point, the professor uses the example of rattlesnakes. She says that the rattlesnakes hunt in the early morning or early evening, when their two main prey, mice and squirrels, are active. By hunting during these periods, rattlesnakes have a greater chance of finding food.

Get Set

A examples of affective memory and objects of attention; how these examples relate to method acting

B **1.** affective memory **2.** emotions **3.** attention **4.** setting **5.** disappointed **6.** winter **7.** shivering

C *Sample Response:* [*Reading and Lecture Topic*] The reading and the lecture are about method acting. [*Relationship Between Sources*] The reading passage explains how method acting provides actors with tools to improve their performances. The professor gives examples about how to use these tools. [*Key Point 1 from Reading*] The first point in the reading passage is that affective memory involves an actor using real memories from life to improve a performance. [*Support 1 from Lecture*] The professor has students remember moments in their lives that are similar to the feelings a character would have, like disappointment. By remembering a real disappointment from their lives, actors can show the character's disappointment more realistically. [*Key Point 2 from Reading*] The second point in the reading is that creating an object of attention helps actors remember the setting of the play. [*Support 2 from Lecture*] The professor explains how just focusing on the temperature of a scene can improve an actor's performance. He uses cold weather as an example, saying that focusing on feeling cold will remind actors to do things that people do to stay warm.

Go for the TOEFL Test

Sample Response #1:

Both the reading passage and the lecture are about assisted migration. The reading defines assisted migration as the practice of moving a species to a new habitat. The professor expands on the topic by describing two animals.

According to the author, assisted migration can be helpful when an organism's original habitat can't provide it with the necessary food supply. The professor supports this by giving the example of the checkerspot butterfly. Due to global warming, the checkerspot butterfly's main food supply became rare in the southern part of its habitat. In order to save the species, scientists relocated the butterflies farther north, where they could find food more easily.

The reading says that animals might benefit from assisted migration when the original habitat doesn't provide satisfactory shelter. The professor supports this by mentioning the North American pika. The professor says that the pika can't find adequate shelter from the cold because there isn't enough snow. By moving the pika to colder areas, the professor suggests that scientists can help it survive.

Sample Response #2:

Checkerspot butterflies are good for assisted migration because they are endangered. Assisted migration is when scientists move animals to live in a new place. The butterflies live in Mexico, but now it's too hot there. In their original habitats, they don't have shelters. The professor says it's too warm there now. The checkerspot butterfly doesn't have a place to live. Moving it will probably save the butterfly. The pika is an animal that lives in the mountains in the United States. It looks like a hamster. It's also good for assisted migration. It's like the checkerspot butterfly, too. Pikas need to hide in the snow. But there isn't enough snow in the mountains where they come from. So the pikas are freezing, and they need to go somewhere that is warmer.

Sample Score #1:

This response scored a 4 because the speaker uses the given time to provide a clear response that appropriately uses transitions and reported speech markers. The speaker organizes his response by defining assisted migration and then describing the two animals mentioned in the lecture. His response shows that he understands what assisted migration is, and he is able to explain why the checkerspot butterfly and the pika are good candidates based on their original habitats. The speaker also uses complex grammatical structures throughout his response.

Sample Score #2:

This response scored a 2 because the speaker gives an incomplete response and provides inaccurate information. The range of vocabulary and sentence structures is limited throughout the response. For example, the speaker uses the same vocabulary and grammatical structure to repeat the information about the checkerspot butterfly's original habitat being "too hot." Furthermore, the speaker says that the checkerspot butterfly is a good candidate because it does not have shelter in its original habitat, which is untrue according to the lecture. The response lacks clear organization and jumps from one topic to another.

Lesson 5: Campus Conversation Questions

Get It Right

Task 1: The busy season at the bookstore is over, and the manager cut back on everyone's hours. The woman could ask the manager for more hours, or she could find another job.   **Task 2:** Can't you just; It might be a good idea just to   **Task 3:** (-) no extra hrs available; (-) pick up hrs only if someone leaves; (-) wait until store gets busy again; (-) no guarantee more hrs will become avail.; (-) off campus; (+) could get job at mall bookstore; (-) no car, needs bus pass (2 wks pay)   **Task 4:** Describe the problem; state which of the two solutions you prefer; explain why   **Task 5:** The woman's problem is that her employer reduced her hours, which means she'll barely make enough money to get by.   **Task 6:** She can keep her job and hope that more shifts become available; She can also get another job off campus.   **Task 7:** I think that getting a different job off campus is the best solution to her problem.   **Task 8:** For one, it's important to save money in case she has an emergency. For example, she might not be able to pay medical bills if she got sick. (disadvantage of other solution); Another reason why I think getting a new job is the best solution is that it is guaranteed to get her more money. She says that the job at the mall pays better than the bookstore job. Also, she can pick a job that gives her enough hours. But the on-campus bookstore may never give her the shifts she wants. (advantage of the speaker's recommendation / disadvantage of other solution)

Get Ready

A Describe the problem.; which of the two solutions you prefer; explain why

B 1. The problem that the speakers are discussing   **2.** The first possible solution   **3.** The second possible solution   **4.** The first supporting detail for the man's recommendation

C 1. Summary of Problem;   **5.** Two Possible Solutions;   **4.** Speaker's Recommendation;   **2.** Reason 1 for Recommendation;   **6.** Supporting Detail 1;   **3.** Reason 2 for Recommendation;   **7.** Supporting Detail 2

D *Sample Response:* The problem that the woman is having is that she's having difficulty studying because her neighbors at her new apartment are too noisy. One possible solution to her problem is studying at the library when her neighbors are being loud. The second possible solution is to move out of the apartment as soon as possible and live in the dorms instead. My recommendation for the woman is to study at the library. This is the best solution for two reasons. First, if she goes to the library when she needs to study, she can maintain her grades and not have to move. By doing this, she will be able to keep her deposit. For students, money is usually hard to come by, so if she can find a way to save money, she should do it. Next, studying at the library is a good idea because she'll have a lot of resources that can help her with studying. This will help her get better grades because she will have access to books that she might need to help her study at the library.

Get Set

A A description of the problem; Which of the two solutions you prefer; An explanation of why you prefer that solution

B 1. fail   **2.** time   **3.** Withdraw   **4.** graduate school   **5.** study group   **6.** office hours   **7.** hurt

C *Sample Response:* [*Summary of Problem*] The man's problem is that he might fail a class. [*Description of Possible Solutions*] He could withdraw from it, but that would show on his transcript and could get his application rejected by grad schools. He could also join a study group and meet with the professor during office hours, but his grades in other courses will suffer if he spends too much time studying for this one. [*Recommendation*] I believe that the man should withdraw from the class. [*Reason 1*] For one, by withdrawing, he'll be able to study more for his other classes. [*Supporting Detail 1*] The man says several times that the other classes are hard, so he is more likely to do well in them with more study time. [*Reason 2*] Second of all, staying in the class will hurt his grades in his other courses. [*Supporting Detail 2*] It's better to withdraw from one class and excel in others than it is to stay in all the classes and do poorly in all of them.

Go for the TOEFL Test

Sample Response #1:

The man's problem is that his computer froze just before he completed a long, important paper. He could take it to a computer repair shop later, but the shop clerk cannot guarantee that the repair will work. The man's other option is to start writing a new paper immediately, but he thinks that the second version will not be as good as the first. In my opinion, the man should start writing a new paper immediately. First, it's possible that the man's first draft is gone for good. If he waits for the computer to get fixed and it doesn't work, he won't get any credit. Second, the man can still produce a good paper. He says that he still has all of his notes, so the most important information is already organized. Even if his new version isn't as good as the first, he'll still be able to get a passing grade.

Sample Score #1:

This response scored a 4 because the speaker provides a complete answer that is well developed. She describes the man's options and clearly states which of the options she prefers. Then, she supports her preferred option by providing two distinct points. The speaker connects the information in her response by using transition language, like "first" and "second." She also uses various grammatical structures and vocabulary choices.

Sample Response #2:

The man's computer stopped working, and he has to turn in an important paper. He should not try to write a new paper, because it will take too long. The man is probably stressed, and I don't think that will help him write the new paper. And his notes were probably on the computer, so he can't even look at those. He will waste his time trying to write a new paper, because it won't be as good as the first one he wrote. That's why he should try just getting the computer fixed. Maybe if he pays extra, the repair shop can finish it early. That way, he can get his paper finished on time and not bother with writing it all over again for no reason.

Sample Score #2:

This response scored a 2 because it is difficult to understand the point that the speaker is trying to make. He states that the man should not try to write a new paper, but he doesn't clearly state what the man should do until the very end of his response. This makes it hard to understand what the speaker's preference is. The speaker's explanation of why the man shouldn't write a new paper is disorganized and hard to follow. He mentions that the man is too stressed and that he doesn't have access to his notes, but he does not develop any of these examples. The speaker also introduces an option that was not mentioned by the speakers (the idea of paying the repair shop extra for fast service).

Lesson 6: Academic Summary Questions

Get It Right

Task 1: The sewing machine was one of the most significant inventions of the nineteenth century, especially when we consider how it impacted Western society.; First, let's look at production rates, which are basically just the rates at which things are made.; Second, because of its effect on consumer prices, the sewing machine also increased access to quality goods. (Sequence words: First, Second)   **Task 2:** Using the points and examples from the lecture; explain two ways   **Task 3:** In the lecture, the professor talks about the impact that the sewing machine had on Western society.   **Task 4:** In the lecture, the professor talks about; The professor mentions; According to the professor; To show this, he gives the example of; The second major impact the professor mentions; The professor suggests

Get Ready

A Using the points and examples from the lecture; explain two processes

B 1. The main topic of the lecture   **2.** The first process used in short-term memory   **3.** An example of the first process used in short-term memory   **4.** The second process used in short-term memory

C 3. Main Topic of Lecture;   **1.** Key Point 1;   **4.** Support for Key Point 1;   **2.** Key Point 2;   **5.** Support for Key Point 2

D *Sample Response:* In the lecture, the professor discusses short-term memory, which is a memory that we remember for a short time only. The professor talks about two processes that we use to create short-term memories. The first process mentioned by the professor is called chunking. This is when we take a long piece of information and break it up into smaller pieces to help us remember. To demonstrate this, the professor talks about remembering phone numbers. She says that we break up long phone numbers into chunks with only three or four digits. We combine those chunks and remember everything. The second process that the professor talks about is the phonological loop. This is when we repeat information in our heads to help us remember. To show how the phonological loop works, the professor talks about remembering the directions to a friend's house. She says we replay the directions over and over in our head so we remember.

Get Set

A How businesses use priming to encourage spending in stores
B 1. spending   **2.** place   **3.** flowers   **4.** fresh   **5.** Presentation   **6.** fruit   **7.** market
C *Sample Response:* [*Main Topic of Lecture*] The lecture is about priming, which is the way that stores influence customers to spend more money. The professor states that there are two types of priming: placement and presentation. [*Key Point 1*] The professor defines placement as the process of putting particular items in a specific area of the store. [*Support for Key Point 1*] He notes a common example, which is when grocery stores place flowers by a store entrance. The flowers make customers think of freshness, which makes the food seem fresh, too. Customers are then more likely to buy the food. [*Key Point 2*] Another way that stores use priming is through presentation. The professor specifies that presentation is how individual items are set up. [*Support for Key Point 2*] He provides apples in a grocery store as an example. They are presented in a creative, colorful, and appealing way. The pretty arrangement of the apples draws customers to them and makes them more likely to purchase the apples.

Go for the TOEFL Test

Sample Response #1:	Sample Response #2:
In the lecture, the professor discusses a phenomenon called colony collapse disorder, which is when honeybee colonies disappear. The professor focuses on the negative impacts of colony collapse disorder on agricultural productivity and food prices. First, the professor points out that bees are important to agriculture because they pollinate crops and allow the crops to reproduce. She adds that common crops like apples and tomatoes rely on bees for a large portion of pollination. The professor says that if bees were to become extinct, it would be very difficult to grow these crops. Next, the professor links the reduction of certain crops to the increase of food prices. She says that when availability of a product decreases, its price actually goes up. She then predicts that if the number of bee colonies continues to decrease, it will be hard for families to buy some foods because they will be too expensive.	The professor talks about disappearing bees. It's called colony collapse disorder. Scientists don't know why it's happening, but it's having a terrible effect so far. There are two results of the disappearing bees that the professor mentions. For example, the professor talks about how bees are important for plants. She says it's affecting agricultural productivity. Now that the bees are disappearing, there probably won't be fruit or vegetables for us to eat anymore. Also, colony collapse disorder is related to high food prices. The professor says that people won't be able to pay as much for food in the future because the bees are disappearing. She mentions a rule that says when availability decreases, prices increase, and that's why. Anything that is pollinated by bees will be too expensive.
Sample Score #1:	**Sample Score #2:**
This response scored a 4 because it gives a complete answer to the prompt in a way that is easy to understand. The speaker organizes his ideas by defining colony collapse disorder and then describing its two consequences based on the professor's lecture. The speaker provides a number of specific details from the lecture and clearly understands how the disappearance of the bees is affecting both agricultural productivity and food prices. The speaker's ideas flow very well due to his use of transition language and citing expressions. He uses a wide variety of grammatical structures and a range of vocabulary.	This response scored a 2 because it is difficult to understand and does not show that the speaker fully understands the concepts presented in the lecture. The clearest ideas presented in the response are those that come directly from the lecture, such as "colony collapse disorder is related to high food prices." The speaker should have expanded on this statement in order to show that she understands how they are related. The speaker's use of language throughout the response is limited. She repeats the same types of sentence structures and does not demonstrate a large vocabulary.

Speaking Review Test

Question 1

Sample Response #1:	**Sample Response #2:**
A person with whom I enjoy talking is my brother, Robert. He's great to talk to for a few reasons. One reason is that he can always cheer me up. For example, last week I was disappointed about a low test grade. But Robert called and told me a few jokes and funny stories. I felt better right away. Another reason that I like talking to Robert is that he gives good advice. During my first year of college, I didn't know which classes to take. I wanted to take a lot of electives because they looked interesting. But Robert advised that I take my required classes first so that I could graduate on time. He was right. If I hadn't taken his advice, I would have spent an extra year in college.	My brother, Robert, is funny. He's older than me, but we still have a lot in common. He's a lot of fun to be around and talk to. I think that's why he has so many friends. Everyone likes talking to him. He's also smart and can help you out with problems or decisions.
Sample Score #1:	**Sample Score #2:**
This response scored a 4 because the speaker makes full use of the 45 seconds provided for the response. The speaker develops the topic by describing two distinct points and supports those two points with personal details. For example, she describes a specific situation in which speaking to her brother made her feel better about getting a low grade on a test. Her vocabulary is varied, and she uses complex sentence structures throughout the response.	This response scored a 1 because it is underdeveloped. The speaker only minimally addresses the points asked about in the prompt and provides few personal details. The response does not make full use of the response time.

Question 2

Sample Response #1:	**Sample Response #2:**
I prefer taking exams to writing essays. I feel this way for two reasons. First, it's easier to identify the right answers on exams. For example, I had an exam on the play *Romeo and Juliet*. I didn't understand all of the play, but I knew which characters did what. Because I understood the basic events, I could identify answer choices that were wrong. The other reason I prefer exams is that they're easier to finish. For example, I had a literature exam that lasted for two hours. When there were only two minutes left, I still had a few questions to answer. I quickly read them and gave my best guesses. But if you run out of time to write an essay, you can't quickly guess the answers. You just have an incomplete essay.	I hate taking exams. You don't get a chance to talk about your own opinion. And they always check on small details. Those are hard to remember sometimes. It's not fair that you can get a bad grade just because you forgot a character's name or what year something happened.
Sample Score #1:	**Sample Score #2:**
This response scored a 4 because the speaker clearly describes his preference between the two choices given in the prompt. He also fully explains his reasoning for this opinion by providing two distinct explanations. Each explanation is followed by a relevant and specific example that serves to further develop his ideas. The speaker's ideas flow well due to his use of transition language, like *for example*, *when*, and *but*.	This response scored a 2 because the ideas are not well developed. While the speaker clearly describes in the first sentence her choice between the two options, she fails to develop her response. The speaker provides only one reason to explain her choice, and her response could have been greatly strengthened by the addition of another reason. In addition, the response is very short.

Question 3

Sample Response #1:	Sample Response #2:
The library announcement says that the third floor will be turned into a silent study area. The reasons for the decision are that some students learn better in quiet areas and that the library staff spends too much time responding to noise complaints on the third floor. The woman thinks that the change is unfair. She gives two reasons to support her opinion. First, she states that the library doesn't have to create a silent study space at all. If students want to study on the third floor and have quiet, they can just wear earplugs. Second, she says that the third floor is the best place for groups of students to meet because it has more space than the dorms. She thinks the library should make the third floor a group meeting space, and that way the librarians won't get noise complaints anymore.	The woman doesn't like the announcement. I think that she's wrong. I think that students should have a quiet place to study. It's not fair to make students wear earplugs just so that they can focus on what they're doing. And even though the students' rooms are too small for meetings, they don't have to meet at the library. They can meet outside or at a café to talk about projects. Libraries are supposed to be quiet.
Sample Score #1:	**Sample Score #2:**
This response scored a 4 because the speaker connects information from both sources. First, the speaker clearly explains the library's plan and describes the opinion of the woman in the conversation. Then, the speaker describes the woman's reasons for holding that opinion using specific details provided in the conversation. Throughout the response, the speaker's use of language is varied in terms of sentence structure and vocabulary. Her pace is good, and she makes full use of the response time.	This response scored a 1 because the speaker does not answer the question asked in the prompt. Rather than describing the opinion of the woman in the conversation, the speaker gives his own opinion regarding the library's plan. While he provides explanations for holding that opinion, the reasons are in support of his own opinion and not that of the woman in the conversation.

Question 4

Sample Response #1:	Sample Response #2:
The reading passage and the lecture are both about living fossils. The author defines a living fossil as an animal that is alive today and that resembles a creature that lived long ago. The author also describes two features of living fossils. In the lecture, the professor discusses the lamprey and two reasons why it is considered a living fossil. First, the passage states that to be a living fossil, a species must have no close living relatives. The professor explains that lampreys are unlike most fish. She also says that there are no fossils to show that lampreys ever evolved into other forms. Second, the passage states that the body forms of living fossils must not have changed. The professor compares modern lampreys to the earliest fossil of a lamprey. She says that even though modern lampreys are slightly larger, the basic structures are almost identical to those of the fossil.	Lampreys are living fossils because they haven't changed. Living fossils don't have close relatives. Lampreys have no jaws or scales, so they're different from other fish. The oldest lamprey fossil is more than 360 million years old. But modern lampreys are usually larger than the oldest lamprey fossil.
Sample Score #1:	**Sample Score #2:**
This response scored a 4 because the speaker effectively uses information from both the reading and the lecture to answer the question in the prompt. The organization of the response makes	This response scored a 1 because it is too short and does not provide enough discussion of major points from the reading and the listening. The speaker also presents facts without describing

(Continued) *(Continued)*

their significance to her argument. For example, she says that lampreys "have no jaws or scales, so they're different from other fish." This sentence supports the idea that lampreys have no close relatives, but the absence of connecting language between the two sentences makes it difficult to understand why she mentions this fact. Due to the shortness of the response, it is difficult to determine the speaker's full range of vocabulary.

it easy to understand, and the speaker uses citing language to effectively describe the source of the information. Furthermore, the content of the response shows that the speaker understands the basic definition of living fossils. The speaker clearly discusses both criteria mentioned in the passage and describes how lampreys meet the criteria.

Question 5

Sample Response #1:

The woman's problem is that she doesn't have time to study for a math midterm the next day and complete a take-home exam that's due the day after that. She could turn in the take-home exam a day late, but her professor will lower her grade. Her other option is to take a makeup test for her math class the next week, but it will be much more difficult than the original test. In my opinion, the woman should turn in the take-home exam on time and take the makeup test. First, the take-home exam is for her major. Getting a bad grade in her major could impact her career in the long term. Second, even though the makeup test will be more difficult than the original, she will have much more time to study. She could even meet with the professor during office hours if she's still struggling to understand the material.

Sample Response #2:

The woman is worried about getting a bad grade. She has two tests but can't study for both. She should take the midterm test later. She can still study for it, and she'll have enough time to finish the take-home exam. Even when I have trouble with a class, I can always study enough to at least pass a test with a week to study.

Sample Score #1:

This response scored a 4 because it addresses all of the points in the prompt in a well-organized fashion. The speaker organizes her response by first describing the problem that the woman in the conversation is having and her two options for resolving the problem. Then, the speaker clearly states a recommendation and provides easy-to-understand and well-developed reasoning for the recommendation.

Sample Score #2:

This response scored a 1 because the speaker does not adequately describe the woman's problem, the two possible solutions, or his recommendation for the woman. The speaker makes a recommendation but fails to explain it, providing only one reason. The response would have been strengthened if the speaker had described the problem and the options available to the woman in more detail. Moreover, the speaker should have provided one more reason to explain his recommendation.

Question 6

Sample Response #1:

In the lecture, the professor explains that the rain forest canopy is so thick that plants underneath it struggle to get light. Because they would be unable to grow without light, plants have adapted to capture more light by growing bigger leaves and climbing tall trees.

First, the professor describes how leaf size affects how much light plants in the understory receive. Plants with larger leaves are more likely to capture some of the light that manages to get through the canopy. She states that the larger a plant's leaves are, the better its chances of surviving.

Sample Response #2:

Trees in the understory don't get enough light to grow. They adapted to get more light. Sometimes plants have larger leaves. If the leaves were small, they would get less light. They also grow around taller trees. Once they grow to a height above the canopy, they have full sunlight.

(Continued)

Next, the professor describes a plant that climbs trees to reach light above the canopy. She explains that a vine called the liana starts growing on the ground but doesn't grow deep roots. It grows vines that reach tall trees and then wrap around them. The vine grows up until it gets to the top of the tree. At that point, it grows away from the tree to get full sunlight.

Sample Score #1:

This response scored a 4 because it clearly summarizes the main idea of the lecture and the two supporting points mentioned by the professor. The speaker effectively paraphrases the information from the lecture by clearly expressing the most important ideas in his own words. He demonstrates a wide vocabulary and uses a number of different types of sentence and grammatical structures.

Sample Score #2:

This response scored a 1 because it fails to provide a complete and accurate summary of the lecture. The response would have been improved if the speaker had organized her response to more clearly show the main idea and two supporting points from the lecture. In addition, the speaker's response leaves out key examples from the lecture, which would have made her response much stronger. The grammatical structures of the response are too simple and demonstrate that the speaker has only a limited ability to speak English in an academic

Audio Script

Listening

Lesson 1

🎧 CD1, Track 4

Narrator: Main Idea and Detail Questions. Get Ready.

Narrator: Listen to part of a discussion in a music class.

Professor: Good morning, class. For today, you all were supposed to read about, uh, the history of the piano. So . . . let's review some of the basic facts. When was the piano invented? Yes, Anna?

Student 1: Wasn't it in the early 1700s?

Professor: That's right. The piano was invented by a harpsichord builder named Bartolomeo Cristofori in Florence, Italy. The, um, harpsichord is an instrument that is similar to the piano . . . it has a keyboard, too. But you don't really need to know about that. OK, when pianos were first invented, only royalty could afford them, right? It wasn't until the 1800s that they started becoming more common in households . . . well, in the households of the wealthy and upper middle class. But still. Yes, Joshua?

Student 2: I'm just curious about why more people were suddenly able to afford them.

Professor: Good question. I think it probably had to do with the fact that the economy of Europe was changing a lot, especially in terms of, um, the distribution of wealth. By the 1800s, a country's riches weren't concentrated in the hands of the royalty—kings and queens. Instead, a lot of people throughout Europe were becoming wealthy, which meant that they had money to spend on luxury items, like pianos. OK . . . now I have a question for *you* all. As the piano became more common in households, what did it come to represent within European cultures?

Student 1: For one, playing the piano well was kind of a status symbol—it was an indication of wealth and education.

Professor: Exactly—and that's a very important point, by the way. I mean, parents started inviting piano instructors into homes to teach children how to play. That's because they knew that being proficient on the piano said something about their standing in the society. But there was more to it than that, wasn't there? It's true that having a piano showed that a family had money. But there were a lot of other reasons that a family would want a piano in its home, right?

Student 2: Definitely. Besides serving as a status symbol, the piano provided entertainment for the household.

Professor: That's it! Think about it—back then, there were no radios, no televisions, and certainly no computers. How do you think families entertained themselves? A lot of the time, it was by performing music together.

Student 1: Right . . . in the reading, it talked about how popular four-hands piano became in households. Oh, uh, four-hands piano—that was when two players sat side by side and played pieces that were specifically written to be played by two people.

Professor: Yes, that's a great example of how the piano had the power to bring families together and provide in-home entertainment.

🎧 CD1, Track 5

Narrator: Main Idea and Detail Questions. Get Set.

Narrator: Listen to part of a discussion in a history class.

Professor: OK, so... . . . let's get started. We know from last time that starting around 3600 BC, bronze was used widely throughout Europe. . . and the Middle East. Can you all think of any examples of what bronze was used for?

Student 1: Well, people in that area used bronze to craft items like knives, cookware, and, um . . . swords.

Professor: Very good. OK . . . this period—when the use of bronze was prevalent, I mean—it's known as the Bronze Age. However, eventually there *was* a transition from the extensive use of bronze to iron. Um, so basically, there was a shift from the Bronze Age to the Iron Age. Does anyone remember when this occurred?

Student 1: Around 1200 BC, right?

Professor: That's about right. It's not clearly defined . . . this is just an approximation of when iron became more commonly used than bronze in Europe and the Middle East. Um, yes, Jessica?

Student 2: Sorry to interrupt. I just have one question. Why did the shift occur in the first place?

Professor: I'm glad that you brought that up because it's actually what I wanted to talk about today. And the answer to this question . . . um, it's not simple. In fact, there are a number of factors that might have contributed to this shift. Let's hear from you all. Any guesses as to why iron surpassed bronze as the metal of choice?

Student 1: Isn't iron superior to bronze in terms of quality? I mean . . . iron *is* stronger than bronze.

Professor: You know, *today* it is . . . but when metalworkers first started working with iron, it wasn't the same as the stuff that we have today. In fact, bronze was harder than early forms of iron . . . which means it lasted for a pretty long time. And in terms of sword-making, which was, of course, an important use of metals back then, bronze was preferred because it held a sharp edge better than early iron. *But* . . . you've hit upon an interesting point. See, while early iron wasn't better than bronze, over time, metalworkers came up with the techniques to make a superior product.

Student 2: What were the techniques?

Professor: Well, the first of these involved how iron is obtained. Like the majority of metals, iron doesn't naturally occur in a pure form. You need to understand that you can't just go and, um, mine a piece of iron. Instead, you'd first have to extract iron ore from the ground. And, uh, in this iron ore, you'd have iron along with a bunch of other substances. Now, to get the iron from the iron ore—that is, to separate the metal from the minerals—it needs to be heated at very high temperatures. Um, if I remember correctly, the melting point for iron is over 1500 degrees Celsius. Unfortunately, the furnaces that metalworkers had back then just couldn't hit those temperatures. It wasn't until they improved their technology—made furnaces that could get extremely hot—that they were able to readily smelt iron ore.

Student 1: Is that all there was to it? They just had to invent furnaces that burned hotter?

Professor: No, definitely not. That was just one step forward for ironworkers. What you need to understand is that pure iron is pretty soft. In its pure state, it wasn't as durable as bronze. However, over time, ironworkers realized that by dissolving small amounts of carbon into iron, they could produce a substance that was significantly harder than iron: steel. This technique of diffusing carbon within iron is called carburization.

🎧 CD1, Track 6

Narrator: Main Idea and Detail Questions. Go for the TOEFL Test

Narrator: Listen to a part of a lecture in a photography class and take notes.

Professor: Good morning, class. This week, I'd like to talk about photography as an art form. But, um, before we delve into the artistic aspects of photography, I want to talk about the birth of photography. What I mean is . . . I want you to know how this technology developed. Unlike other art forms, like, say, painting or sculpture, photography is rather new. In fact, the very first permanent photograph wasn't created until 1826 by a French scientist named Joseph Nicéphore Niépce. And as we'll learn today, this breakthrough was the result of several centuries' worth of research.

OK, in ancient times, many scientists explored optics. That's the, uh, the study of light, basically. This study led to the invention of a device called the camera obscura. These devices have probably been around since around the fourth century BC. Anyway, camera obscuras are basically darkened structures . . . like a small room or even a box. The walls of the structure are solid . . . you know, to keep out light. And the only light that *does* enter comes through a small hole located on one of the walls. Due to the laws of optics, what happens is that the scene outside of the box is projected onto the inside wall of the structure. It's amazing . . . the color and the perspective of the scene are maintained perfectly. For the purpose of this class, you really don't need to know the exact mechanics of why this occurs. What you *do* need to know is that this practice— projecting a scene exactly as it appears onto a different surface—was an important precursor for modern photography.

So . . . for several hundred years after its initial invention, scientists continued to improve the camera obscura. For example, scientists discovered that making a larger hole in the wall produced a clearer image. Additionally, a smaller, more, um, portable version of the camera was created. But even then, they were still a ways off from having anything close to photography as we know it today. I mean, sure, the camera obscura was able to project a scene onto a different surface . . . but it wasn't *captured* on that surface.

The next step was finding a way to create a permanent image. And the first advance in this direction didn't occur until 1727. That was when a German professor named Johann Schulze accidently stumbled upon the first photosensitive compound. What's a photosensitive compound? Well, it's a material that changes when it's exposed to light. In other words, it's sensitive to light. In Schulze's case, he was experimenting with different types of silver salts. He observed that certain salts—like silver nitrate and, um, silver chloride—darkened when exposed to light. You all see why that's important, right? I mean, if you have a photosensitive material, there's a chance you can capture an image on it.

So . . . Schulze didn't end up doing anything with his discovery. But it inspired a lot of other scientists. For example, throughout the 1790s, an English photography pioneer named Thomas Wedgwood covered different materials with silver nitrate. For example, he put the silver nitrate on pieces of leather and glass . . . stuff like that. Anyway, he then placed these materials inside the camera obscura and projected images onto them. What do you think the result of this was? Of course! He was able to create a photograph on the surface of the material. But there was a catch . . . Wedgwood didn't have a way of preserving, or fixing, the image. So when the piece of leather or whatever was exposed to light later, the entire thing would turn dark, and the photo was lost.

Obviously this was a problem . . . and it was one that Joseph Nicéphore Niépce was determined to overcome. He experimented with different types of photosensitive compounds and eventually found success with bitumen-coated paper. Bitumen is a sticky liquid that is found in petroleum, and like silver salts, it's photosensitive. So Niépce took this photosensitive paper and he put it in his camera obscura. After projecting an image on the paper for eight hours, he washed it in lavender oil in order to remove the unexposed bitumen. As a result, he fixed the image and created the first permanent photograph!

Narrator: Now answer the questions. You may use your notes.

Lesson 2

🎧 CD1, Track 15

Narrator: Purpose and Inference Questions. Get Ready.

Narrator: Listen to part of a conversation between a student and a clerk at the registrar's office.

Clerk: Good morning. How can I help you?

Student: Hi . . . um, I kind of have a special situation and, well, maybe you can help me.

Clerk: Do you need help adding or dropping a class?

Student: It's not really a problem. OK, so I'm taking three classes this semester. But there's a fourth one that I'm *really* interested in. It's in the physics department.

Clerk: I'm not sure I understand. I mean, the maximum course load is four classes per semester. That means you can take up to four classes. So if you're interested in taking the physics class, all you have to do is sign up for it—assuming that you've taken the prerequisites . . . and that the class isn't full.

Student: It's just that . . . well, the three classes that I'm enrolled in are pretty difficult. *And* they all count toward my major . . . and, um, and I really want to be careful with my GPA.

Clerk: Your grade point average? Is your GPA low?

Student: Not at all—an A average, actually. And I want to keep it that way.

Clerk: So . . . ?

Student: So my advisor warned me about putting too much pressure on myself by taking a class that isn't even for my major. What I'd really like to do is just sit in on the physics class.

Clerk: Hmm . . . there is one option that I *think* might be good for you. Have you ever heard of auditing?

Student: I . . . I don't think so. What is that?

Clerk: It's an enrollment option. Um . . . when you audit a class, you basically attend the lectures. But you don't have to do any of the coursework. Also, you don't get a grade for it. Even buying the book is completely optional.

Student: Wow! That sounds perfect for me. Um . . . so how would I go about doing that?

Clerk: First of all, you need to fill out the class registration slip just as you would for any other class. So you include your name and student ID number. And you'll also write the course number and professor's name on there. On the far right of the slip, there's a little box that says "add," "drop," and "audit." You'll want to mark "audit."

Student: OK. I just submit the slip here and that's it? I can audit the class?

Clerk: Not quite. After you fill out the slip, you need to give it to Professor, um . .

Student: Professor Yang—that's the professor who's teaching the course.

Clerk: OK . . . so you'll take it to Professor Yang and ask her to sign it. Get the signature and bring it back here. Oh, but you'd better hurry. You know, today's the last day you can sign up for audits . . . and we close in just an hour.

Student: Got it—I know what I need to do. I certainly hope she's in her office!

🎧 CD1, Track 16

Narrator: Purpose and Inference Questions. Get Set.

Narrator: Listen to part of a conversation between a student and a chemistry professor.

Student: Hi, Professor Walker. I'm surprised—and so glad— you're here! Um . . . well, your office hours are on Wednesday from two to four o'clock, right?

Professor: Well, yes . . . but hey, if this is important, come in and take a seat. No sense waiting. I'm available anytime I happen to be in my office—regular hours or not.

Student: Thanks! And yes, it's important. I promise I won't take too much of your time.

Professor: OK . . . so do you have questions about the midterm? Several students stopped by to ask me about that.

Student: No, it's not about the midterm. I wanted to talk to you about your grading policy. Um, in the syllabus, it says that you'll deduct a point from our final grade for each unexcused absence. You said only three excused absences are allowed.

Professor: Yes, that's correct. I'm sorry, have you been absent this semester?

Student: Well, two weeks ago, I missed two classes. I was *really* sick with the flu.

Professor: Oh, right, I remember that. But—and correct me if I'm wrong—those were excused absences. So . . . there's nothing to worry about.

Student: OK. The problem is, I'll be absent for three days later in the semester. I, um, I'm going to a conference about biotechnology. I signed up for it earlier this semester, and . . . well, I wasn't exactly planning on getting sick with the flu.

Professor: Biotechnology?

Student: Yes, it's my major.

Professor: Is that a fact? I didn't realize that. But can't you just go back and forth between class and the conference? I mean, I doubt that you'll be in sessions all day long, right?

Student: I would if it were local, but . . . well, this conference, I'm actually flying to attend it . . . it's a pretty big deal.

Professor: Ah, right . . . understood.

Student: Anyway, it's important because it deals directly with my thesis topic. Since the conference is for school, I was wondering . . . is there any way we could figure something out? I mean, I really don't want my grade to suffer. But I really have to attend the conference.

Professor: Well, I made that rule for a reason. The fact is, it's *hard* to learn the material completely when you're gone a lot. But since your absences are related to academics, I suppose I can give you a break this time. Although, I have to tell you, if you miss more than those we've discussed, you'll get a lower grade.

Student: Thank you *so* much. Um, is there something I should do? To make it official about the days I have to miss?

Professor: Yes, um . . . please provide me with a justification that I can put on file. All you have to do for that is—do you have a professor in the biology department who's helping you plan for the conference?

Student: Yeah, Professor Montgomery is my thesis advisor. He's actually going to make a presentation at the conference.

Professor: Perfect. Just write a short note for me explaining the reason for your absences. Then have Professor Montgomery sign it.

Student: Great. You don't need anything else?

Professor: No, nothing else. Although . . . I'll be curious to know how your conference goes. I think there are a lot of ways that it could relate to our chemistry class, don't you think?

Student: Definitely! I'll make sure to come talk to you when I come back. I'll tell you all about it. But I guess I should get going . . . I'll get you the justification during our next class.

🎧 CD1, Track 17

Narrator: Purpose and Inference Questions. Go for the TOEFL Test.

Narrator: Listen to part of a conversation between a student and a librarian and take notes.

Librarian: Hi, there. Can I help you with something?

Student: Um . . . yes. I want to find out if a movie is checked out or not. I think it's called *Planetary Paths*.

Librarian: Well, let me look that up. Hmm, unfortunately, I don't see any videos in our collection called *Planetary Paths*. However, there *is* one called *Planets and Their Paths*. Could that be it?

Student: Yes, that's it. I'm sorry—I must have gotten the name mixed up.

Librarian: No problem. So . . . according to our records, it is available. Do you want to check it out right now? I'll just need your student ID, and I can take care of that for you.

Student: Well . . . the thing is, I need the movie for next Wednesday. And I was under the impression that students can only check out videos for up to three days.

Librarian: Yes, according to the library's borrowing policy, students can only keep videos for three days. Today's Tuesday . . . so . . . Tuesday, Wednesday, Thursday . . . you'd have to return it on Thursday.

Student: That's what I thought. I guess I'll wait to check it out. I just hope it's here when I come back!

Librarian: Um . . . if you don't mind me asking, why do you need it on Wednesday?

Student: Actually, Professor Harmon does . . . she's in the astronomy department. Anyway, she wants our class to watch it on Wednesday because she'll be going to a conference. So she wanted me to come down here and make sure it was available.

Librarian: Wait, so it's actually a professor who needs the movie?

Student: Uh-huh. Wait a second—since it's for a professor, is there any way that I can check it out for a longer time?

Librarian: Professors are actually allowed to keep movies for up to two weeks.

Student: Oh, I didn't know that. But that's great . . . I mean, I can just check it out under Professor Harmon's name, then, right?

Librarian: Well, um, it doesn't really work that way. If Professor Harmon were to come down here, we could check it out to her. But I can't check something out to a student in her name. It's against library policy.

Student: Oh, I guess that makes sense. But . . . well, what do you think I should do? I know Professor Harmon really wants us to watch the movie on Wednesday. And it would just be such a shame if someone else ends up checking it out.

Librarian: The best thing to do is probably have Professor Harmon come to the library and check it out.

Student: It's just . . . I know that she's really busy preparing for her conference. What if she lends me her faculty ID? Could I check it out for her then?

Librarian: No, I'm afraid that's not possible. Although . . . well, what we *could* do is reserve the movie in her name. We don't allow students to reserve films, but professors do it all the time. And that way, no one else could check it out before Wednesday.

Student: But she would still have to come and check it out herself, right?

Librarian: Yes, that's the only way.

Student: OK, well, given the situation, I think that's probably the best solution. How do we do that? Um, reserve the movie for her, I mean. Do I need to bring her a form?

Librarian: Actually, we went paperless last year. And anyway, I'll handle everything on my end. Then, when Professor Harmon has time, she can check it out. So you might tell her that it's ready for pickup.

Student: I will—in fact, I'll run down to her office right now and tell her. Thanks a lot for helping me out. I really appreciate it, and I know Professor Harmon will, too.

Narrator: Now answer the questions. You may use your notes.

Lesson 3

🎧 CD1, Track 26

Narrator: Function and Attitude Questions. Get Ready.

Narrator: Listen to part of a discussion in a sociology class.

Professor: We've been talking about theories that try to explain the causes of crime. In particular, we spent some time discussing the classical school of criminology. I mentioned that while it does have some valid points, it's, well . . . it's a very dated view and one that most people today, me included, might question. Now, with the classical view behind us, let's move on to a more modern approach. And, um, so . . . yeah, let's move on. Yesterday, I asked you to do some research about the broken windows theory. Did everyone complete the assignment? Yes? Great. Let's do a quick review. So, um . . . who came up with the theory? Leah?

Student 1: Wasn't it James Wilson and George Kelling?

Professor: That's right. And what does the theory predict? Somebody else, please.

Student 2: OK, basically, it states that when a neighborhood appears to be lawless, it *becomes* lawless. Like, if a community is dirty or run-down, people assume no one cares about it.

Professor: Good. And this attitude that no one cares about the neighborhood leads to a rise in crime. So let's talk about their famous example, the broken window. Say if a building has a broken window and nobody ever takes the time to fix it, people in the area will think that authorities are not paying attention. They start thinking that they'll probably get away with acting lawlessly, and people might start engaging in more serious crimes . . . like theft. Before you know it, the area could become crime-ridden. All because of one broken window. But this is just one example. What else could serve as a broken window, in this sense?

Student 1: How about litter or graffiti?

Professor: Litter or graffiti can also have a "broken window" effect. And I can think of a really famous instance in which this was the case. So . . . when you were researching, did anyone come across the New York City example? Ben?

Student 2: Yeah, I read about that. Um, in the 1980s, New York City had a big problem with crime, especially in the subways. There was graffiti everywhere, and people would always get on the train without paying the fare.

Professor: That's right. Crime was a *major* problem. Then, in 1985, the city hired George Kelling—that was one of the creators of the broken windows theory—as a consultant. Under Kelling's advisement, the city cleaned up the graffiti in the subways. Several years later, by 2001, crime in the New York City subways had decreased significantly. Because of these great results, the broken windows theory became more famous, and people began to accept it. Yes, Leah?

Student 1: Couldn't it work the other way? Like, maybe neighborhoods with more broken windows and things like that are areas with more crime to begin with? I . . . it just seems to me that we're ignoring other factors here.

Professor: Very possible. But at least in New York City, implementing cleanup policies helped curb crime quite a bit. It's hard to argue with those results.

🎧 CD1, Track 27

Narrator: Listen again to part of the discussion. Then, answer the question.

Professor: Let's do a quick review. So, um . . . who came up with the theory? Leah?

Student 1: Wasn't it James Wilson and George Kelling?

Professor: That's right. And what does the theory predict? Somebody else, please.

Narrator: Question two. Why does the professor say this?

Professor: Somebody else, please.

🎧 CD1, Track 28

Narrator: Listen again to part of the discussion. Then, answer the question.

Professor: They start thinking that they'll probably get away with acting lawlessly, and people might start engaging in more serious crimes . . . like theft. Before you know it, the area could become crime-ridden. All because of one broken window.

Narrator: Question three. Why does the professor say this?

Professor: All because of one broken window.

🎧 CD1, Track 29

Narrator: Listen again to part of the discussion. Then, answer the question.

Student 1: Couldn't it work the other way? Like, maybe neighborhoods with more broken windows and things like that are areas with more crime to begin with? I . . . it just seems to me that we're ignoring other factors here.

Narrator: Question four. Why does the student say this?

Student 1: . . . it just seems to me that we're ignoring other factors here.

🎧 CD1, Track 30

Narrator: Function and Attitude Questions. Get Set.

Narrator: Listen to part of a conversation between a student and a sociology professor.

Student: Excuse me, Professor Dawes. Is it OK if I come in?

Professor: Of course, Jessica. How are you? How's your paper coming along?

Student: That's what I was hoping to talk to you about. I'm kind of drawing a blank. I was . . . um, well, maybe you could suggest something to get me started. I hope I'm not being a burden . . .

Professor: Are you kidding? I wish more students would ask for my input on this project. I'd be glad to brainstorm with you. Um . . . is there a topic that you're particularly interested in?

Student: I guess, well, I was sort of thinking about yesterday's lecture . . . that stuff about cultural diffusion.

Professor: OK . . . there's plenty you could write about on that topic. And as far as I know, no one else is planning to write about that. Do you have a good understanding of what cultural diffusion is?

Student: I think so. It's, um . . . well, OK, every culture has a set of traits, things like food that people of that culture eat or the clothing that they typically wear. And those traits originate in a culture region. When the traits of a culture start spreading away from the culture region, that's . . . that's called cultural diffusion. Is that right?

Professor: Wow! So you didn't do the reading, huh? So . . . next, you need to think about what angle you'd take, um . . . what aspect of cultural diffusion you'd want to write about. Here's a thought—what if you looked at different theories that explain patterns of cultural diffusion?

Student: Like what?

Professor: OK, there's one theory that predicts that cultural diffusion occurs most in areas with a lot of immigrants. We talked about it briefly in class. Don't you remember?

Student: Um . . . sort of. You gave New York City as an example, right?

Professor: Right. You know, maybe you could research how cultural capitals like New York experience cultural diffusion. You could talk about how both direct and *in*direct cultural diffusion occur there.

Student: Sorry? Um, I think maybe I was out the day we talked about that. Could you . . . ?

Professor: Oh, I don't think we got to talk about this in class. Basically, direct cultural diffusion is when people from two cultures come into close physical contact. And because of that contact, the cultural traits are exchanged—diffused. Look at the diversity of food options in New York City, for example. The spread of all those different types of foods, which are essentially cultural traits, is a result of the close contact between all those cultures.

Student: Oh, I get it . . . and I'm guessing indirect diffusion would be when cultural traits are spread between cultures that *aren't* close to each other.

Professor: That's right. Indirect diffusion occurs when the traits of one culture are spread to another place through an intermediary.

Student: Like the, um, like the Internet?

Professor: Yes, precisely. You know, I wish we had more time to talk about this in class . . . I think everyone would find it really fascinating. Anyway, I do have some good books on this topic at home. I'll bring them to class next time so you can take a look at them. Could you . . . maybe just send me an e-mail to remind me . . . or I'll forget.

Student: OK. I'll be sure to do that. Thanks for your help. I really appreciate it.

🎧 CD1, Track 31

Narrator: Listen again to part of the conversation. Then, answer the question.

Student: That's what I was hoping to talk to you about. I'm kind of drawing a blank. I was . . . um, well, maybe you could suggest something to get me started. I hope I'm not being a burden . . .

Professor: Are you kidding? I wish more students would ask for my input on this project.

Narrator: Question one. Why does the professor say this?

Professor: Are you kidding?

🎧 CD1, Track 32

Narrator: Listen again to part of the conversation. Then, answer the question.

Professor: Wow! So you didn't do the reading, huh? So . . . next, you need to think about what angle you'd take, um . . . what aspect of cultural diffusion you'd want to write about. Here's a thought—what if you looked at different theories that explain patterns of cultural diffusion?

Narrator: Question three. Why does the professor say this?

Professor: Here's a thought—

🎧 CD1, Track 33

Narrator: Listen again to part of the conversation. Then, answer the question.

Professor: Right. You know, maybe you could research how cultural capitals like New York experience cultural diffusion. You could talk about how both direct and *in*direct cultural diffusion occur there.

Student: Sorry? Um, I think maybe I was out the day we talked about that. Could you . . . ?

Professor: Oh, I don't think we got to talk about this in class. Basically, direct cultural diffusion is when people from two cultures come into close physical contact.

Narrator: Question four. Why does the student say this?

Professor: Sorry? Um, I think maybe I was out the day we talked about that.

🎧 CD1, Track 34

Narrator: Listen again to part of the conversation. Then, answer the question.

Professor: Indirect diffusion occurs when the traits of one culture are spread to another place through an intermediary.

Student: Like the, um, the Internet?

Professor: Yes, precisely. You know, I wish we had more time to talk about this in class . . . I think everyone would find it really fascinating.

Narrator: Question five. What can we infer about the professor when he says this?

Professor: You know, I wish we had more time to talk about this in class . . . I think everyone would find it really fascinating.

🎧 CD1, Track 35

Narrator: Function and Attitude Questions. Go for the TOEFL Test.

Narrator: Listen to part of a lecture in an anthropology class and take notes.

Professor: OK . . . last time, we brought up the subject of dynasties in ancient India. Now, a dun—um, sorry, a *dyn*asty is a series of rulers that all come from the same family. It was often the case, in a lot of places, that a single dynasty would rule for many, *many* years. That was certainly true with the Chola dynasty. So before I go on . . . what can you tell me about the Chola dynasty. Have any of you even heard of it? Yes, Alex?

Student: Um, this might seem kind of random, but . . . Rajaraja—he was one of the famous leaders of that dynasty, wasn't he?

Professor: I'm impressed. Yes, Rajaraja was probably the most well-known emperor of that dynasty. How, um, how did you hear about him?

Student: I have this video game, and he was one of the characters in the story. It was kind of a, I don't know, like a historical game.

Professor: Interesting . . . so I guess some video games *do* have educational value, then. Anyway, let me just give you a brief background. The Chola dynasty ruled from about 850 until the late thirteenth century. And one of the really fascinating parts about them was that their empire was *huge*. They were originally from the southeast coast of India, but they came to rule all of south India, as well as Sri Lanka, the Maldives, and even a part of Java. Um, Java . . . that's an island in Indonesia.

Now, think about it . . . with the exception of south India, all of the places I just mentioned are islands. The Cholas were able to conquer these places because they had a really powerful navy. That navy was originally built by a really powerful emperor, um . . . Alex just mentioned him—Rajaraja.

OK . . . I'm going to stop here because . . . well, because you'll read all about Rajaraja and the rise of the Chola dynasty in the textbook. And I'd like to focus on something that's *not* covered in the text: the *cultural* contributions of the Cholas.

So one cultural area in which the Cholas really, um, well, left their mark was in the arts . . . and especially literature. OK, what you have to understand is that the Cholas succeeded in uniting a bunch of different villages and areas in south India under one ruler . . . so then, um . . . what happens when people stop spending their time fighting amongst themselves? And at the same time, the leaders encourage things like the arts and education? Well, the people have time to dedicate themselves to more . . . um, scholarly pursuits . . . like writing. Now, the Chola rulers were big supporters of literature—they loved it. One way that we know this is because we've found references to many works of literature in historical records left behind by the Cholas. And it's not just that they enjoyed reading literature, but they actually encouraged its creation by acting as patrons for writers. What that means is that they would provide financial support to their favorite writers. Because of this support, famous Indian poets were able to write their great masterpieces. One thing, for sure, is that the literature created under Chola rule is considered today among the most important in Indian literature.

OK . . . so obviously, Indian literature would have been really different today without the Cholas. But that's not it. The Cholas also had a significant influence on the architecture of India. At the request of Chola leaders, hundreds—I'm sorry, *thousands*—of beautiful stone temples were built throughout India. The temples . . . they, they were amazing. I mean, they featured really complicated decorations that were carved into stone. And, mind you, they were often carved out of granite, which was just a common type of stone in the region. But the thing about granite is, well, it's a really hard stone . . . so it's hard to cut into with any accuracy. As you can imagine, it took incredible skill to make the temples. Just amazing. Oh, and, uh, and something else that the Cholas are known for, in terms of architecture, is creating the *tallest* temples of the time. For example, in 1010, Rajaraja, the leader we talked about earlier, well, he commissioned the construction of a temple that was sixty meters tall. Now, that may not seem very tall compared to the skyscrapers we see nowadays, but back then, it was quite an achievement to build a temple so tall. And that temple is actually still standing today, one thousand years after it was first constructed.

Narrator: Now answer the questions. You may use your notes.

Lesson 4

🎧 CD1, Track 44

Narrator: Organization and Connecting Content Questions. Get Ready.

Narrator: Listen to part of a lecture in a geology class.

Professor: The next topic we'll be focusing on is mass wasting, or, as some people call it, mass movement. Both terms refer to the same thing, but for the sake of clarity, let's just stick with "mass wasting" for this class. OK . . . so what *is* mass wasting? It's any instance in which rock or soil shifts to a lower elevation due to gravity. And by that, I mean it moves from a higher place on the earth's surface to a lower place. So everybody's clear on that basic definition? Good, so keep that in mind as we talk about a few different types of mass wasting—the, um, two main types being flow and creep.

OK, so flow—what you need to know about flow is that it happens really fast. Examples of flow would be landslides, mudslides, and even rockfalls. You all know what each of those are, right? For those of you who don't, let's just go over it really quickly. A landslide is when you have a slope and a large amount of earth on it moves downward. A mudslide is similar, except it specifically involves the movement of mud, not just dry earth. OK, and a rockfall is when a rock or rocks fall from a high place. Now, I want to clarify something here. Notice that landslides and rockfalls are a little different. Of course, they are both types of flow, but there's definitely a distinction between the two. A landslide involves the downward movement of a large amount of soil or rock. A rockfall, however, is when a large chunk of rock falls independently from a cliff. So . . . it's not the *amount* of earth moving, but the fact that both events occur pretty quickly.

Now, let's move on to the second type of mass wasting, um, creep. OK, if we're going to compare flow and creep, one major basis for comparison is the speed at which they occur. As I said before, flow happens pretty quickly. In contrast—and as you can probably guess from the name—creep occurs rather slowly. But it involves the same thing, the, um, downward movement of earth over a large area. What causes creep? There are several factors . . . like the, um, the freezing and thawing of soil in winter and spring can create soil creep. Um, and that's because it destabilizes the soil. Animals grazing on the land can contribute to it as well. Also, know that creep is usually responsible for the gentle slope of hills.

🎧 CD1, Track 45

Narrator: Organization and Connecting Content Questions. Get Set.

Narrator: Listen to part of a lecture in an engineering class.

Professor: So at the end of the last lecture, we started talking about nanotechnology. And I got e-mails from *at least* five of you last night asking about exactly what it's used for . . . so I get the sense that it wasn't totally clear. Plus, I know we didn't really get to talk about it that much, so . . . OK. What nanotechnology is, um, it's the field of science that deals with using and, um, and changing matter on a very small scale—the, um, nanoscale. This . . . this needs some further explanation.

Um, when we talk about measurements, we tend to think in terms of meters, centimeters, and millimeters. And we usually stop there, maybe because we don't really deal with stuff that's smaller than a millimeter. But the materials that we're talking about in nanotechnology are actually much smaller than a millimeter. For example, molecules are small—no, tiny—units of matter that you can't even see without a special microscope. Just one molecule is one-billionth of a meter. Let me put it this way: the head of a pin is about, what, a millimeter across, right? Well, you can fit one million of these molecules on the head of one pin! That's the scale that nanotechnology deals with. Uh-oh, I'm still seeing a lot of confused faces. You know, maybe the best way to explain this is by talking about some of the everyday products that make use of nanotechnology.

Let's start . . . yeah, let's start with a very basic example. It's something that many of you probably use every day—um, sunscreen. You'd never guess, but many types of sunscreen today use nanoparticles. All those are are tiny chemical compounds that scientists create by working with molecules.

The idea is that the size of these particles makes them easier to rub into your skin. And that means that you have better protection from the sun. In the past, sunscreen formulas used larger particles, and they didn't rub into your skin as easily. That's why—and some of you might remember this—in the past, sunscreen stayed on the surface of your skin, and you'd get that white tinge. But you don't see that so much anymore. Today, sunscreen blends more easily and is more effective, and it's all thanks to nanotechnology.

Um, oh, here's another good example: clothing. I bet you never thought much about scientists messing with your clothes—am I right? Well . . . they do. In fact, recently, scientists have started putting *layers* of nanoparticles—there's that term again—on cloth. For those of you who forgot, nanoparticles are extremely small chemical compounds. OK, but how—um, I mean, *what*—is the purpose of this? See, the nanoparticles provide UV protection. Um, it provides protection from the harmful rays from the sun. Scientists are even experimenting with nanoparticles to make clothes more stain resistant! They've figured out how to add tiny nanoparticles to your clothing that repel water and other materials that could stain clothes. These examples might be surprising, especially because, usually, when you hear about nanotechnology, it's in reference to application in the medical or industrial fields. But it just goes to show you how much this field is expanding, not to mention the potential it has to really improve our daily lives.

🎧 CD1, Track 46

Narrator: Organization and Connecting Content Questions. Go for the TOEFL Test.

Narrator: Listen to part of a discussion in a biology class and take notes.

Professor: Last time, we started talking about birds. Now, we know that these are amazing creatures—for one, they can fly, which in itself is pretty fascinating. We talked about some species that migrate over hundreds of miles . . . all without getting lost. I'd like to know how many of you can do that. I know I couldn't. OK . . . today . . today, I want to look at a more specific feature of birds. But first, let's just review. So . . . what makes a bird a bird? Just, um, think about the basic features of birds that we talked about last time. Roberta, what do you think?

Student 1: Um, all birds have wings and feathers, right?

Professor: That's right . . . all birds have both wings and feathers, but *not* all birds can fly. But we'll . . . we'll talk about that some more today. Um, another defining feature is that all birds lay eggs. So . . . OK . . . those three things—um, wings, feathers, eggs—those are the defining characteristics of birds.

OK, good . . . um . . . well, as I mentioned before, not all birds can fly, but many of them *do* fly. Why am I bringing this up again? Because that's what we're talking about today: bird flight. I mean, birds are basically flying machines—they are built for flying. And I want to talk about some of these specially designed features that allow birds to fly. OK, what do you think these features might be? Let me give you a hint: Roberta already mentioned one of them.

Student 2: Do you mean feathers?

Professor: That's right . . . *all* birds have feathers. And feathers serve a number of important functions when it comes to flight. For one, birds, at least those that fly, have a special kind of feathers called contour feathers. These feathers are very rigid, and that quality helps birds achieve lift.

Student 1: Sorry, but what is lift, exactly?

Professor: What is lift? Say you're flying a kite . . . lift is the force that results when air moves over and under the kite. As a result, the kite moves upward, away from the ground. Does that make sense? I mean, that's all you really have to know—that lift helps objects or animals move upward. So like I was saying, the rigidity of the feathers on the wings allows the birds to get lift, which is, of course, a key part of flying, wouldn't you say? I mean, if you can't even get off the ground, well, good luck with flying.

All right, now, birds also have contour feathers on their tails. And those feathers, the tail feathers, serve a different purpose. They help the bird steer. That means that a bird has some control over what direction they go in when they fly.

Um . . . now, feathers are *not* the only part of a bird that is built for flying. Can anyone think of something else?

Student 1: Well, the bird's skeleton is pretty lightweight. I bet that has something to do with why birds are able to fly.

Professor: Yes, it certainly does. In reality, flying birds have a lot of hollow bones . . . so they don't weigh much. Interestingly, the non-flying bird species, like penguins, generally have heavier skeletons. And some birds have bones that are even lighter than their feathers!

Student 2: Excuse me, Professor. I don't know if this is related, but I've read that birds actually have fewer bones than a lot of other animals.

Professor: That's correct. In fact, consider this: adult humans have 208 bones. Now, doves, which are a very common type of bird, have only twenty-seven bones!

Anyway, before, I was saying that the bones themselves are lightweight, right? And like Ralph just said, birds actually have fewer bones than many other animals. These features—the hollow bones and relatively small number of bones—mean that birds that fly have a pretty low body weight. And this makes it possible for the bird to fly because, as you might guess, it takes a lot less energy and effort to keep a light object in the air as opposed to a heavy one.

Narrator: Now answer the questions. You may use your notes.

Listening Review Test

🎧 CD2, Track 2

Narrator: Listening Review Test

Narrator: Part 1, Listening 1. Listen to a conversation between a student and her international business professor. Take notes.

Professor: Hi, Diana. What can I do for you?

Student: Hi, Professor Bloom. Um, look, I was wondering if I could talk to you about the final project for your international business class.

Professor: Of course. Um, I'm guessing you need help with research. I can probably suggest a couple of books, but, um . . . can you remind me what your topic was again?

Student: Well, I appreciate that, but what I really wanted to talk about is the format of my project. So, you know, everybody had the choice between writing a paper individually or doing a group project?

Professor: Right. I'm trying to remember . . . are you doing a group project?

Student: Yes, I'm working with Sam, Jared, and Abby. But I'm not so sure it's a great idea anymore. I was hoping . . . um, I wonder if it would be OK for me to switch and do a paper instead.

Professor: Well . . . I don't understand, Diana. Is there some sort of problem with your group?

Student: No, not at all! In fact, my group is great. When we're able to get together, we do good work. The thing is . . . well, my schedule just isn't very flexible. See, I work at the Blue Café most nights. Unfortunately, the only time that all three of them are available is in the evenings, when, um—

Professor: When you're working.

Student: Uh-huh. Honestly, I would love to do my project with them, but my schedule makes it really hard. And because that's the case, I think doing an individual project would be easier for all of us.

Professor: Well, one issue is, um, well, they were depending on you to do a portion of the project. Will they be able to finish the project on time if you drop out of the group now?

Student: I think it should be fine—I mean, we haven't gotten that far, anyway.

Professor: But have you already spoken with them about this?

Student: Oh, yes, yes, I . . . I've already talked to them. In fact, we all decided that this was probably the best way to go.

Professor: So they're OK with it? Good. I mean, as long as your group members have agreed to it, I don't really have a problem with it, either. Um, but assuming that they still plan on working together, may I suggest that you give them whatever research you've already prepared for the group topic? I'm sure they'll appreciate it, especially since they'll have one less person to divide their work amongst now.

Student: Oh, of course! I already e-mailed them all of my notes and a list of the sources I had planned to use. Hopefully that will be helpful.

Professor: I'm sure it will be. Um, OK, now that we have that straightened out, I'm wondering, have you given any thought to a topic for your paper?

Student: Yes, well, I have an idea, but I don't know . . . um, I want to write about the kinds of conflicts that international businesses face.

Professor: Hmm . . . that's a pretty broad topic. Maybe you can narrow it down by focusing on one particular problem?

Student: Well, I kind of wanted to concentrate on cultural differences—like how international businesses deal with cultural differences. What do you think? Is that OK?

Professor: I think that's great. Actually, I read a book about this recently. Basically, the author described how businesses that have international ties deal with cultural differences. It's funny, because I think it's something that business owners don't really think about when they're making the decision to expand into a foreign country.

Student: Good . . . so you said there are books written on the subject, right? Because, well, my hesitation in picking that as a topic is that I haven't found a lot of good sources for it.

Professor: Yes, definitely. There's the book I just mentioned, and a couple of articles also come to mind. I can't think of the titles at the moment, but I'll look into that and send you an e-mail with the titles and authors. You should be able to find all of it in the library.

Student: Great . . . I appreciate that. I guess I'll go down there now and see what else I can find on my topic so I can get started on my paper. Thanks for your help!

🎧 CD2, Track 8

Narrator: Listening 2. Listen to part of a lecture in a management class and take notes.

Professor: Good morning, class. Um . . . OK, today we're gonna talk about flextime. Flextime is a scheduling system that . . . well, it gives full-time employees some *flexibility* when they're deciding on their work schedules. So it's not just the typical nine-to-five workday that most people are so used to. I'm gonna guess that you probably haven't had a flextime schedule, since most of you haven't worked a full-time job yet. But maybe if you talk to your parents or some of your friends, you'll find somebody who has flextime. Anyway, in most cases, an employee can't just decide that they want to work a flextime schedule. It's really up to management to say yes or no. And since we're talking about management in this class, it's important to understand flextime if you ever want to manage a business.

Let's start with, um . . . let's start by describing different types of flextime schedules. The first type is called a condensed schedule. Under a condensed schedule, an employee still works the full forty hours a week. But instead of working those hours over five days, which is typical, they work them over three or four days. So, um, the weekly hours are condensed into fewer days, right? Let me just give you an example of a condensed schedule. Um, as I said before, a conventional schedule for an office job would be Monday through Friday, from nine in the morning to five in the afternoon. Now, a condensed schedule might mean that the person works only four days a week—let's say Monday through Thursday—from 8 a.m. to 6 p.m. That's, um, that's a ten-hour workday.

So that's one kind of flextime schedule. Another type of flextime schedule is called an altered schedule. With an altered schedule, employees work eight hours a day, five days a week. But instead of coming in at 9 a.m., like they would with a traditional work schedule, they come in either earlier or later than that. And their day ends according to when they come in. So maybe an employee will choose to come in at 7 a.m., and they'll work a full eight hours, so they get to leave at 3 p.m. This could be every day or only certain days of the week.

OK, so those are two types of flextime schedules—the, um, condensed schedule and the altered schedule. If that's clear, let's go ahead and move on. OK, next, we need to talk about the pros and cons of a flextime system. Imagine that you are the manager of an office and you're trying to decide whether flextime is a good way to go. You *have* to think about the possible advantages and disadvantages, right? Let's start with advantages. First of all, say you allow your employees to work flexible schedules because of, maybe, family obligations. Um, for example, imagine a household in which both the parents work full-time from nine to five. But their kids are in school, and school hours are from 8 a.m. to 3 p.m. every day. With this schedule, getting the kids to school in the morning is no problem, but picking them up after school might be difficult. So maybe the mother decides to start a flextime schedule, from seven to three. That way, the father can take their kids to school in the morning, and the mother can pick them up in the afternoon. In this case, using flextime is convenient. Now, if you're a manager, and you allow an employee to have flextime to accommodate family obligations, that employee will probably appreciate the flexibility quite a bit. As a result, you are more likely to retain those employees—you'll build loyalty.

But flextime is not a perfect system. In fact, there are times when flextime could make life more difficult for you as a manager. For example, let's say you're trying to hold a staff meeting. It could be hard to schedule a meeting that everyone is able to attend if different employees are working different hours. Also, it might be harder for you to oversee your employees' work if they are not always in the office at the same time that you are. And one more thing is that it might be difficult for your employees to work in teams—to work together on different projects—if they are in and out at different times. As a manager, you'd have to weigh the pros and cons and just figure out what works best for your company.

🎧 CD2, Track 15

Narrator: Listening 3. Listen to part of a discussion in an oceanography class and take notes.

Professor: OK, everyone, today we're going to discuss a new topic in oceanography—vertical migration, or, to be more specific, diel vertical migration. And as you may know, "diel" is from the Latin word for "day." So based on that, what does *diel* vertical migration probably mean? Yes, um, Tom?

Student 1: Well, I imagine it refers to some kind of movement in the water? Maybe from the coastline to, um, open sea—um, you know, away from the coast.

Professor: It does involve movement in the water, so you're definitely on the right track. But remember, it's called vertical migration, so it refers to up and down movement. Um, so just to give you a clear definition, diel vertical migration is when organisms in the ocean move from deep zones to shallow zones. Oh, and one more thing that I want to add to that definition is that this doesn't just happen in oceans. Scientists have actually observed vertical migration in lakes as well. Rachel, did you have a question?

Student 2: It's just, well, earlier you mentioned a term . . . "diel."

Professor: Oh, that's right. So vertical migration refers to movement from deep to shallow water. And "diel" just means that it occurs daily based on the time of day. Is that more or less

clear? So, for example, during the day, animals like squid stay in the deep part of the water. Then, after it gets dark, they rise—um, migrate—to shallower waters. That's diel vertical migration. Now, why the squid—or any animal, for that matter—engages in diel vertical migration is what I want to focus on next. Before I move on to that, does anybody have any questions? Tom?

Student 1: In the example you just mentioned, with the squid, you said that the animal stays in deep water during the daytime and moves to shallow water at night. I'm wondering . . . is it ever the other way around? Like, do animals ever stay in shallow parts of the water in the daytime and move to deeper water only when it's dark?

Professor: Actually, they do. What you just described is called reverse migration. I'm, um, trying to think of an example of an organism that does that, but . . . I'm going to have to get back to you on that. That just goes to show you, reverse migration is pretty rare. That's why I can't think of an example—there just aren't that many animals that do that. Anyway . . . *why*? That's the question I, uh, want to answer. Why do animals engage in diel vertical migration? Any guesses?

Student 2: There's one thing that comes to mind. Um, maybe by staying in the depths of the ocean during the day, animals are safer. Because it's dark down there, isn't it?

Professor: Yes, very. And you're definitely onto something, but you've only explained one part. You, um, you explained why animals stay in the depths during the day. But what about . . . why do they migrate up at night?

Student 1: To get food, right?

Professor: That's it! OK, so here's how it works. As Rachel mentioned, it's dark in the deep parts of the ocean, and frankly, there isn't much to eat down there. But by staying there during the day, organisms avoid detection from predators. Um . . . but there's a problem here. They can't stay down there forever or they won't be able to find food. So . . . they rise to shallower waters, where there's more food. And they do this at night, when it will be harder for predators to see them. It's a pretty good strategy, huh? OK. Good . . . OK, so that's one reason for diel vertical migration, and it's related to survival by avoiding predators. But there's another reason that I want to mention. Let me start by asking, um . . . OK, what happens if you go to the beach and you spend too much time in the sun?

Student 1: You get sunburned?

Professor: Right . . . because the sun's rays are strong, and they can damage our skin. And it may be hard to believe, but this is true for animals, too, including fish. The fact is, for many organisms, the light intensity near the surface of the water is just too strong. It would hurt them if they stayed there all day long. So what do they do? They move to the deeper zones, where the light intensity isn't so strong. Then, at night, when there is less light and the shallower zone is more comfortable, they move up.

🎧 CD2, Track 22

Narrator: Part 2, Listening 4. Listen to part of a conversation between a student and an employee at the housing office. Take notes.

Student: Hi. I, um, I have some questions about housing.

Employee: Well, you're in the right place. What can I help you with?

Student: OK, since this academic year is almost over, everybody's talking about arranging housing for *next* semester. The thing is, everyone I know is planning on living in the dorms again, and . . . what I want to know is, is there a way that I can apply to live *off* campus?

Employee: Um . . . what year are you?

Student: I'm a first-year now, but I'll be a second-year student next semester.

Employee: I see. I hate to be the bearer of bad news, but off-campus housing is reserved for third- and fourth-years. So it's not an option for you.

Student: I was afraid of that. See, I live in a single room in the dorms now, but it's just too loud for me. It's really distracting, and, more importantly, it's really affected my grades this year. I mean, usually I'm a straight-A student. But this semester, I earned three Bs and one C. That's . . . that's the first C I've ever gotten. And it's all because it's next to impossible to study in my dorm room.

Employee: Is the issue that your neighbors are too loud? I mean, we have policies about loudness in the dorms. Officially, quiet hours are from midnight to 7 a.m. If the people in your dorm aren't following the rules, they can get punished by the university.

Student: No, it's not that at all. Nobody ever made noise during quiet hours. It's just that, in order for me to study, I need complete silence, you know. Even the sound of people talking in the next room just kills my concentration.

Employee: Hmm. Well, have you tried studying in the library? A lot of students find that it's easier to study in a library environment. It's a lot quieter than the dorms, for sure.

Student: I know, but . . . well, I usually can't start studying until pretty late at night, when the library's already closed. Plus, I guess I just prefer to study at home. I think that, with my study style and my schedule, it's just better if I live alone off campus. If you don't mind me asking, why is it that only third- and fourth-years are allowed to live off campus?

Employee: There are a couple of reasons, actually. For one, living on campus is just more convenient for underclassmen. I mean, that way you're much closer to your classes, the dining halls, and all the other campus facilities. Most students, especially those in their first and second years, have enough to worry about. By being on campus, they're close to services when they need them. Also, the university really prefers that students live in the dorms for two years because of the social environment. In the dorms, you get to meet people who are in the same situation that you're in. In that way, you have a lot of support from other students and friends.

Student: You're definitely right that there are benefits—being close to things and having your friends around. It's just too bad. I think I'd be able to get better grades if I had my own quiet space for studying.

Employee: Well, there *is* the Quiet Dorm. Have you thought about applying to live there?

Student: I don't think I've heard of that. What's the Quiet Dorm?

Employee: It's a special dormitory on campus especially for students like you, who need a silent space to study in. If you decide to live there, you have to sign a contract that basically promises that you won't make any excessive noise—that means no music and no loud talking. Keep in mind, there's a resident advisor there at all times to enforce the rules.

Student: Wow! That sounds perfect for me. How can I apply to live there?

Employee: You just need to fill out this special housing form. Here, let's see . . . OK, here's a copy. You fill this out and bring it back to us.

Student: Great. And how long do I have to wait to find out if I can live there or not?

Employee: We'll make the announcement the same time as other housing decisions—in two weeks.

Student: OK . . . I'll fill it out now, then. Thanks for all your help!

🎧 CD2, Track 28

Narrator: Listening 5. Listen to part of a discussion in a biology class and take notes.

Professor: Good afternoon, class. So, um, today we're going to discuss biotoxins. Um, in particular, we're going to talk about the uses of biotoxins. But I'm, um . . . I'm getting ahead of myself here. First, let's talk about exactly what a biotoxin is. Can anybody give us a definition? Cynthia?

Student 1: It's a poison, isn't it? Something that causes physical harm to anybody or, um, to anything that comes in contact with it.

Professor: Well, that's a good definition of a toxin, but remember, we're talking about *bio*toxins. Here's a hint: "bio" comes from the Greek term for "life."

Student 2: So a biotoxin is a poison that's created by something that's alive?

Professor: Yes, that's correct. So let me just give you a really common example of a biotoxin. How many of you have been . . . been stung by a bee? A lot of you, right? Well, when a bee stings you, it, um, it injects a biotoxin into you. Of course, the venom from a bee sting is just a minor biotoxin. I mean, it hurts you, but for most people, a bee sting does not cause long-lasting harm. OK, those of you who have been stung by a bee—most of you, I think—um, you would probably agree that it wasn't pleasant. I mean, bee stings hurt! And they're supposed to—bees use that biotoxin to protect their hives. But what happens when humans use biotoxins produced by other organisms? Can biotoxins ever be used to improve life for humans? The answer, we're finding, is yes. Today I'm mostly interested in talking about how biotoxins are used in medicine, and I think you'll all be surprised by the ways that scientists and doctors use biotoxins for medical purposes! Um, how many of you have heard of botulism? OK, for those who don't know what botulism is, it's a really serious illness. It's, um, it's caused by bacteria that produce the botulinum toxin. So, according to our definition, botulinum is a biotoxin, right? I mean, I know it's weird to think of bacteria as living organisms, but technically they are. Um, anyway, this biotoxin can be pretty dangerous. Um, in some circumstances, it can lead to death. But amazingly, scientists have discovered how to use botulinum to *cure* illness, if you can believe that.

Student 1: Excuse me, Professor, but how is that possible?

Professor: Well, let me explain. There are actually different kinds of the botulinum toxin. The type that medical researchers are interested in is called botulinum toxin type A. So what they found was, they take botulinum toxin type A and they, um, basically dry it and, um, purify it. And really, don't worry about the process itself—just know that by processing botulinum toxin type A in this way, it's possible to create medicine.

Student 2: Uh, medicine for what?

Professor: I was just getting to that. So this medication, it can be used to effectively cure migraines. Um, those are . . . they're basically severe headaches, and people who suffer from them often experience nausea and other symptoms, too. OK, where's the proof? Well, there have been several clinical trials. In one study, researchers found that study participants who took this drug made from botulinum toxin type A, they had *significantly* fewer headaches every month. So it seems that this drug is effective! OK, that's just one example, though. Can you think, um . . . well, have you heard of any other medicinal uses of biotoxins?

Student 2: Now that you mention it, I remember reading an article recently that's sort of related. Um, according to the article, researchers were studying the effects of a biotoxin made by a certain type of snail. I don't remember what the snail was called. But scientists are studying the biotoxin to see if it can be used as a painkiller.

Professor: That's a great example! Um, if I'm not mistaken, the snails you're referring to are called cone snails. And their venom, called conotoxin, is really dangerous. But as Steve said, medical researchers are finding out how we can use this venom as a powerful painkiller.

Student 1: I don't get it . . . we already have a bunch of different kinds of painkillers, don't we? What's so special about this one?

Professor: Good question. For one, it's a lot more powerful than the other painkillers that are currently available. All you need is a tiny dose and the pain is gone!

🎧 CD2, Track 35

Narrator: Listening 6. Listen to part of a lecture in an astronomy class and take notes.

Professor: Today we're going to learn about the climate of Mars. Some of you may be wondering why scientists would study such a thing. Why is the climate of Mars important to us on Earth? Well, there are a couple of reasons. For one, the climate of Mars can tell us quite a bit about our own climate. You see, Mars, like Earth, has seasons and weather patterns. So by observing the climate of Mars, we can learn about our own climate patterns. And another thing . . . it's, um, well, studying Mars's climate might help us figure out whether there was ever any life there. But . . . um, don't worry about these issues right now, because we *won't* be addressing them today. For today, I really just want you all to understand the basic features of the Martian climate.

OK . . . so we're talking about Mars's climate. Why don't we begin by . . . by talking about one of the more general aspects of

its climate—its seasons. Just like Earth, Mars has four distinct seasons. However, the season lengths on Mars are quite different than on Earth. In fact, the seasons on Mars are actually twice as long as Earth's seasons. Why is that? Here's the short explanation: as a lot of you probably know, Mars takes twice as long as Earth does to go around the sun. Um . . . so that means that Mars years are about twice as long as Earth years. In other words, for every two Earth years, one Mars year goes by. Logically, this also means that the seasons on Mars are twice as long as Earth's. Though, really, for the purposes of this class, you don't have to know why the seasons on Mars are longer than those on Earth. All you have to know is that they are about twice as long as Earth's seasons.

Uh, let's move on. So what about the temperatures on Mars? Well, like Earth, Mars is warmer at its center, along the equator. And it's colder at its . . . at its poles. Um, poles, of course, are the extreme northern and southern ends of a planet. Like, on Earth, we have the north and south poles, and *both* of these places are really, really cold, right? So determining the temperature on Mars really depends on the time and place the temperature is taken. Say you measure the temperature along the equator of Mars in the middle of summer. You'd find that the temperature can reach up to twenty degrees Celsius at noon. However, if you measured the temperature at the same time of day, but at Mars's poles, you'd get readings as low as negative 153 degrees Celsius. Just to help you understand how cold that is, consider this: the coldest temperature ever recorded on Earth was negative 89.2 degrees Celsius. I mean, that's a sixty-degree difference! And what can we tell from these temperatures, then? Well, I think we can all say with complete certainty that Mars is a very cold planet. And according to scientists, it will only continue to get colder.

Now I want to talk about another aspect of Mars's climate, and it's one that might actually help you understand the effects of temperature change on Mars—it's, uh, winds. So . . . the average wind speed on Mars is around thirty-two kilometers per hour, but they have been measured up to ninety-six kilometers per hour. Right now, a lot of you are probably thinking, "So what?"—and rightly so. I say that because, well, these speeds aren't anything spectacular. Indeed, Earth's wind speeds are similar. However, there *is* something remarkable that happens when the winds pick up—when they start blowing faster. Since most of Mars is covered in dust, when the winds pick up, it results in enormous dust storms. Amazingly, these dust storms have been known to cover most of the planet! Recently, though, scientists have seen fewer dust storms. They aren't sure exactly why this is happening, but one guess is that it is because the planet is getting colder. This hypothesis is based on, um . . . OK, typically if there is less heat, the air doesn't move around nearly as much. So colder temperatures on Mars would mean less wind and, as a result, fewer dust storms.

Speaking

Lesson 1

🎧 CD2, Track 43

Narrator: Get Ready Sample Response

Respondent: One type of music that I really enjoy listening to is jazz. I like jazz music for a number of reasons. First of all, it helps me relax. For instance, during exam week, I'm usually really tense and stressed out. But I always put on jazz when I come home from the tests. As I listen, I can actually feel my body and mind relaxing! Additionally, I like jazz because it helps me bond with other people. Take my older brother, who introduced me to jazz when I was only eight years old. Last month, we went to see a jazz show live. Not only was it a great show, but I got to spend some time with my brother. Enjoying the show together helped me feel closer to him!

🎧 CD2, Track 44

Narrator: Get Set Sample Response

Respondent: An activity that I like to do is ride my bike. I enjoy riding my bike for two reasons. First of all, it's a really inexpensive way of getting around compared to other types of transportation. For example, in order to ride the bus, I'd have to pay one dollar for every trip that I make. Some days, I take several trips by bus. Off the top of my head, it would probably cost me about $300 to ride the bus to and from school each semester! But this isn't a problem if I ride my bike, since it's always free. The next reason I like riding my bike is because it's a good way to get exercise. Before I began riding my bike, I was really out of shape. In fact, when I first started riding, it really made me exhausted. But as I rode more and more, I got in better and better shape. And best of all, since I started riding my bike, I've lost ten pounds!

🎧 CD2, Track 46

Narrator: Speaking Task 1: Go for the TOEFL Test, Sample Response #1

Respondent: Two places that I have traveled to are Hong Kong and Miami. These two trips were different in at least two ways. First of all, the food in each country was completely distinct. In Hong Kong, I ate a lot of noodle dishes that had soy sauce. On the other hand, I ate a lot of spicy foods in Miami, like tacos. Another way that my trips to each country were different was the general pace of life. I found that in Hong Kong, people walked faster and always seemed to be in a rush to get somewhere. In Miami, people walked pretty slowly and were not as rushed. Life there seemed to be more relaxed in general.

Narrator: Speaking Task 1: Go for the TOEFL Test, Sample Response #2

Respondent: I've been to New York City and to Paris. New York City is very big, like Paris. There are so many people in both places. And they're both really expensive. I spent a lot more money in both places than I thought I would. Also, New York City has the Statue of Liberty. It is very tall, and many people visit it. When I went, I waited in line for three hours. That's a long time. Paris doesn't have the Statue of Liberty. Paris has the Eiffel Tower.

Lesson 2

🎧 CD2, Track 48

Narrator: Get Ready Sample Response

Respondent: While some people may think it's a bad idea to work during college, I think it's a good idea. I hold this belief for two reasons. First, I think it teaches you how to manage your time. For example, before I got a part-time

job, I used to waste a lot of time watching television. Now that I work, I realize how precious my time is, and I follow a strict schedule. That way, I can fulfill my academic and work commitments. Next, I think working in college is a great way to be independent. A lot of people I know depend on their parents for money, but not me. By working, I am able to earn my own money and determine exactly how I spend it.

🎧 CD2, Track 49

Narrator: Get Set Sample Response

Respondent: I know that some people think it's good to learn by making your own mistakes, but it's my belief that it's best to learn from the mistakes of others. I feel this way for a couple of reasons. First of all, it saves time. For example, my older brother, Randy, recently made the mistake of procrastinating on a school project. The problem was that he waited too long to start writing an important term paper. He ended up missing the deadline as a result. Since he told me about this, I now know never to procrastinate. I don't have to waste my time learning this lesson on my own. In addition, learning from the mistakes of others is less stressful. I know when my brother missed his deadline, he was really upset. By learning from his mistakes, I avoided all the stress that would have come if I had made the mistake myself.

🎧 CD2, Track 51

Narrator: Speaking Task 2: Go for the TOEFL Test, Sample Response #1

Respondent: While some people think that there are no benefits to watching television, I disagree because I've found that watching television can be both educational and relaxing. To start with, a lot of television shows are actually educational. For example, my favorite shows are about astronomy and biology. By watching these shows, I have a better understanding of these fields. Plus, the shows feature the latest discoveries, so I have access to recent research. Next, watching television is relaxing, which is very beneficial. No matter how stressful my day is, I always feel better after watching a half hour of television. Because I've had the chance to unwind, my mind is clear when it's time to do homework, so I can do a better job.

Narrator: Speaking Task 2: Go for the TOEFL Test, Sample Response #2

Respondent: Everybody knows that watching television is really bad for you. I don't even know how watching a lot of TV is good. For one thing, it makes you lazy because you will not want to go outside to do anything. You will just stay inside all day long and watch all your favorite shows. And you'll probably eat a lot, too. So it makes life bad. TV has too many commercials, so it's boring, too. I can't even tell what the commercials are for. Sometimes I see a commercial and I don't know what product they are talking about.

Lesson 3

🎧 CD2, Track 54

Narrator: Get Ready Listening Passage

Narrator: Now listen to two students as they discuss the announcement.

Speaker 1: Did you hear about the mandatory advisory meetings? We have to see our advisors twice a semester.

Speaker 2: I heard that. But I already see my advisor at least twice a semester. I think it's a great idea for everyone.

Speaker 1: Really? I'm busy, so it's hard to make time for my advisor. I don't think it's that helpful.

Speaker 2: Oh, I disagree. I wouldn't be graduating this year if it weren't for my advisor. Last year, she noticed that I never took a required writing course. I just forgot to sign up for it my freshman year. But I can't graduate without it. I took it last semester, but only because she noticed it. Without her, I'd be taking that course next fall.

Speaker 1: OK, I can see why that's useful. But do you really need two visits to check on required courses?

Speaker 2: Maybe not. But that's not all we talk about. I've gotten a lot of good career advice from my counselor. She's helped me figure out where I should apply for jobs after graduation. She's even written me a letter of recommendation. I wouldn't have gotten all that with just one meeting a semester.

Narrator: The woman expresses her opinion of the announcement by the advising department. State her opinion and explain the reasons she gives for holding that opinion.

🎧 CD2, Track 55

Narrator: Get Ready Sample Response

Respondent: According to the announcement, the City College advising department is going to require students to meet with their advisors twice a semester instead of just once.

The college is doing this so that students will know which courses to take and also to help advisors get to know students better. The woman thinks that the change is a great idea. For one, the woman would not be graduating on time without her advisor's help. She forgot to enroll in a required writing course her freshman year. But her advisor noticed that mistake, and the woman was able to take the course without delaying her graduation. The woman also says that her advisor has helped with her career. The advisor suggested places for the woman to apply and has written her a letter of recommendation. The woman believes that she wouldn't have gotten that help with just one meeting a semester.

🎧 CD2, Track 56

Narrator: Get Set Listening Passage

Narrator: Now listen to two students as they discuss the announcement.

Speaker 1: Wow. According to this announcement, the computer lab is charging students five cents for every page they print.

Speaker 2: Really? Does it say why?

Speaker 1: Yeah, it has a couple of reasons. For one, it says that the cost of ink and paper is too high to let students print for free. Which makes sense, I guess. The ink for printers is pretty expensive. And there are a lot of students who print papers and research there.

Speaker 2: But it's totally unfair. We already pay for printing. Every student in this college is charged a technology fee with their tuition. So every semester, you and I and every other

student here pay for the right to use the computer lab. The cost of whatever we print should be covered by that fee.

Speaker 1: You've got a good point. But at least the money they save will go toward updating the computers and software.

Speaker 2: I don't know if that's necessary, either. I mean, ninety percent of students use the computer lab for performing research and typing up papers. The fact is, you don't need the newest computer or expensive new software to do that. You just need a computer that works well.

Narrator: The woman expresses her opinion of the university's plan to change its printing policy in the student computer lab. State her opinion and explain the reasons she gives for holding that opinion.

🎧 CD2, Track 57

Narrator: Speaking Task 3: Go for the TOEFL Test

Narrator: Now listen to two students as they discuss the announcement. Take notes.

Speaker 1: Did you hear that first-year students can't get single rooms anymore?

Speaker 2: Oh, really? I hadn't heard that. Too bad for the new students, I guess.

Speaker 1: Actually, I think it's a smart decision. I've lived in the dorms for my entire university education, and I had roommates every year until now. And to be honest, my upper-level chemistry classes are so much harder than the ones I took as a first-year. I'm glad I have a room to myself so I can study whenever I need to. But first-year courses don't require the same amount of studying.

Speaker 2: That makes sense. But what about students who just aren't very social? Shouldn't they be able to ask for a single room?

Speaker 1: I thought about that. But your freshman year can be pretty rough, and that would be worse if you lived alone. I was so nervous when I first got here. I was even afraid to go to class. But my first roommate, Carol, became my best friend. If I hadn't known her, I don't know if I would have made it through that first year. I might have moved and gone to a university closer to my family and friends.

🎧 CD2, Track 58

Narrator: Speaking Task 3: Go for the TOEFL Test, Sample Response #1

Respondent: The notice from the Office of Residential Life states that freshmen cannot get into single rooms at City University. The reasons for the decision are that upperclassmen need their own rooms because they take more difficult classes and that freshmen benefit from having roommates. The woman says that the decision is a smart one. She mentions two reasons why she supports the decision. First, she states that her upper-level chemistry classes are much harder than her freshman courses. If she didn't have her own room, she'd have trouble studying as much as she needs to. Second, she explains that if she hadn't lived with a roommate her freshman year, she might have left the university. The woman had been nervous and afraid until she became friends with her roommate. That friendship helped her finish her first year at the university.

Narrator: Speaking Task 3: Go for the TOEFL Test, Sample Response #2

Respondent: I think the university made a good decision. Upper-level students deserve the privacy more than incoming students. When my friend Max was in his third year of university, he always said he was happy to have a single room. His classes were really hard. In my opinion, first-year students don't really have to worry about really hard classes. Another reason is that first-year students need to be social. If they are shy, they will have trouble if they live in a single room. Maybe they will leave the university and study somewhere closer to their families, like the lady said.

Lesson 4

CD3, Track 4

Narrator: Get Ready Listening Passage

Narrator: Now listen to part of a lecture in a biology class.

Professor: Deserts have very little water, which is why many desert creatures take on specific adaptations to survive. So consider the coyote, which is basically a wild dog. But it can survive in the driest deserts of Central and North America. So how do coyotes do it? Well, they're omnivores that will eat anything. They eat plants, fruits, and vegetables when they're available. They hunt large animals as a pack or small rodents as individuals. And they'll even eat any dead animals they come across. By eating whatever food is available, coyotes are able to take in enough liquid and food to survive.

But rattlesnakes, on the other hand, can't tolerate such a diverse diet, and they can only hunt to survive. Rattlesnakes live solely on small animals like squirrels and mice. But the squirrels hide in shade during the day, and the mice come out only at night. If rattlesnakes hunted only during the day, they'd miss half of their food source. So they hunt in the early morning and early evening, when the squirrels and mice they depend on are beginning or ending their periods of activity. That doubles their chances of finding sufficient food sources.

Narrator: The professor describes the diets of desert coyotes and rattlesnakes. Explain how their diets relate to the adaptations of desert animals.

CD3, Track 5

Narrator: Get Ready Sample Response

Respondent: The reading passage and the lecture are both about adaptations of desert animals. The reading describes two types of adaptations, and the professor gives examples of two animals that each use one of the adaptations mentioned in the reading.

First, the reading passage states that some desert animals will eat any plant or animal they can. The professor uses coyotes, a type of wild dog, as an example of an animal that uses this adaptation. She explains that coyotes will eat fruit, vegetables, small or large prey, and even dead animals. Having a diverse diet allows coyotes to survive in deserts.

The second adaptation mentioned in the reading is that some animals hunt in the early morning and early evening to catch prey that is active during the day or night. According to the professor, rattlesnakes are an example of animals that use the

second adaptation. The professor says that rattlesnakes depend on squirrels and mice for food but that these prey are active at different times. By hunting in the early morning and night, rattlesnakes have twice as many chances to catch these animals.

CD3, Track 6

Narrator: Get Set Listening Passage

Narrator: Now listen to part of a lecture in a theater class.

Professor: Now that you know what some of the tools used in method acting are, you need some examples of how you can use them. Start with affective memory—it's a powerful device that really improves your display of emotion. So let's say your character just received disappointing news. Maybe she's a queen who just found out her army lost a battle. Of course, no one here could possibly know what that feels like. But we *do* all know how it feels to be disappointed. Think of any time you failed to reach a goal, like a role you didn't get or a class that you did poorly in. Let yourself feel the disappointment again. You won't just be pretending to be a disappointed queen anymore—you'll *actually* feel disappointed. And I promise, you'll be far more convincing than someone who's just pretending.

Of course, not all method-acting tools require that you recall sad memories. An object of attention, for example, just makes the world your character lives in more real to you as an actor. And when it's more real to you, it's more real to your audience. Let me give you an example. If a play takes place outdoors in the winter, then the cold weather would be a good object of attention. With every action, you'd be focusing on how it feels to be cold and how it changes your behavior. So at all times, you might be rubbing and blowing on your hands to keep warm, or shivering.

Narrator: The professor describes examples of affective memory and objects of attention. Explain how these examples relate to method acting.

CD3, Track 7

Narrator: Speaking Task 4: Go for the TOEFL Test

Narrator: Now listen to part of a lecture in an environmental science class and take notes.

Professor: Many scientists are still undecided about whether assisted migration is a good idea. But considering early research, I think we need to acknowledge the advantages of such projects. Take the checkerspot butterfly, for example. The butterfly's original habitat is along the Pacific coast of Mexico and California. However, because of global warming, the butterfly's main food source has become increasingly difficult to find in the southern range of its habitat. As you can guess, this has caused its numbers to start falling at an alarming rate. To save the checkerspot butterfly, researchers began to relocate large numbers of them farther north. Now the butterfly is thriving in the northern areas, and that is because of assisted migration.

Another animal that might benefit from assisted migration is the North American pika, which is a small, hamster-like creature. Pikas live in the mountainous regions of the western United States. Again, global warming has started to affect the pika, but in a different way than the checkerspot butterfly. See, during the winter, pikas seek shelter under the snow, and that's how they keep warm. But because temperatures are getting warmer in a lot of places, there isn't as much snow. So the pikas don't have any protection during cold snaps, and they're freezing to death. To help the North American pika, scientists have considered relocating it to colder areas with more snow. They think this would help the creatures survive during the cold season.

CD3, Track 8

Narrator: Speaking Task 4: Go for the TOEFL Test, Sample Response #1

Respondent: Both the reading passage and the lecture are about assisted migration. The reading defines assisted migration as the practice of moving a species to a new habitat. The professor expands on the topic by describing two animals.

According to the author, assisted migration can be helpful when an organism's original habitat can't provide it with the necessary food supply. The professor supports this by giving the example of the checkerspot butterfly. Due to global warming, the checkerspot butterfly's main food supply became rare in the southern part of its habitat. In order to save the species, scientists relocated the butterflies farther north, where they could find food more easily.

The reading says that animals might benefit from assisted migration when the original habitat doesn't provide satisfactory shelter. The professor supports this by mentioning the North American pika. The professor says that the pika can't find adequate shelter from the cold because there isn't enough snow. By moving the pika to colder areas, the professor suggests that scientists can help it survive.

Narrator: Speaking Task 4: Go for the TOEFL Test, Sample Response #2

Respondent: Checkerspot butterflies are good for assisted migration because they are endangered. Assisted migration is when scientists move animals to live in a new place. The butterflies live in Mexico, but now it's too hot there. In their original habitats, they don't have shelters. The professor says it's too warm there now. The checkerspot butterfly doesn't have a place to live. Moving it will probably save the butterfly. The pika is an animal that lives in the mountains in the United States. It looks like a hamster. It's also good for assisted migration. It's like the checkerspot butterfly, too. Pikas need to hide in the snow. But there isn't enough snow in the mountains where they come from. So the pikas are freezing, and they need to go somewhere that's warmer.

Lesson 5

CD3, Track 11

Narrator: Get Ready Listening Passage

Narrator: Listen to a conversation between two students.

Speaker 1: Hi, Sarah. Are you ready for the big test today?

Speaker 2: No, not at all. I tried to study all week, but I just couldn't concentrate.

Speaker 1: Really? That's surprising. You're such a good student. What happened?

Speaker 2: Well, it's this new apartment building that I moved into. The people who live there are just way too loud. I can't think with so many noisy neighbors. I'm starting to worry about my grades for this semester. I mean, if I can't study all year, I'm going to fail.

Speaker 1: That's awful. What are you going to do?

Speaker 2: I don't know. I guess I could study at the library when my neighbors are being too loud. But the problem is, I have to drive to campus to get to the library. And that means I have to pay for parking, too. I don't really have the time or money to do that every day, you know?

Speaker 1: That's true. Parking can get pretty expensive. And you live so far from campus, so it probably takes you an hour to drive there and back, doesn't it?

Speaker 2: Yeah, it does. So that's making me think that I should just move out of the building as soon as possible and get back into the dorms.

Speaker 1: That sounds like a good idea. I mean, if your neighbors are that bad, you should get out of there before your grades start to drop.

Speaker 2: Unfortunately, it's not that simple. See, I had to pay a deposit when I moved into that apartment. You know, just in case there's any damage to the carpet or anything like that when I leave. But if I move out early, the landlord will keep my deposit. And it's not a small amount of money. I'd hate to lose it if I don't really have to. It feels like a waste.

CD3, Track 12

Narrator: Get Ready Sample Response

Respondent: The woman's problem is that her neighbors at her new apartment are so noisy that she has difficulty studying. She could study at the library when her neighbors are noisy, but the drive would take a long time and she would have to pay for parking. She could also move out of her apartment and back into the dorms, but she would lose her deposit on the apartment. In my opinion, moving out of her apartment is the best solution. I believe this for two reasons. First, she won't be able to study as much if she drives to the library. That's because every time she drives back and forth from the library, she loses time that she could have spent studying. Second, her top priority should be her grades, not her finances. In the end, getting poor grades would have a larger effect on her life than losing the deposit on her apartment.

CD3, Track 13

Narrator: Get Set Listening Passage

Narrator: Listen to a conversation between two students.

Speaker 1: Joe, you look worried. Is everything OK?

Speaker 2: Honestly? Not really. I just got my grade on my midterm, and I failed it horribly. I don't know if I'll be able to pass this class now.

Speaker 1: I'm sorry to hear that. But don't feel too bad. It was a pretty hard test, and there's still half the semester left. I'm sure you can turn things around.

Speaker 2: Thanks, but I don't know. All of my classes are so hard this semester. I just didn't have enough time to study for it.

I had my chemistry midterm the day before. And I had to write a ten-page paper for my literature class over the weekend. By the time I got finished with all of the other tests and projects, I couldn't catch up on this class.

Speaker 1: Wow, it seems like you're really busy. I know that nobody likes to do it, but maybe you should withdraw from this class.

Speaker 2: I could do that. But we're pretty far into the semester now. If I withdraw, it'll show on my academic record. And that doesn't look good. After all, I want to get into graduate school next year, and having a withdrawal on my transcript could get my application rejected.

Speaker 1: Oh, I didn't even think of that. Well, there's a study group for this class, you know. We meet after each session for about an hour. And I'm sure Professor Smith would be happy to help you out during his office hours. If you really need to pass, I think that would do it.

Speaker 2: Yeah, I bet that would help my grade a lot. But the fact is, I can't spend that much time studying for just one class. Like I said, all of my courses this term are really challenging. If I spend all my time studying for this class, my grades will drop in the other ones. And that would hurt my grad school application, too.

Narrator: The students discuss two solutions to the man's problem. Describe the problem. Then, state which of the two solutions you prefer and explain why.

🎧 CD3, Track 14

Narrator: Speaking Task 5: Go for the TOEFL Test

Narrator: Listen to a conversation between two students.

Speaker 1: Hi, Charles, good to see you. How are you doing?

Speaker 2: Hi, Beth. I'm really stressed out, actually. The worst thing happened to me last night. My laptop froze just when I was about to finish my final paper for our history class. You know, the one that determines a third of our grade? I worked on the computer for hours last night, but I couldn't get it working again.

Speaker 1: Oh no! That's terrible! Can you take it in to a computer repair shop? Maybe someone there can get it working again or at least find your paper on the hard drive.

Speaker 2: That's the first solution I thought of, too. I called a computer repair shop this morning, and the clerk said I could bring my laptop in later today. He's seen problems like this plenty of times and said that sometimes they can get the computer up and running just like it was before. But he also told me that sometimes they have to reinstall the operating system, and that would erase everything on my computer, including the history paper. But I won't know if they can fix my computer until tonight.

Speaker 1: But the paper is due tomorrow afternoon. What will you do if the computer repair shop can't fix the computer or save your paper? Will you just write a new paper in the computer lab?

Speaker 2: I could try to do that. But that's a long paper. If I'm going to start all over and get it done before tomorrow

afternoon, I'll have to start right away. In fact, I won't even have time to take the laptop into the repair shop. I mean, I have all of my notes, but it'll still take more than one day to type it all up again. And even if I do finish it again, I doubt it will be as good as the first draft. I have been working on that paper for weeks. There's no way it will get as good of a grade, and I can't afford to do poorly on a paper that's so important.

Narrator: The students discuss two solutions to the man's problem. Describe the problem. Then, state which of the two solutions you prefer and explain why.

🎧 CD3, Track 15

Narrator: Speaking Task 5: Go for the TOEFL Test, Sample Response #1

Respondent: The man's problem is that his computer froze just before he completed a long, important paper. He could take it to a computer repair shop later, but the shop clerk cannot guarantee that the repair will work. The man's other option is to start writing a new paper immediately, but he thinks that the second version will not be as good as the first. In my opinion, the man should start writing a new paper immediately. First, it's possible that the man's first draft is gone for good. If he waits for the computer to get fixed and it doesn't work, he won't get any credit. Second, the man can still produce a good paper. He says that he still has all of his notes, so the most important information is already organized. Even if his new version isn't as good as the first, he'll still be able to get a passing grade.

Narrator: Speaking Task 5: Go for the TOEFL Test, Sample Response #2

Respondent: The man's computer stopped working, and he has to turn in an important paper. He should not try to write a new paper, because it will take too long. The man is probably stressed, and I don't think that will help him write the new paper. And his notes were probably on the computer, so he can't even look at those. He will waste his time trying to write a new paper, because it won't be as good as the first one he wrote. That's why he should try just getting the computer fixed. Maybe if he pays extra, the repair shop can finish it early. That way, he can get his paper finished on time and not bother with writing it all over again for no reason.

Lesson 6

🎧 CD3, Track 18

Narrator: Get Ready Listening Passage

Narrator: Listen to part of a lecture in a psychology class.

Professor: Short-term memory is memory that lasts for a brief period, usually fewer than thirty seconds. We use short-term memory often for tasks like remembering phone numbers, people's names, or directions to a location. Without being consciously aware of it, our brains employ two processes for short-term memory. These processes are called chunking and the phonological loop.

First, let's examine chunking. Chunking is the process of taking a long piece of information and breaking it up into smaller pieces. These "chunks" are then recalled as whole pieces of information. This way, you don't have to remember all the information at once. A great example is when you need to remember a telephone number. As you listen, you hear "four, one, five," and then a few more numbers—"five, five, five"—and a final set of numbers, "nine, two, eight, six." Your brain registers each set as a whole and puts them all together afterward.

A second process of short-term memory is the phonological loop. Uh, in a phonological loop, we replay information over and over again in our minds. Imagine that you're getting directions to a friend's house, but you don't have a pen. Your friend tells you to take a right, then turn left, drive two miles, and then take the third left. To keep track, your brain makes a phonological loop. You repeat this information over and over again in your head until you don't need it anymore.

Narrator: Using the points and examples from the lecture, explain two processes that humans use for short-term memory.

🎧 CD3, Track 19

Narrator: Get Ready Sample Response

Respondent: The lecture is about short-term memory. The professor discusses two different ways our brains create short-term memories: chunking and the phonological loop.

According to the lecture, chunking is when we break up a long piece of information into smaller pieces. To illustrate how this works, the professor gives an example of how we use chunking to remember telephone numbers. Usually, we divide the long number into three smaller sections. The professor says that by breaking up the information into these "chunks," it helps us remember it more easily. The second method mentioned in the lecture is the phonological loop. The professor explains that this is when a person repeats information over and over again in the mind. The example given in the lecture is of directions to a place. Our brains use the phonological loop to repeat the steps over and over again, which helps us remember them.

🎧 CD3, Track 20

Narrator: Get Set Listening Passage

Narrator: Listen to part of a lecture in a marketing class.

Professor: When you go shopping, you may think you are in total control of what you buy. However, the reality is more complicated. The fact is, retailers encourage you to spend money in their stores every day. This process is called priming. Now, there are two main ways in which stores prime customers: placement and presentation.

First, let's take a closer look at placement. Placement is when certain products are deliberately put in a certain area. Here's an example: have you ever walked into your local grocery store and seen bunches of fresh, beautiful flowers by the door? OK. This is placement in action. By setting flowers next to the entrance, the store owners are leading us, the consumers, to believe that the food in the store is also fresh, fragrant, and beautiful. You are more likely to buy food that is fresh and smells great, right? Thus, the placement of the flowers *primes* us to spend money.

Placement is just one way to prime a customer, however. Presentation is another form of priming. What do I mean by

presentation? Well, presentation is the way in which items are arranged in a store. Consider fresh produce, like fruits and vegetables. We may find apples neatly stacked in wooden barrels, lined up in different colors. The barrels remind us of a farmers' market or farm, which in turn, makes us think of nature and freshness. The bright colors draw our eye to the apples. It's almost like a piece of art that has been carefully crafted by store employees. A lot of thought and creativity is required to create those displays! We constantly encounter presentations like this as a type of priming, and we spend more as a result.

Narrator: Using the points and examples from the lecture, explain how businesses use priming to encourage spending in stores.

🎧 CD3, Track 21

Narrator: Speaking Task 6: Go for the TOEFL Test

Narrator: Listen to part of a lecture in a biology class.

Professor: In recent years, honeybee colonies have been disappearing at an alarming rate—and scientists still aren't sure exactly why it's happening. This phenomenon is called colony collapse disorder, and it has some very serious consequences. In particular, colony collapse disorder affects agricultural productivity and food prices.

OK . . . when I say agricultural productivity, I mean how much food farmers are able to grow. To understand the impact of colony collapse disorder on agricultural productivity, we need to examine the role of bees in agriculture. Bees pollinate flowering plants, which is to say that they help the plants produce fruit or vegetables. In this way, bees are an important part of the growth cycle for many crops that we rely on for food. In fact, common foods like apples, peaches, and tomatoes rely on bees for up to one-third of their total pollination. So if bees keep on disappearing, we're going to see a reduction in how much of these foods farmers can grow. That means that many of our favorite foods will become harder to grow and will be less plentiful.

This decrease in crops is actually related to a second consequence of colony collapse disorder that I want to talk about today: its effect on food prices. As I just explained, colony collapse disorder leads to a decrease in agricultural productivity, right? Unfortunately, that means that food prices would probably go up by a lot. This is due to the simple economic rule that when the availability of an item decreases, its price *increases* dramatically. So if bee colonies continue to disappear, we could expect that families would find it difficult to afford certain food items because many foods—those pollinated by bees—would become too expensive.

🎧 CD3, Track 22

Narrator: Speaking Task 6: Go for the TOEFL Test, Sample Response #1

Respondent: In the lecture, the professor discusses a phenomenon called colony collapse disorder, which is when honeybee colonies disappear. The professor focuses on the negative impacts of colony collapse disorder on agricultural productivity and food prices. First, the professor points out that bees are important to agriculture because they pollinate crops and allow the crops to reproduce. She adds that common crops like apples and tomatoes rely on bees for a large portion of pollination. The professor says that if bees were to become extinct, it would be very difficult to grow these crops. Next, the professor links the reduction of certain crops to the increase of food prices. She says that when availability of a product decreases, its price actually goes up. She then predicts that if the number of bee colonies continues to decrease, it will be hard for families to buy some foods because they will be too expensive.

Narrator: Speaking Task 6: Go for the TOEFL Test, Sample Response #2

Respondent: The professor talks about disappearing bees. It's called colony collapse disorder. Scientists don't know why it's happening, but it's having a terrible effect so far. There are two results of the disappearing bees that the professor mentions. For example, the professor talks about how bees are important for plants. She says it's affecting agricultural productivity. Now that the bees are disappearing, there probably won't be fruit or vegetables for us to eat anymore. Also, colony collapse disorder is related to high food prices. The professor says that people won't be able to pay as much for food in the future because the bees are disappearing. She mentions a rule that says when availability decreases, prices increase, and that's why. Anything that is pollinated by bees will be too expensive.

Speaking Review Test

🎧 CD3, Track 24

Narrator: Review Test Question 1, Sample Response #1

Respondent: A person with whom I enjoy talking is my brother, Robert. He's great to talk to for a few reasons. One reason is that he can always cheer me up. For example, last week I was disappointed about a low test grade. But Robert called and told me a few jokes and funny stories. I felt better right away. Another reason that I like talking to Robert is that he gives good advice. During my first year of college, I didn't know which classes to take. I wanted to take a lot of electives because they looked interesting. But Robert advised that I take my required classes first so that I could graduate on time. He was right. If I hadn't taken his advice, I would have spent an extra year in college.

Narrator: Review Test Question 1, Sample Response #2

Respondent: My brother, Robert, is funny. He's older than me, but we still have a lot in common. He's a lot of fun to be around and talk to. I think that's why he has so many friends. Everyone likes talking to him. He's also smart and can help you out with problems or decisions.

🎧 CD3, Track 26

Narrator: Review Test Question 2, Sample Response #1

Respondent: I prefer taking exams to writing essays. I feel this way for two reasons. First, it's easier to identify the right answers on exams. For example, I had an exam on the play *Romeo and Juliet*. I didn't understand all of the play, but I knew which characters did what. Because I understood

the basic events, I could identify answer choices that were wrong. The other reason I prefer exams is that they're easier to finish. For example, I had a literature exam that lasted for two hours. When there were only two minutes left, I still had a few questions to answer. I quickly read them and gave my best guesses. But if you run out of time to write an essay, you can't quickly guess the answers. You just have an incomplete essay.

Narrator: Review Test Question 2, Sample Response #2

Respondent: I hate taking exams. You don't get a chance to talk about your own opinion. And they always check on small details. Those are hard to remember sometimes. It's not fair that you can get a bad grade just because you forgot a character's name or what year something happened.

🎧 CD3, Track 27

Narrator: Question 3

Narrator: The third floor of the library will be turned into a silent study area. Read the announcement about the change. Read the announcement in 45 seconds. Begin reading now.

Narrator: Now listen to two students as they discuss the announcement.

Speaker 1: Anne, you heard that the library turned the third floor into a silent study area, right? Our study group will have to meet somewhere else from now on.

Speaker 2: I did hear that. But I think it's totally unfair. I mean, I understand that some people study better when it's quiet. But those students can just wear earplugs if they want to study on the third floor. The library doesn't have to create a space that's completely quiet just for them.

Speaker 1: You have a good point. But I think that people complained about groups talking there. The librarians were spending too much time responding to the noise complaints.

Speaker 2: But that's my other point. The third floor is the best place for groups of students to work together. After all, we all live in the dorms, and our rooms are way too small for group meetings. But the third floor has couches and large tables, so of course people meet there. Instead of making it a silent area, they should make it a group meeting space. Then the librarians wouldn't have to respond to noise complaints, because everyone there would be in a group.

🎧 CD3, Track 28

Narrator: Review Test Question 3, Sample Response #1

Respondent: The library announcement says that the third floor will be turned into a silent study area. The reasons for the decision are that some students learn better in quiet areas and that the library staff spends too much time responding to noise complaints on the third floor. The woman thinks that the change is unfair. She gives two reasons to support her opinion. First, she states that the library doesn't have to create a silent study space at all. If students want to study on the third floor and have quiet, they can just wear earplugs. Second, she says that the third floor is the best place for groups of students to meet because it has more space than the dorms. She thinks the library should make the third floor a group meeting space, and that way the librarians won't get noise complaints anymore.

Narrator: Review Test Question 3, Sample Response #2

Respondent: The woman doesn't like the announcement. I think that she's wrong. I think that students should have a quiet place to study. It's not fair to make students wear earplugs just so that they can focus on what they're doing. And even though the students' rooms are too small for meetings, they don't have to meet at the library. They can meet outside or at a café to talk about projects. Libraries are supposed to be quiet.

🎧 CD3, Track 29

Narrator: Question 4

Narrator: Read a short passage about living fossils. Begin reading now.

Narrator: Now listen to part of a lecture in a biology class.

Professor: Now, when you think of a fossil, what comes to mind? Probably dinosaurs or some other animal that's not around anymore, right? Well, that's not the case with living fossils. Take the lamprey, for example. A lamprey is a unique animal. It's a kind of fish, but it doesn't have any scales or a jaw. The lamprey's body is basically a long tube with a flat, round mouth. Doesn't sound like a fish you'd see in an aquarium, does it? It has no close relatives today. Also, there are no fossils to show that other types of fish evolved from lampreys at one point. They are the only creatures of their kind, and they have been for a long time.

OK, so the earliest fossil of lampreys comes from about 360 million years ago. And do you know what that fossil looks like? A long tube with a flat, round mouth. That's right. It looks just like the lampreys of today. Now, the fossil from millions of years ago is slightly smaller than modern lampreys. But that's just a size difference—the actual form of the body has not changed at all. They have the same bone structure, the same gills, the same jawless mouth. So basically, if you compared the skeleton of a small modern lamprey to that ancient fossil, you'd pretty much be looking at the same thing.

🎧 CD3, Track 30

Narrator: Review Test Question 4, Sample Response #1

Respondent: The reading passage and the lecture are both about living fossils. The author defines a living fossil as an animal that is alive today and that resembles a creature that lived long ago. The author also describes two features of living fossils. In the lecture, the professor discusses the lamprey and two reasons why it is considered a living fossil. First, the passage states that to be a living fossil, a species must have no close living relatives. The professor explains that lampreys are unlike most fish. She also says that there are no fossils to show that lampreys ever evolved into other forms. Second, the passage states that the body forms of living fossils must not have changed. The professor compares modern lampreys to the earliest fossil of a lamprey. She says that even though modern lampreys are slightly larger, the basic structures are almost identical to those of the fossil.

Narrator: Review Test Question 4, Sample Response #2

Respondent: Lampreys are living fossils because they haven't changed. Living fossils don't have close relatives. Lampreys have

no jaws or scales, so they're different from other fish. The oldest lamprey fossil is more than 360 million years old. But modern lampreys are usually larger than the oldest lamprey fossil.

🎧 CD3, Track 31

Narrator: Question 5

Narrator: Listen to a conversation between two students.

Speaker 1: Hey, Marie. Is everything OK?

Speaker 2: Honestly, I'm a little worried. I have a take-home exam due in two days for my history class. I haven't even started on it, and it's definitely going to take me a few hours to finish it.

Speaker 1: Well, you still have two days, right? That's enough time to work on it, isn't it?

Speaker 2: Under normal circumstances, it would be. But I also have a midterm tomorrow for my math class. Between the two, I don't know when I'll have time to prepare for my midterm and finish my take-home exam.

Speaker 1: Oh, that might be tricky. I know—is there any way you could turn in your take-home exam later? That way, you can focus on studying for your math test today. And once you finish your math midterm, you can work on your take-home exam.

Speaker 2: I could, but the professor has already said that he'll give extensions only if we can prove that we had some sort of emergency—like we were extremely ill or something like that. Otherwise, he'll take off a full letter grade for every day that it's late. And since history is my major, I really don't want to jeopardize my grade.

Speaker 1: Oh, that would be bad. Maybe, I don't know, could you talk to your math professor and take the test later?

Speaker 2: I know she's holding a makeup test a week from tomorrow. But the makeup test has to be different than the test tomorrow so that students don't share the test questions. And she warned us that the makeup test is going to be much, much harder than the one tomorrow. I really struggle in that class already. I don't know if I could pass the harder version of the test.

🎧 CD3, Track 32

Narrator: Review Test Question 5, Sample Response #1

Respondent: The woman's problem is that she doesn't have time to study for a math midterm the next day and complete a take-home exam that's due the day after that. She could turn in the take-home exam a day late, but her professor will lower her grade. Her other option is to take a makeup test for her math class the next week, but it will be much more difficult than the original test. In my opinion, the woman should turn in the take-home exam on time and take the makeup test. First, the take-home exam is for her major. Getting a bad grade in her major could impact her career in the long term. Second, even though the makeup test will be more difficult than the original, she will have much more time to study. She could even meet with the professor during office hours if she's still struggling to understand the material.

Narrator: Review Test Question 5, Sample Response #2

Respondent: The woman is worried about getting a bad grade. She has two tests but can't study for both. She should take the midterm test later. She can still study for it, and she'll have enough time to finish the take-home exam. Even when I have trouble with a class, I can always study enough to at least pass a test with a week to study.

🎧 CD3, Track 33

Narrator: Question 6

Narrator: Listen to part of a lecture in a biology class.

Professor: The upper layer of a rain forest, called the canopy, consists of a dense layer of branches and leaves that stem from tall trees. The canopy is so thick that very little sunlight gets through to the layer below, the understory. This presents quite a problem to smaller plant life because growth without sunlight is nearly impossible. Nevertheless, plants manage to grow and thrive beneath the canopy. This success is the result of a variety of plant adaptations, including the ability to increase their leaf size and climb trees, that allow the plants to capture more light.

The majority of plants in the understory have adapted by increasing their leaf size. The reason is quite simple. Plants can benefit only from sunlight that hits their leaves. So in sunny regions, leaf size doesn't matter as much. But in the understory, a plant with small leaves is unlikely to receive any of the little sunlight that passes through the canopy. Plants that grow large, wide leaves, however, are able to cover a larger area and absorb any light that manages to get through. The bigger its leaves are, the more likely a plant is to survive in the understory.

Of course, not all plant life simply adjusts to the low levels of available light. Others do whatever it takes to get above the canopy, where full sunlight is available. A type of vine, the liana, takes this approach. When it first sprouts on the ground, the liana grows very shallow roots and spreads vines out toward surrounding trees. Once a tree is located, the liana wraps its vines up and around that tree, climbing toward the top of the canopy. Because the liana is supported by the larger tree, it doesn't waste resources on a large root system. All its energy is spent on climbing higher. Upon reaching the canopy, the liana branches out and away from the support tree to gather unobstructed sunlight.

🎧 CD3, Track 34

Narrator: Review Test Question 6, Sample Response #1

Respondent: In the lecture, the professor explains that the rain forest canopy is so thick that plants underneath it struggle to get light. Because they would be unable to grow without light, plants have adapted to capture more light by growing bigger leaves and climbing tall trees.

First, the professor describes how leaf size affects how much light plants in the understory receive. Plants with larger leaves are more likely to capture some of the light that manages to get through the canopy. She states that the larger a plant's leaves are, the better its chances of surviving.

Next, the professor describes a plant that climbs trees to reach light above the canopy. She explains that a vine called the liana starts growing on the ground but doesn't grow deep roots. It grows vines that reach tall trees and then wrap around them. The vine grows up until it gets to the top of the tree. At that point, it grows away from the tree to get full sunlight.

Narrator: Review Test Question 6, Sample Response #2

Respondent: Trees in the understory don't get enough light to grow. They adapted to get more light. Sometimes plants have larger leaves. If the leaves were small, they would get less light. They also grow around taller trees. Once they grow to a height above the canopy, they have full sunlight.

Academic Word List

academic**ⓐ** / ækədemɪk, ækədemɪkli /**ⓑ** (academics)

ADJ ⓒ (ADJ n) Academic is used to describe things that relate to the work done in schools, colleges, and universities, especially work which involves studying and reasoning rather than practical or technical skills.

Their academic standards are high.

*I was terrible at school and left with few academic qualifications.***ⓓ**

academically ADV

He is academically gifted.

ⓐ the word you are looking for
ⓑ how it sounds
ⓒ type of word (e.g. noun, adjective, adverb, etc)
ⓓ example sentence

The following 570 words are of the most common word families found in academic texts. These are important to learn and know to ensure academic success. Use the *Collins Cobuild Advanced Dictionary* to find definitions, different forms of words, see authentic sample sentences, learn pronunciation, and much more!

Coxhead Academic Word List*

abandon	affect	approximate
abstract	aggregate	arbitrary
academy	aid	area
access	albeit	aspect
accommodate	allocate	assemble
accompany	alter	assess
accumulate	alternative	assign
accurate	ambiguous	assist
achieve	amend	assume
acknowledge	analogy	assure
acquire	analyze	attach
adapt	annual	attain
adequate	anticipate	attitude
adjacent	apparent	attribute
adjust	append	author
administrate	appreciate	authority
adult	approach	automate
advocate	appropriate	available

aware
behalf
benefit
bias
bond
brief
bulk
capable
capacity
category
cease
challenge
channel
chapter
chart
chemical
circumstance
cite
civil
clarify
classic
clause
code
coherent
coincide
collapse
colleague
commence
comment
commission
commit
commodity
communicate
community
compatible
compensate
compile
complement
complex
component
compound
comprehensive
comprise
compute

conceive
concentrate
concept
conclude
concurrent
conduct
confer
confine
confirm
conflict
conform
consent
consequent
considerable
consist
constant
constitute
constrain
construct
consult
consume
contact
contemporary
context
contract
contradict
contrary
contrast
contribute
controversy
convene
converse
convert
convince
cooperate
coordinate
core
corporate
correspond
couple
create
credit
criteria
crucial

culture
currency
cycle
data
debate
decade
decline
deduce
define
definite
demonstrate
denote
deny
depress
derive
design
despite
detect
deviate
device
devote
differentiate
dimension
diminish
discrete
discriminate
displace
display
dispose
distinct
distort
distribute
diverse
document
domain
domestic
dominate
draft
drama
duration
dynamic
economy
edit
element

eliminate	final	incline
emerge	finance	income
emphasis	finite	incorporate
empirical	flexible	index
enable	fluctuate	indicate
encounter	focus	individual
energy	format	induce
enforce	formula	inevitable
enhance	forthcoming	infer
enormous	found	infrastructure
ensure	foundation	inherent
entity	framework	inhibit
environment	function	initial
equate	fund	initiate
equip	fundamental	injure
equivalent	furthermore	innovate
erode	gender	input
error	generate	insert
establish	generation	insight
estate	globe	inspect
estimate	goal	instance
ethic	grade	institute
ethnic	grant	instruct
evaluate	guarantee	integral
eventual	guideline	integrate
evident	hence	integrity
evolve	hierarchy	intelligent
exceed	highlight	intense
exclude	hypothesis	interact
exhibit	identical	intermediate
expand	identify	internal
expert	ideology	interpret
explicit	ignorant	interval
exploit	illustrate	intervene
export	image	intrinsic
expose	immigrate	invest
external	impact	investigate
extract	implement	invoke
facilitate	implicate	involve
factor	implicit	isolate
feature	imply	issue
federal	impose	item
fee	incentive	job
file	incidence	journal

justify
label
labor
layer
lecture
legal
legislate
levy
liberal
license
likewise
link
locate
logic
maintain
major
manipulate
manual
margin
mature
maximize
mechanism
media
mediate
medical
medium
mental
method
migrate
military
minimal
minimize
minimum
ministry
minor
mode
modify
monitor
motive
mutual
negate
network
neutral
nevertheless

nonetheless
norm
normal
notion
notwithstanding
nuclear
objective
obtain
obvious
occupy
occur
odd
offset
ongoing
option
orient
outcome
output
overall
overlap
overseas
panel
paradigm
paragraph
parallel
parameter
participate
partner
passive
perceive
percent
period
persist
perspective
phase
phenomenon
philosophy
physical
plus
policy
portion
pose
positive
potential

practitioner
precede
precise
predict
predominant
preliminary
presume
previous
primary
prime
principal
principle
prior
priority
proceed
process
professional
prohibit
project
promote
proportion
prospect
protocol
psychology
publication
publish
purchase
pursue
qualitative
quote
radical
random
range
ratio
rational
react
recover
refine
regime
region
register
regulate
reinforce
reject

relax	site	terminate
release	so-called	text
relevant	sole	theme
reluctance	somewhat	theory
rely	source	thereby
remove	specific	thesis
require	specify	topic
research	sphere	trace
reside	stable	tradition
resolve	statistic	transfer
resource	status	transform
respond	straightforward	transit
restore	strategy	transmit
restrain	stress	transport
restrict	structure	trend
retain	style	trigger
reveal	submit	ultimate
revenue	subordinate	undergo
reverse	subsequent	underlie
revise	subsidy	undertake
revolution	substitute	uniform
rigid	successor	unify
role	sufficient	unique
route	sum	utilize
scenario	summary	valid
schedule	supplement	vary
scheme	survey	vehicle
scope	survive	version
section	suspend	via
sector	sustain	violate
secure	symbol	virtual
seek	tape	visible
select	target	vision
sequence	task	visual
series	team	volume
sex	technical	voluntary
shift	technique	welfare
significant	technology	whereas
similar	temporary	whereby
simulate	tense	widespread

*Please note, there is no direct correlation between the words found on the TOEFL Test and those found on the Coxhead Academic Word list. This list has been included only as a reference for vocabulary commonly found in academic texts.